Television

A WORLD VIEW

Television

A WORLD VIEW

WILSON P. DIZARD

SYRACUSE UNIVERSITY PRESS

First Edition 1966

FOR
EDWARD R.
MURROW

Preface

Within the next decade television will become the most influential mass media outlet in most parts of the world. My purpose in this work is to survey the present condition and the future implications of this development, with particular emphasis on its effect on American world leadership.

Several of my fellow workers in the vineyard of mass-media studies have tried to explain TV's influence, relying heavily on sociological and psychological approaches. The most provocative of these theorists is Marshall McLuhan of the University of Toronto, whose ideas other academicians have tried to sweep under the faculty-lounge rug because of the unorthodox (and often hyperbolic) way in which he expounds them. Useful work has been done by Dallas Smythe of the University of Saskatchewan, Henri Dieuzeide of *l'Institut National pédagogique* in Paris, and Rev. Neil Hurley, an American Jesuit sociologist. These men are exploring the frontiers of a new age where global television will serve (in McLuhan's phrase) the world village. One of my purposes is to provide students of this subject with an over-all view of the current television scene throughout the globe.

I hope, too, that the work will be useful to the American television industry, particularly in enlarging its perspective of the medium's world role. For the present, the industry views overseas television almost exclusively in terms of an export market. This is a legitimate part of our national interest, but it is also a limited one. The long-range American role in international TV is going to be determined primarily by the attitudes and the action of the domestic TV industry. It is unrealistic and potentially dangerous to suggest, as some have, that the government should extend its regulatory control over U.S. television activities to the international field. The problem lies in the structure and quality of the medium here at home. If the industry, using publicly owned frequencies, cannot fulfill its primary commitment to the needs of a rapidly changing U.S. social order, then we cannot expect the United States to have much influence on the medium's world role.

Finally, I hope that the work will prove useful to laymen concerned about our future in a world where the tides of social and political pluralism threaten to undermine the structure of an evolving world order. Our national ability to communicate effectively with three billion members of alien cultures is crucial in this process. Television, bringing the sights and sounds of our dialogue to Everyman's front parlor, is the most dramatic advance in mass-media technology since the invention of the printing press. Its capabilities are directly relevant to our national effort to build a stable democratic world order. The medium itself is neutral: it can be used to transmit the dialogue of free men building such an order or the commands of a dictator trying to prevent it. If my survey has any pretensions, they lie in the direction of attempting to influence a positive American response to this particular challenge.

I have tried to cover the field with some thoroughness, but, inevitably, there are gaps. Television's world-wide growth is a fast-moving phenomenon that will not stand still long enough to permit a panting researcher to pin down a definitive statistic or a trend as firmly as he would like. Despite the growing importance of the subject, academic studies of it are virtually nonexistent. I have had to rely heavily on U.S. and foreign trade publications and on personal contact with television practitioners here and abroad. It has been my good fortune to observe TV operations in over twenty countries in recent years and to meet with many talented people in the profession here and abroad. I refrain from attempting to list them for fear of slighting some. However, I must pay posthumous tribute to the late Edward R. Murrow, who encouraged me to write this book and to whom it is dedicated.

I am indebted also to my former colleagues on the staff of the Center for International Studies at the Massachusetts Institute of Technology for their advice and encouragement while I was a Research Fellow there during the 1962/63 academic year. My thanks go to the information staffs of the British Broadcasting Corporation, the Independent Television Authority, and the Center for Educational Television Overseas in London, the European Broadcasting Union in Geneva, the Japanese Broadcasting Corporation, the German Information Office in New York, the Ford Foundation, and to the British, Australian, Yugoslav, Venezuelan, Chinese, Japanese, and Malaysian embassies in Washington, all of whom answered my requests for facts and figures with care.

My wife, Lynn, was, as always, immensely helpful in editing copy for the work. To our boys—John, Stephen, Wilson and Mark—my thanks for their interest and comments.

I have previously discussed some of the ideas in this book in articles in the following journals: *Journal of Broadcasting*, *Problems of Communism, Television and Adult Education*, and *Television Quarterly*.

Finally, it should be noted that, despite the assistance I have received from many sources, the accuracy of the information and the validity of the opinions in this work are my responsibility alone. The work does not necessarily reflect the official points of view of the United States Information Agency or of the U.S. government.

WILSON P. DIZARD

Washington, D.C.
September 1965

Contents

Television
A WORLD VIEW

1

Small Screen,
Big World

In George Orwell's vision of 1984, conformity and fear are symbolized by ever-present television screens controlled by Big Brother. The vision is only partly prophetic. We probably have the wit and the will to avoid the political tyranny Orwell described. We may be less skillful in coping with the brash, ubiquitous power of television.

Long before 1984, television will be the world's most influential mass communications medium. It is already establishing its primacy in the industrialized West and in Japan; the rest of the world is catching up quickly. Television stations in over 90 countries today serve an audience of over 750 million persons. By the early 1970's this audience will have doubled in size as national networks expand to cover all but the most isolated areas. Regional and intercontinental networks will be commonplace, making possible electronic links anywhere on earth. TV's influence will stretch from Minsk to Manila, from London to Lima, and on to the Nigerian upcountry city of Kaduna where even now bearded camel drivers and local tribesmen sit in fascinated harmony before a teahouse television set watching "Bonanza."

By 1975, television will be an integral part of a vast international communications network built around computers and space satellites. These machines will provide any kind of data instantaneously in all parts of the world to meet the needs of the new information explosion. They will carry a dialogue of experts

1

speaking the international language of technology, and that dialogue will affect the prospects for a more stable world order. Television can be the sight-and-sound interpreter of the dialogue, making it understandable to everyone. Properly used, television can be the forum of a new age of interdependence, the only mass medium fully capable of crossing geographical, cultural, and political barriers to link men and nations in an evolving world community.

The alternative is a world struggling to meet its informational needs largely through traditional means. This is a losing race. Books and other written materials reach no more than half the earth's population. The other half is still functionally illiterate. Outside Europe, Japan, and the United States, newspapers are an insignificant media factor. The film medium has developed primarily as an entertainment spectacle. Only radio is still expanding at a rate which begins to match present-day mass communications needs.

Where does television fit into the pattern? At one extreme are those who conjure up Orwellian prospects of large screens feeding the mindless mass with doublespeak or, at least, Dick Van Dyke comedies. At the other extreme are the Pollyanna believers in television as an instrument for bringing people together in some sort of electronic Chautauqua. The broad confusion of intensely propounded evaluations suggests the need for consensus. For the present, we have a stunning means of reaching one another without a clear idea of what it signifies for us. The situation recalls Thoreau's doubts about building telegraph lines to Texas before one decides what to say to Texans. Television has materialized so quickly from a fast-moving technological revolution that we have not had a reflective chance to define its purpose and set its goals, here or abroad.

We can be sure only that television is here, and that there is going to be more of it very soon. Whatever its long-range implications, TV will soon be the first medium to be shared and understood by virtually everyone on earth. André Malraux once summarized the internationalization of culture by describing a film in which a Swedish actress playing a Russian heroine works for an American director to draw tears from the Chinese. But motion-picture films pale before television's unique sight-and-sound ability to bring both reality and fantasy directly to Everyman. Never was a single emotion shared by so many people as on the day in November, 1963, when three hundred million persons on four continents watched the televised funeral of a martyred American president. Television is not only a recorder of events in a revolutionary age; it is, by its persuasive immediacy, a major tool for shaping the age. Presenting with electronic impartiality not only reality but also the fantasies which cushion us from reality, it is the ultimate instrument of both confrontation and escape. Television serves this double function with a subtlety that makes it the despair of those who try to define its purposes.

The United States has a direct stake in these answers. Our influence in television is primal; more than any other nation, we have set its standards and its pace. Television abroad is often a reflection, or at least a caricature, of our own. To walk into a Tokyo television station is to see American TV with slanted eyes. The comparison is not always favorable. "The future television men are gradually emerging," a London critic declared in a 1959 survey of British TV. "They will be brash, tabloid, half-American, lively and unscrupulous."[1] The distrust of television voiced by American intellectuals is echoed in scores of other countries whose intelligentsia see American TV as a new form of cultural imperialism. But they are in the minority. Most of the world loves Lucy—and other familiar TV personalities who light up the screens. The United States is the largest exporter of television programs: in 1965, almost eighty million dollars' worth of shows were sold to television stations in ninety countries. Through this flood of programs, ranging in quality from the very best to the worst, we send out a forceful image of ourselves and our society.

Another U.S. influence in this field has been the increasingly successful efforts of American industry to gain control over television outlets abroad. Led by the three major networks, U.S. firms own or are affiliated with television interests in over thirty countries. The export market is increasingly important for the American TV industry. In 1965, the industry earned an estimated 125 million dollars in overseas sales of programs, equipment, and other services. For some parts of the industry—notably the production of television films—the overseas market means the difference between profit and loss on its operations.

Important as our economic involvement is, it is only part of the larger question of what role television may play in strengthening—or undermining—America's position in world affairs. Ten years ago the question would have been frivolous. At that time, TV was an entertainment medium for the middle class in the United States and a few other rich countries, generally expected to trickle down to the rest of the world in a generation or two. Events have caught up with cautious projections. Television is no longer a Western monopoly, with a Japanese extension. In a decade it has spread from a few hundred transmitters grouped largely in the North Atlantic area to over four thousand stations on five continents. It covers all of Latin America and the Middle East. In the Communist bloc, it is the most rapidly expanding mass medium, a new weapon in the regimes' propaganda arsenal. Over half of the new African nations have added television to their list of chauvinistic prestige symbols. In South Asia and the Far East, only a handful of smaller countries—Burma, Cambodia, Laos, and Ceylon—have resisted the introduction of television. For the rest of the so-called underdeveloped countries, television is perhaps the most readily available and prominently visible of the amenities of political independence and economic promise of things to come.

Equally significant is the rapid development of regional and intercontinental networks. The earliest and most successful of these has been in operation in Europe for over a decade. It is the pacesetting Eurovision network of a thousand stations in seventeen countries connected in a four thousand-mile relay. In Eastern Europe a similar Communist network, Intervision, links stations in seven countries. Geographical and political difficulties have inhibited the development of similar connections in other parts of the world. By 1975, however, such regional links will be commonplace. Five Central American nations already operate a network which will one day be part of a Latin American chain stretching from the Rio Grande to the Strait of Magellan. In the Far East, Japanese interests are promoting the idea of an "Asiavision" network linking cities from Tokyo to Karachi. Arab nationalists, led by the United Arab Republic's Gamal Abdel Nasser, see a television network as a powerful stimulus to Arab unity. Even African leaders, beset by post-independence political and economic turmoil, talk expansively of continent-wide television within the next decade.

The most dramatic of these international links is the one made possible by the American-built communications satellite system scheduled for full operation in 1967. The high-flying "comsats" will be utilized mainly for telephone, teletype, and other circuits now serviced by wireless or cable connections. However, they will also have the capacity for transmitting television sight-and-sound throughout the world. Such programs have been a reality since July, 1962, when the first experimental telecasts were exchanged between the U.S. and Western Europe. By 1970, successors to these pioneering satellites will be transmitting to Japan and Latin America and most of the world. It is an amazing record for a communications medium that was little more than a laboratory model twenty years ago.

Americans are beginning to ask questions about our part in this development. Most of the discussion so far has centered around the allegedly baleful influence of our television program exports. This concern is justified because much of what foreigners see on their TV screens is, directly or indirectly, American. Increasingly television is becoming the most widespread and effective portrayer of the United States to hundreds of millions of people abroad. For almost four decades, Hollywood was the main source of the world's ideas about the U.S. and its people. The movies' fictionalized portrayal of our life set the tone for two generations. Television has now taken over much of Hollywood's role. It reaches a larger world audience in a single day than Hollywood ever did in a week. Furthermore, television presents current reality as well as fiction-drama.

Obviously it makes a difference to Americans how we project ourselves. Debate over the validity of our television image has been inconclusive, clouded by hyperbole and weakened by unsupported speculation. "History has known few nobler or more selfless actions than the generosity which America has shown to other nations during the last twenty years. But one cannot wonder whether the good that has been done by the program of foreign aid is not in danger of being undone by the image of America as it appears in program after program on the television screens of the world."[2] The words are those of Sir Hugh Carleton Greene, director-general of the British Broadcasting Corporation, speaking to an American audience in 1962. The American television industry, ever sensitive to its own image, usually reacts with pained surprise to such charges. The tendency is to assume that they cannot be true. Witness the Radio Corporation of America's Robert Sarnoff: "The wide popular favor American TV enjoys, and the belief that wholesale exposure of foreign audience to impressions of America is on balance a blessing, however mixed, leads to the verdict that American commercial TV showings currently are more helpful than harmful in creating favorable attitudes towards the United States."[3]

Both Messrs. Sarnoff and Greene compel attention because they are dealing with the most visible part of U.S. television activity abroad. As we shall see later, some of our exported shows serve us badly, others serve us well, and most are so bland that it is almost impossible to assign a value to them. Whatever their influence, they are, in fact, only a small part of the American stake in overseas television. It would be a mistake to ignore them, and a mistake to let them block our view of the larger U.S. commitment. It is time for a longer look at the political, economic, and cultural aspects of the medium as they relate to our national interests.

American television is entering a new stage in its development, the third since it burst out of its laboratory cocoon thirty years ago. Television became technically feasible in the 1930's, largely due to research investment by leading U.S. broadcasters and manufacturers. These same men had a curiously limited view of the medium's potential. They visualized television as a diversion for an upper-income audience. Their ideas about programing centered around cultural uplift—plays, poetry readings, and sopranos singing German *lieder*. Much of their inspiration came from Great Britain, where the British Broadcasting Corporation's infant television service was transmitting stiffly cultural shows. ("The BBC begins its program day with a lecture on how to stuff a field mouse," said comedian Fred Allen at the time, "and continues in the same vein for the rest of the day.") Money was another factor in limiting the early exploitation of television. Radio was in its gold-rush period. The broadcasters did not want to abandon it for the uncertain—and expensive—prospects of television.[4] Founders of American television were strangely unprepared to meet the consequences of their technical achievements.

Commercial and artistic shortsightedness continued into the postwar period. With radio still booming, broadcasters were inclined to let their television interest build up gradually around an upper-income audience. It gradually became apparent that they had misjudged their medium and its seductive appeal. The television audience of the late forties started at the bottom of the income scale, bulged out in the middle and contracted at the top. Suddenly, the networks realized the prospects for sending sight-and-sound sales messages into tens of millions of front parlors. The new gold rush was on. The second phase of U.S. television—its dominance by the commercial networks—came in with a roar. No longer a cultural theater, television was the biggest pitchman of all time, and the program pattern was shaped accordingly. In Frank Lloyd Wright's phrase, the medium was designed to provide chewing gum for the eyes.

Television is too brash and potent a force, however, to be trapped forever between soap commercials. Although the pattern of network control may seem as solid and unyielding as ever, there are forces at work that promise a new, diversified approach. The most important of these can be summarized in three sets of initials: UHF, ETV, and STV. UHF is the ultra-high-frequency broadcast band, capable of adding thousands of new channels to the very-high-frequency band now used mainly for commercial broadcasting. ETV is the growing network of community and school educational stations. STV is subscription television, the system for supplying special programs to home receivers on

a closed circuit for a fee. Individually, none of these developments represents a threat of any seriousness to the networks.
Taken together, they add up to a significant modification of
American television. Network broadcasting will continue to
dominate, but a new diversification of resources will be available
to the American public. Commercial networks and their affiliated
stations may be expected to use their vast political and economic
power to resist such diversification. A pungent example of this
use of power took place in November, 1964. In league with
motion-picture interests, California broadcasters successfully
propagandized for a state constitutional amendment which, in
effect, prohibited pay-TV operations in the state. (The amendment was declared unconstitutional by the State Supreme Court
in 1965.) The broadcasters' determination to outlaw a legitimate
private business to protect their own interests is less a sign of
hypocrisy than of desperation in the face of unaccustomed outside
competition.

Current changes in domestic television have important implications for our stake in international TV. As long as American
television is controlled by a few large commercial interests, it
cannot reflect the medium's full potential in our society. Diversification will strengthen this potential not only at home but also
abroad. At present, our direct involvement in overseas television
primarily consists of selling programs to foreign stations. This
is a legitimate activity, but it need not be the only one or even
the most important one. We could and should embrace the full
spectrum of television's potential as the first world-wide mass
medium of communication. Shipping "The Beverly Hillbillies"
films to the Nigerians is only a narrow beam in the spectrum.
Our interests cannot be adequately reflected by three New York
networks or by Washington bureaucrats. We need a dynamic,
diversified pattern in which the medium fully serves a democratic
civilization at home and an evolving world order abroad.

There has been too much parochial concern about the American "image" we project through television. Our foreign viewers

spend relatively little time in judging us. Most of the time they are judging themselves and their own societies. The distinction is fundamental. Perhaps the hardest lesson we have had to learn in our postwar experience as a world leader is simply that the long-range acceptance of our leadership role depends far more on what foreign peoples think of themselves than on what they think of us. Our overconcern for our own image conceals, often badly, a desire to get rubber-stamp approval for ourselves and our policies. Only in recent years have we come to realize that our best hope lies in getting world opinion to see its own interests clearly in the hope that they will be identified, at least partly, with our own. In a world that is at once increasingly pluralistic and interdependent, our leadership role will be circumscribed by our ability to recognize and act in accord with its pluralism and interdependence.

The lesson is applicable to new television developments. More than any single medium, TV has an uncanny power to identify and define for people the world around them. It can do this truthfully, or falsely, or somewhere in between. Whatever the circumstances, its impact is enormous. Americans have had almost two decades of daily experience with this phenomenon; most of the rest of the world is just beginning to experience it. Television is developing abroad primarily as an entertainment medium as it did in the United States. However it would be a mistake to underestimate its political, social, and economic force.

Any mass medium that can command the attention of hundreds of millions of people for four to six hours a day is, per se, a political factor. It becomes more so when it involves a relatively cheap instrument, usually located in a place of honor in individual homes, whose only minimal demand on its audience is the ability to see and hear.

Most governmental leaders around the world underestimated television's political potential when it was first introduced. They were inclined to dismiss it as an innocuous entertainment device. There were, however, exceptions—and they have included some of the most powerful political leaders of our time. The first such leader to recognize TV's possibilities was Adolf Hitler. He encouraged experiments in television, with emphasis on large-screen projections in theaters where people could gather to see and hear him speak. On at least one occasion before the war, Hitler made an important government announcement to just such an audience.[5] The German leader was not able to develop his theories about television after 1939 because of other wartime demands on German technology. However, dictators since then have shown how television can be adapted to totalitarian regimes. The most striking example has been Fidel Castro. Television has been a major weapon for propaganda and political intimidation in his regime. Other Communist leaders were slower to recognize the propaganda potential of TV. Josef Stalin was almost totally disinterested in the medium. His successors have taken a different attitude, encouraging the use of television both as an ideological tool and as a conspicuous example of the good life of the post-Stalin period.

In the free world, the political potential of television has been exploited by such charismatic leaders as Charles de Gaulle and Gamal Abdel Nasser. In France, activities of the state-controlled network center around the personality and policies of the head of state. Most French leaders have used the medium since 1950, but none has utilized it as frequently or as effectively as Charles de Gaulle. The French people's dominant image of their leader is *le grand Charles*, peering through a TV screen and exhorting Frenchmen to their national duties. In the United Arab Republic, Colonel Nasser took an early interest in television. The original Nasserite coup in 1952 involved the traditional seizure of radio stations; there was no television in Egypt at the time. Once he was firmly established in office, Nasser revived dormant plans for an Egyptian television network. In half a dozen years, he built up the most extensive service of any developing country in Asia and Africa. In between entertainment shows, UAR television has the dual political purpose of projecting the benevolent image of Gamal Abdel Nasser and of giving his countrymen a new sense of unity by bringing to them the sights and sounds of national development. It is good television—and good propaganda.

These are outsized examples of television's direct political impact. In most countries, the impact has been less spectacular, but equally significant. As in the United States, more people every day are getting their facts and opinions from television than from any other medium. There is considerable evidence that this trend is developing more rapidly abroad than it did here. It was not until 1963 that most Americans named television as their chief source of information. (More important, perhaps, is the fact that they also listed it as their most trusted information source.) Thus it took television almost fifteen years to overtake the traditional influence of other U.S. media.[6] This growth pattern seems to be accelerated abroad. Surveys in such disparate countries as Sweden and Japan indicate that, in less than a decade after television was introduced, it has become the most influential mass medium.

Political leaders are aware of the facts and are adjusting their political style accordingly just as their American counterparts did a decade ago. Election campaigning abroad is increasingly geared to the requirements of television. Between elections, politicians have learned the value of keeping themselves and their assorted good works before the TV cameras. There is every reason to believe a report that in 1959 a newly constructed superhighway in Italy was dedicated five times on television by the incumbent government. Such events form a far larger portion of the foreign viewers' diet than they do here. Television is the new electronic soapbox in scores of countries, and woe to the politician who scorns pancake make-up while playing his role as a man of the people.

Politically, however, television also has some of the qualities of an iceberg. Its visible portion involves the campaign speeches, groundbreaking ceremonies, and other events which are—with certain trimmings—simply an electronic reporting of traditional activities. More important is that part of the medium's political impact that is less visible but, like the underside of an iceberg, still very much present. This is its influence as a shaper of the social patterns that are the raw material of political change.

Here TV's influence, both present and potential, is truly revolutionary. Its base is television's natural affinity with the aspirations of the newly affluent postwar middle class in the U.S., Europe, and Japan—and by extension to the rest of the world which aspires to affluence. All the mass media have been redirected to serve this postwar phenomenon. Television alone has shown an ability not only to serve the emerging affluent masses but to become, in a very short period of time, the instrument for setting the pace of their aspirations by defining standards and visualizing them in an attractive, compelling way. This has been television's *raison d'être*, the root cause and justification for its popularity and growth. The flickering screen is, for hundreds of millions of ordinary people, the sight-and-sound confirmation of what, in fantasy or fact, they will ever want or need on earth.

"What sort of world are they shown?" asks a British television critic. "It is not a violently crude world; in all sorts of obvious ways, it is a very decent world. It is a bright world and a congenitally innocent world, a world prior to the knowledge of good and evil, in which all the young girls have that wonderful Jamesian exclamation mark between their eyebrows . . . and even the middle-aged fathers look no more than nicely weathered. . . ."[7] His definition does not cover all that is shown on television, but it offers a good rule-of-thumb reason why people are drawn to television in the first place. It defines the common denominator of television's appeal, and offers a starting point for measuring its weight in world communications.

Television has developed primarily as a commercial medium. This was to be expected in the United States and a few other countries, notably in Latin America, where broadcasting was traditionally a private venture. Elsewhere, however, broadcasting was a state monopoly without commercial connections. Theoretically, television should have followed in the established pattern; significantly, it did not. The reasons are complex. Economics played a large role. So did the shortsightedness of politicians who regarded television in its early days as a toy that did not merit their attention. At present, television systems in over fifty countries are controlled, in whole or in part, by private interests under state supervision. Commercial advertising is carried by all but a handful of the world's ninety-five television systems. As a result a large measure of program control rests with men who instinctively understand the middle-class aspirations of their audience and who cater to their desires in programing as well as in advertising.

The shift away from state-directed television broadcasting toward commercialism began in the early 1950's. The event that triggered the shift was the British government's decision to introduce commercial television in competition with the government-chartered BBC. Within a few years, dozens of other countries adopted similar arrangements. The focus of overseas television moved from the measured beat of government control to the quick step of commercialism. The change confirmed the effectiveness of American-style broadcasting both as a revenue producer and as a highly acceptable form of entertainment and persuasion. Increasingly television became, in critic Richard Schickel's phrase, the visceral medium before which we are all children.

Television sets the pace for a new order of public expectations. The politicians have little choice but to accommodate to it. This is most evident in Western Europe where the decline of the old-line ideological parties from the Fascist right to the Communist left can be measured to a large degree by the fact that they are out of step with the new order. Even moderate leftist parties like the British Labor party have had to face the consequences. The working-class voter now prefers to stay home and watch the "telly" rather than to attend political meetings or even to regard politics with anything near the personal involvement that his father did. Labor leader Ian Mikardo summed up his party's 1959 electoral setback by saying: "We were defeated by 'Maverick'." His comment was hyperbolic, but there is little doubt that television confers a political advantage on middle-of-the-road and conservative parties. Their emphasis on normalcy and never-had-it-so-good-ism is supported not only by their own TV electioneering but in the commercial programs that surround such appeals. The commercial shows, after all, say much the same thing.

Television's influence on mass attitudes is having its effect on the structure of power at the top. We have seen this happen in the United States; increasingly it is taking place abroad. Commenting on the changing patterns of leadership in Britain after introduction of commercial TV, social critic Anthony Sampson noted in 1965:

> It is hard to recall what Britain was like eight years ago, before that first television toothpaste advertisement and the whole noisy invasion of jingles and ephemeral fame that followed it. Television broke through the high walls that separate British institutions from one another, and dragged almost everyone into its studios. It knocked down its own wall between private and public enterprise and turned the BBC, most influential of the nationalized industries, inside out. The young New Boy Net took over the keys to promotion, salesmanship and fame. They demolished much of the status of the existing Old Boy Networkers, and have built up their own jolly show-biz parade, with teen-agers and David Frost of TW3 as their pacemakers—a parade that any strong silent man joins at his peril.[8]

Television is changing not only the rituals of politics, but also its conditions. Americans could easily be blinded to the political significance of television by the bread-and-circus glitter we pour over it. The time has come for us to take a hard look at this new force overseas and to establish our national responsibilities toward it. This involves, first of all, studying the many facets of television abroad and determining where our interests lie.

The most comprehensible aspect of world television for us concerns those countries which are closest to us politically and culturally, namely, the industrialized nations of Western Europe and, in the Far East, Japan and Australia. Here is where the medium's middle-class impact compares most nearly with our own experience. We are inclined naively to jump to the illusory conclusion that television in these countries is "just like ours." A great deal of it is—to our credit and to our detriment. But the differences are as important as the similarities. Japanese television has its full quota of cowboys, monster serials, and quiz shows. But it also sponsors an educational television effort that is years ahead of anything planned in this country. British television has all the American video trimmings. But it also has a ruling Labor party which proposes to use television intensively as a national educational resource, up to the university level. Other Western European countries import hillbilly serials from New York, but they also plan, through their Eurovision network, to transmit the sights and sounds of their free society to TV viewers in Communist Eastern Europe. We have every right to be humble before these facts.

The key political fact is that Western Europe, Japan, and Australia are our major allies in the effort to defend the peace and to lay the groundwork for a more viable world order. We must eventually include everyone in this undertaking, but we begin with these nations. Since they are not slavish allies, we will influence them only to the degree that we maintain an effective dialogue with their leaders and the people who elect them. Here is the framework in which we measure the American national interest in television as the most important communications medium in the industrialized world. We have hardly begun to construct this framework, much less act on it.

The difficulties of properly using our dialogue with our industrialized allies are plentiful. Yet they pale before the prospects we face in coping with the rise of television in the so-called developing countries of Asia, Africa, and Latin America. Here we start with a psychological handicap. Going by the ground rules governing the rich and the poor, these countries are not ready for the middle-class gift of television: they cannot afford it, they do not need it, and they do not understand it. Such an attitude tells much about our residual legacy of Puritan disapproval of people who enjoy what they should not. It does not take a great deal of hindsight to understand why over sixty so-called underdeveloped countries now have television systems, and why the rest of them will have it in a few years.

In the first place, the timing was right. Television became a technological possibility during a period when scores of nations achieved independence. In the tumult of new freedom, everything was promised and everything seemed possible. It did not take long to shuck off these illusions and to modify the plans for steel mills, jet planes, and other chimeras. But there were a few prestige items available. Television was one of them. A small TV transmitter has a price-tag well under a million dollars; the big international electronics companies were usually ready to extend credit against the day when local television became a more profitable business for them. In one provincial Philippine city, a television station began operations serving a total of six sets. In most of these countries, however, there was a sufficiently affluent class in the major cities to support a station. This group shared its TV programs with bedraggled audiences gathered in teahouses or village squares to watch "Huckleberry Hound," "The Fugitive," "Dr. Kildare," and other popular imports.

However, television is not a quaint irrelevancy in Asia and Africa. It has a political role to play in these areas as important as its role in our dialogue with other Western nations, for it has the potential ability to accelerate the pace of development in poorer nations. Here its educational force can be truly revolutionary.

The proper use of radical new educational techniques—television included—is a crucial need for emerging countries. In developed societies, schooling takes on the aspect of a consumer good; we do not have to relate the study of Shakespeare's plays to the growth of national output. The poorer nations are obligated to regard their educational effort as a major capital investment. For the next generation at least, the problem is that of determining how to do this quickly and efficiently. Seen in this light, educational television may be the social and economic bargain of the century for the new nations of Asia and Africa. Despite expensive installations, it may be the cheapest per-capita-cost way of using x resource of teachers to get y amount of facts and z degrees of twentieth-century attitudes into the minds of half the world's population now living in ignorance and poverty.

The most obvious need is for childhood education. Under present development plans a few underdeveloped countries will achieve universal education during the next generation. Most of the rest will require two generations or more. The bottlenecks in teacher training, school construction, and equipment are compounded in many countries by ill-advised reliance on traditional Western educational methods. However well such methods have worked in Europe and America, they need to be profoundly modified for the newer nations. The need is for effective educational shortcuts to eliminate a massive inventory of social and technological illiteracy. Shortcuts exist, and they are mainly the product of Western technology. They involve the whole range of audio-visual techniques, television included, which have given new pace and dimension to modern education in the West. There is, in fact, little hope that the educational needs of the new nations can be met without a generous application of these techniques.

Beyond the primary education of children, the re-education of entire societies must be considered. This includes "adult education" as we use the phrase to mean supplementing earlier education. It also means providing the masses of Asia, Africa, and Latin America with a comprehensible image of their new societies. For most of them, the idea that they are citizens of a new country is largely irrelevant to their day-to-day lives. Their social loyalties are to a caste, clan, village, or religion. Most of the shining development plans drawn up in the capital city run against this stubborn fact. The older Western symbols of nationalism—flags, anthems, parliaments, and the like—are meaningless or inadequate to the task of establishing national identity. What is needed is what television and its audio-visual allies can best provide, namely a dramatic visualization of nation building brought directly to every corner of the country in terms that can be understood by everyone. Television can show its audience the rest of the world beyond their borders, relating it to their own lives. It can tell its audiences that they have a stake in the new order, and demonstrate to them that the best of their older traditions can be preserved and enhanced through change. The medium's potential as a nation-building instrument has only begun to be explored, but it may well prove to have revolutionary implications for all the developing world.

Television offers no panaceas for poorer nations. It is easy enough to install an impressive TV system under the banner of national development. It is considerably more difficult to provide the will or the expertise to utilize the system effectively. In too many Asian and African nations, television is a frivolous boondoggle, designed primarily to satisfy the gadget-mindedness of the elite class. In other countries, it is being incorporated into the propaganda apparatus of the area's proliferating dictatorships. There is little reason to believe that most Asian and African leaders are ready to recognize television's educational value, over and above its undoubted advantages for publicizing their own activities.

The United States has a political stake in seeing that television's possibilities as a development tool are fully explored. This involves our broad interest in bringing about a greater measure of stability in Asia and Africa. It also affects the efficiency of our economic and technical assistance to these countries. If twenty years of trial-and-error operations in the field have taught us anything, it is that the impact of our efforts is in direct ratio to the local level of social and technological literacy. By default or design, television will affect this ratio. It can be used as a conscious instrument of development, a sight-and-sound classroom whose students are shown reality and their relation to it. Or it can be a powerful incitement to further unrest in poor countries by fueling already-overdeveloped expectations without explaining how they can be realistically satisfied. The "revolution of rising expectations" becomes the revolution of rising frustrations, a time of troubles with no foreseeable end.

Among the industrialized countries, the United States has the broadest experience and resources to effect a decision. Although educational television (ETV) has not reached its full potential here, no other nation has experimented so intensively with its possibilities. Most other Western countries have national school systems; their tendency has been to settle on one type of educational TV and stay with it. The U.S. experience encompasses thousands of school systems experimenting with ETV at all levels. Beyond its value for American education, our ETV is a storehouse of information for educators from Asia, Africa, and Latin America. Our experience cannot be exported wholesale, but (to cite only one example) the pacesetting South Carolina state education department's use of television to reach deprived children in rural areas offers useful lessons for any underdeveloped country.

The United States has already taken the lead in exporting techniques abroad. For over a decade, American ETV stations have been a mecca for foreign educators interested in the subject. Since 1960, American pilot program assistance to ETV efforts in underdeveloped countries has been increasing rapidly. The Ford Foundation took an early lead with projects in India and in Latin America. The only training school for TV educators in the developing world is being operated under American sponsorship in the Philippines. More significantly, since 1963, the U.S. government's technical assistance program has included funds for ETV projects in developing countries. These efforts are still modest in scope, especially when measured against the problems with which they are intended to deal. Their usefulness lies in setting a new pace for educational development in the poorer countries.

To summarize, the United States has a stake in overseas television whether we recognize it or not. It affects us at many different levels, and it will do so increasingly during the coming decade. Television will be the most important mass medium of information and persuasion in a world we hope to lead out of the slough of nuclear fear, economic poverty, and political disorganization. Television is not an electronic salvation device. However, it would be shortsighted to underestimate its influence as the most effective sight-and-sound instrument of mass confrontation yet invented by man. Not the least of our attitudes in approaching this fact should be humility. We need to remind ourselves that our new television contact with the rest of the world must be a two-way conversation, not a smug preachment.

A positive U.S. policy on international TV will be difficult to develop. The medium in this country is dominated by commercial interests, supported by a strong tradition of freedom from government interference. An enlightened U.S. approach to television opportunities abroad will have to be guided by a consensus between industry and government. Public opinion must also participate, including one group that has heretofore played a marginal role in television's development. These are the intellectuals, most of whom have written off television as a low-grade abomination. Their apprehensions are understandable, but they abdicated their responsibilities too early.

It is time for the intellectuals to get back into the fight. Television is changing rapidly here and abroad. The American stake in its future cannot be left to men for whom it is primarily a profit-and-loss item. There is room for everyone concerned with the quality of our society at home and with its obligations abroad. There is no reason why television today has to be a parody of its great promise. The improvements needed lie largely in the realm of ideas and imagination. With network commercialism now challenged by ETV, pay-TV and smaller UHF stations, the chances for getting a true competition of talents in television are brighter than ever. The alternative is for the intellectuals to retreat further from their role as explainers and interpreters of a complex society and its needs.

As Marya Mannes has pointed out: "The intellectual (by whom I mean a man whose entertainment is his intelligence) will ignore television at his peril and pay for this in the end by having to speak to people incapable of understanding him, to teach people distracted by trivia and corrupted by commerce: a people abandoned to the cheapest use of a great medium."[9]

Our national impact on world television will depend primarily on the quality of our domestic use of the medium. We live in a glass-house culture, watched by everyone. Through television, we will be seen more often by more hundreds of millions of people than ever before in history. What they see and what they think about our televised image will, in large part, set the tone for our world leadership in the coming years. We would be foolish to measure television's impact by any smaller yardstick.

In the following chapters, we will use this yardstick to measure our prospects—and potential pitfalls—in international television. First, however, it will be useful to put the subject into historical perspective by reviewing the circumstances of television's growth abroad since the 1930's.

2

Up from
Alexandra Palace

The Topsy-like growth of television has made it the mass media success story of the postwar age. It is a story with many facets. These include stunning technical achievements, showmanship, high finance, and low politics, all tied in with the phenomenon of a world in rapid social transition.

Unfortunately for future chroniclers of our age, television has no dramatic single event to mark its beginnings, no "What hath God wrought" or "Mr. Watson, come here," to give it a convenient, memorable schoolboy's peg on which to hang its entry into history. If a date and place had to be selected, the date would be November 2, 1936, and the place the British Broadcasting Corporation's experimental television studio at Alexandra Palace on the northern edge of London. The occasion was the inauguration of the first public television broadcasting service in the world. The broadcasts were intended to test two technical systems for transmitting television images. The first system, a mechanical device to record and receive the pictures, had been developed by John Baird, a brilliant and somewhat impractical Scottish inventor. Baird had been working on television developments for over a decade before the Alexandra Palace tests. The second system, using newly developed electronic methods of transmission and reception, came from the research laboratories of the Marconi-E.M.I. Television Co., a subsidiary of two large British electrical companies. For three months, the two systems were tested in transmissions from the tiny studios.

Among the first performers to step before the primitive cameras were an unknown actress named Greer Garson and a well-known playwright, George Bernard Shaw.

In February, 1937, the BBC announced that it had selected the Marconi-E.M.I. system for its future transmissions. It was a tribute to the engineering skill of two Marconi-E.M.I. engineers, Isaac Shoenberg and Charles S. Franklyn. The system they developed, using a 405-line picture standard, is still in use in Britain and many other countries to this day.[1] The Alexandra Palace experiments were the culmination of half a century's search for a practical TV system by scientists of a half-dozen nations. They included the German, Paul Nipkow, who developed the first device for mechanical scanning of images in 1884; the Russian, Boris Rosing, designer of the first system using a cathode ray tube as a receiver in 1907; and Vladimir Zworykin and Philo Farnsworth of the United States, who brought the potential of all-electronic television to working reality during the early 1930's.

The United States was by far the most active area of experimentation; by 1932, the Federal Radio Commission had authorized twenty-five experimental television stations. Earlier the Bell Telephone Company had demonstrated wire-circuit television by transmitting pictures from Washington to New York.

However, television developed slowly, inhibited by the lack of a clear-cut government policy on technical standards, the fiscal setbacks of the Depression, and the broadcasting industry's concentration on its profitable radio operations.[2] It was not until 1940 that the Federal Communications Commission (FCC), successor to the Radio Commission, approved a plan for commercial television broadcasting. In July, 1941, the National Broadcasting Company (NBC) and Columbia Broadcasting System (CBS) began station operations in New York on a fifteen-hour weekly schedule. Within a year, eight other commercial stations went on the air; only six of them continued to broadcast throughout the war. By the end of 1944 the three pioneers in broadcasting—NBC, CBS, and DuMont—had stepped up their programing in anticipation of television's postwar expansion.

The expansion was a long-awaited one for American electrical equipment and broadcasting companies that had invested millions of dollars in television experiments before the war in hopes of commercial reward. RCA claimed in an FCC hearing in 1940 that it had spent ten million dollars since 1934 on television; CBS put its television expenses at a million dollars a year.[3] In May, 1945, the FCC defined its policy on postwar television in a decision that set the tone and pattern for American television—and for a good part of the rest of the world. All of the channel allocations were to be commercial, with only minor consideration for educational or other public-service uses of television. (It took seven years for the FCC to make a decision on the allocation of channels for educational stations.)

Meanwhile, a powerful range of economic and political interests were involved in the licensing procedures for the 400 channels initially allocated by the FCC. By September, 1948, 106 stations had begun broadcast operations when the commission declared a "freeze" on the construction of new stations because of technical problems involving signal interference by stations in the same area. The freeze lasted until 1952. It had the effect of slowing down, but not stopping, the postwar spurt in American television. Television stations were operating in almost all major cities, providing vast audiences their first experiences with a medium that was destined to have an important influence on their lives.

There was very little doubt that American television would be developed primarily on a commercial basis. There was, however, considerable doubt about the pace of this development, centered largely around the question of whether television set sales would be extensive enough and whether advertising could cover the high cost of television programing. Television was considered a medium for the upper and upper-middle income classes. This thesis was quickly disproved as television began to attract a mass audience from the middle and lower-middle income groups, with large segments of the rock-bottom income groups represented. TV set production went from 178,000 in 1947 to 6,000,000 in 1952; by the end of 1952, there were over 20,000,000 sets in use. Television had found its first mass market and a highly successful operating formula. More significantly, this growth signalled the fact that television had a social dynamic all its own, that it would develop rapidly under the prodding of commercial interests, and that it would not be denied its role as a revolutionary new mass medium.

Meanwhile, other countries were watching the American experience for clues to the development of their own television operations. Because of postwar political and economic dislocations, their progress in this field was to be considerably slower than in America. A few were able to resume their prewar operations on an experimental scale. The British began telecasting, after a seven-year hiatus, in June, 1946. (At the time there were only 1,300 sets in operation, compared with 20,000 before the war.) Britain's postwar economic difficulties inhibited the production of television receivers and other equipment; it was not until the end of 1951 that the number of receivers reached the million mark.[4] With this increase went a radical change in the composition of the BBC's audience. As in the United States, it was heavily weighted in favor of lower-income, lower-education groups. A BBC survey made in 1950 showed that 70 percent of its total television audience was not educated beyond the age of fifteen.[5]

Across the Channel, the French had resumed telecasting soon after the liberation of Paris in 1944. The only other country which maintained scheduled television operations before 1950 was the Soviet Union. The Russians had begun scheduled television services in 1938 in Moscow utilizing equipment bought from the Radio Corporation of America. The station resumed telecasts on a limited scale in 1946.

With the stepping up of the pace of economic development after 1950, dozens of other countries examined the possibilities of getting into the television sweepstakes. Their plans ranged from the modest to the grandiose; in most cases, expectations ran ahead of the economic and technical realities. These realities were deeply involved in the question of who would control television in the thirty or more countries which were planning such operations by 1950. At first, there seemed little doubt as to the answer. Television was, like radio, a "natural" government monopoly and, like radio, would be developed under strict government control. In 1950, television was destined to follow the historical pattern of radio. In fact, however, this did not happen. Only a handful of the more than ninety countries with television operations in 1965 had state-controlled, noncommercial television. Of the rest, about half had a television system controlled directly by the state but permitting some form of commercial participation. In the remaining countries, television operated either as a wholly commercial operation or as a combination of state and commercial operations.

This development has been an important one not only in setting the pattern of world television but also in defining the American relationship to television abroad. The reasons for the strong upsurge of commercially oriented television varied from country to country but, in each instance, the harsh economic facts of developing and maintaining television operations played an important role. Most governments quickly found out that they could not afford television as a budgetary item. In many cases, they had supported their radio operations from a license fee on each home receiver. The economics of television would not, however, permit such a simple solution unless license fees were raised to the point where television would be permanently restricted to an upper-income audience.

Significantly, the few countries that elected strict state monopoly of their television operations have been those where the medium has developed proportionately more slowly. For most other countries, the problem resolved itself into developing a suitable formula for combining government control over television with some form of commercial operations to sustain the operation. The ratio between government and private control was determined, in most cases, by the pressure of political and economic forces, guided by men who recognized the high stakes involved in the control of the new medium. This resulted in a wide variety of formulas. They ranged from complete commercialization of television with only nominal government supervision as in Iran, Luxembourg, pre-Castro Cuba, and the

Philippines to some form of state control with limited use of commercials as in Italy, Finland, and Spain.

Although many countries were impressed by the commercial success of American television, few of them adopted the American pattern outright. Most governments took their cue from the European countries whose experience in state monopoly broadcasting was closer to their own. It has been the European rather than the American example which has set the specific pattern of television's administrative development throughout the world. It will be useful to examine the growth of television in key European countries, operating under systems which range from strict state control of the medium to uninhibited commercial operations.

The first of these groups have been those countries which developed television primarily as a noncommercial state monopoly, following the tradition set thirty years earlier in radio broadcasting. Among the European countries which followed this course were France, Norway, Sweden, Denmark, Switzerland, and the Netherlands. The French took a strong stand in favor of state-controlled television during the postwar debate on the reasons for the French defeat in 1940. Investigations showed that in the prewar period private radio stations, like the French press, had been manipulated by political and economic groups to the detriment of national interests. In 1946, all French political parties, from the Communist to the Catholic MRP, supported legislation nationalizing all French radio and television facilities. The initial result was to purge French broadcasting of its collaborationist taint and to give it a more "national" appeal.

However, the French moved slowly in expanding their TV system. This was partly due to the government's decision to give priority to the rehabilitation of the national radio network during the late 1940's. At the end of 1952, France had only sixty thousand TV sets in operation, giving it the lowest ratio of sets per family of any European country. It was not until 1954 that the French National Assembly approved a five-year television plan for Radiodiffusion Télévision Française, providing for a network of forty-five transmitters.[6] These plans developed slowly, however, due to the Assembly's reluctance to appropriate sufficient funds to carry them out.

French television's development was also hampered by charges and countercharges over the alleged use of the nationalized radio and television network for political purposes. Radiodiffusion Télévision Française was under the direct control of the Ministry of Information. Under successive postwar governments it exercised its right to guide the content of French broadcasting, particularly on sensitive political matters. The most often cited example of this guidance is French broadcasting's handling of the Algerian war during the 1950's; French television did not, according to its critics, carry a single program about the conflict between 1956 and 1959.[7]

Charges of alleged consorship continued after General Charles de Gaulle became head of state in 1958. With a significant part of the press opposed to his policies, the new President turned to television as a means for projecting his forceful personality and policies to the people. (For more detailed discussion of de Gaulle's use of television, see Chapter 6.) Largely as a result of this decision, French TV was given a new lease on life in the form of expanded technical facilities, a bigger budget for program operations, and a larger audience to serve. In April, 1964, a long-delayed second network was inaugurated.

The new role assigned to television by the Gaullist government led to increased criticism that the medium was being used primarily as a political weapon against the opposition. Although the government ignored the charges, it took steps in 1963 to reorganize the structure of French broadcasting. In part the move was made to disarm critics of Gaullist television. However the main purpose was to give French radio and TV a stronger competitive position in attracting the attention of its audience. In opening the National Assembly debate on the government's proposals in 1964, Minister of Information Alain Peyrefitte acknowledged that the state-operated radio system had lost half its listening audience in the previous fifteen years to private stations broadcasting from Luxembourg, Monaco, and other nearby areas. Television, he warned, was threatened with the same competition.[8]

The government's bill, approved by the Assembly in June, 1964, transferred radio and television activities from direct control of the information ministry to an autonomous organization, L'Office de Radiodiffusion Télévision Française (ORTF). An eighteen-member board of directors, equally divided between government and public members, was given authority to set ORTF's broadcasting policy, with the Ministry of Information limited to an advisory role. The bill had a number of provisions which indicated the government's willingness to meet the "censorship" charge. One such provision requires that future government programs should be specifically identified as such. However, critics of Gaullist broadcasting policies were not completely mollified by the new legislation. They noted that ORTF's director-general, who would be responsible for day-to-day broadcasting activities, was a government-appointed official whose term of office was not specified, thus making it possible for the government to replace him at will.

Despite such criticisms, ORTF represented an important move away from the traditional French government control over broadcasting activities. In 1965 another change was also imminent as the government officially considered a proposal for introducing commercial advertising on French television. Although the number of French television receivers had risen above the five million mark, the seventeen-dollar annual license fee collected from each set owner was insufficient to finance the costs of the expanding TV network. ORTF had inherited a debt equivalent to thirty million dollars when it assumed control of broadcasting operations a year earlier.

A French decision to permit television advertising would undoubtedly strengthen the pressures for a similar move in other countries that have clung to the concept of noncommercial nationalized television. It would add to the pressures already generated by the American example and, perhaps more strongly, by the 1954 British decision to establish a commercial second network in competition with the venerable BBC.

This event marked a turning point in the development of television abroad. The BBC was the monumental, and certainly most successful, example of the social and political benefits of a government-created public monopoly in radio and television. It was, moreover, the best-known broadcasting system in the world, largely as a result of the effectiveness of its wartime short-wave broadcasts. BBC radio was the model on which the broadcasting systems of a score of countries were organized over a period of thirty years. It was assumed that British television would also be a BBC monopoly after the war, as it had been before 1939. However, within a few years, the very ramparts of state-created monopoly television had been breached, revolutionizing broadcasting in Britain and in dozens of other countries. A new and potent argument for commercial television was introduced throughout the world: If the British can do it, why can't we?

Commercial television in Britain resulted from a remarkable performance in political lobbying by a small group of Conservative members of Parliament, discreetly aided by a coalition of advertising and industrial interests who recognized the economic potential of commercial television. They first advanced their views on commercial broadcasting in hearings before the Labor government's commission on broadcast policy during the late 1940's. Predictably, the commission recommended that the BBC continue its monopoly position in both radio and television.

The supporters of the BBC monopoly included all of the Labor party leadership and most of the Tory leadership. They dominated the subsequent parliamentary debate on the subject in 1951; only two Conservative backbenchers spoke in favor of commercial TV during the debate. However, the commercial television proponents controlled the Conservative party's broadcast study group. This advantage proved decisive for their position when the Conservative party, under Winston Churchill's leadership, ended Labor's five-year reign in the general elections of October, 1951. The study group prepared a government white paper, issued in

May, 1952, which suggested that "provision should be made to permit some element of competition" in British television. The statement, cautious as it was, marked the Churchill government's commitment to commercial television. Thus, a political maneuver permitted less than a dozen Conservative MP's (out of a total of 320 Conservatives in Parliament) to commit their party and the government to commercial television.[9]

The vote also reflected the general anti-BBC bias of Winston Churchill. Along with other Conservatives, Churchill believed that the Labor party victory over his party in 1945 was caused in part by BBC favoritism toward the Laborites in its broadcasts and commentaries. Years earlier Churchill had supported the idea of sponsored BBC programs; in 1929 he had sent a letter to the BBC's director, Sir John Reith, offering to pay one hundred pounds "from my own pocket for the right to speak for half an hour on politics. How ashamed you will all be in a few years for having muzzled the broadcast." Churchill was no great proponent of commercial TV (which he characterized as a tu'penny Punch and Judy show) but he was interested in giving the BBC some competition.

The Conservative's surprise decision on commercial television served to rally the defenders of the BBC's monopoly to latter-day action. They represented the overwhelming majority of Establishment opinion in Britain, from archbishops to university dons, in temporary league with commercial groups such as the managers of motion picture and legitimate-theater enterprises who feared the effects of commercial television on their own enterprises. In June, 1952, this coalition formed the National Television Council as the organizational center for their lobbying efforts.

It was a propitious moment to defend the BBC and to attack the alleged horrors of commercial television. Not only was the BBC's reputation at an all-time high as a result of its excellent coverage of Queen Elizabeth's coronation, but there had been a sharp reaction against the manner in which American television had handled the films of the coronation telecast a few hours after the event. British newspapers were filled with sensationalized accounts of how one American station had interrupted the Westminster Abbey communion service to advertise bed sheets, while another network featured the antics of its mascot, a chimpanzee named J. Fred Muggs, during its coronation coverage.

J. Fred Muggs was a potent if unwilling ally of the proponents of a continued BBC monopoly for many months, but his coronation role was no match for the formidable strength of economic forces supporting commercial television. These commercial interests—including advertising agencies, television equipment suppliers, and consumer goods manufacturers—provided the financial aid and organizational talent for a mass lobbying organization, the Popular Television Association (PTA), designed to whip up popular support for what they termed "competitive television."

The PTA's themes were a combination of high-minded warnings about the dangers of the BBC's monopoly to freedom of expression in Britain together with promises that commercial television would be more interesting to watch than the BBC. Occasionally their argumentation was specious and sometimes below-the-belt. One PTA lecturer went out of his way to suggest BBC dullness by noting that its programs were used by mental hospitals to soothe their patients. Another speaker informed church groups that commercial television could spark a religious revival in Britain as it had (he claimed) in the United States. The BBC was the worst kind of monopoly, said one Major C. H. Tait at a PTA-sponsored meeting, because "it set out unashamedly to make people think, and from that it was only a short step to telling them what to think."[10]

Perhaps the shrewdest of the arguments advanced by commercial TV advocates was their promise to avoid the alleged excesses of American television. The bill authorizing commercial TV sought to minimize such excesses by placing the proposed new stations under the control of an Independent Television Authority (ITA), a public corporation. The authority would own and operate the new system's transmitting facilities, renting them to independent program companies. Advertising sold by these companies would be strictly controlled by ITA regulations; all such advertising would be limited to short "spot" announcements placed between programs.

Supported by more reluctant than enthusiastic votes, the bill creating the Independent Television Authority became law in July, 1954. The first commercial station went on the air in September, 1955, and immediately captured the lion's share of the TV audience in the London area. In the following months, other commercial stations began their transmissions and their commanding audience lead over local BBC stations. It would be seven years before the BBC could claim, temporarily, a popularity lead in the weekly "Top Twenty" programs.[11] By 1963 there were fifteen commercial companies sharing the equivalent of a quarter billion dollars in revenues from programs that reached over 90 percent of British homes.

Television no longer marched to the measured pace set by the Establishment. It now moved forward with a brisk, noisy quick-step, piped to the tunes of a thousand commercial jingles. Its program pattern was dominated by light entertainment shows encompassing imported Hollywood cowboys, glint-eyed detectives, quiz programs, vaudeville turns, and soap operas, all eagerly cheered on by the growing numbers of British families who watched the "telly" every night. Their frothy TV diet was occasionally made more substantial by the addition of cultural programs that were almost always well produced and sometimes self-consciously artistic. A good example of this was the presentation of *Electra* in the original Greek. This and other uplift exercises drew predictably small audiences; they did not notably challenge commercial TV's steady hold on at least 60 percent of the British TV audience. As revenues continued to soar, one station proprietor declared that his TV franchise was a license to print money.

There was, however, a day of reckoning for all this success. The original 1954 commercial television act was limited to a ten-year period. Anticipating a parliamentary review of the entire television structure, the Conservative government set up a public investigation committee in 1960 headed by Sir Harry Pilkington, a prominent glass manufacturer. The committee's report, issued in 1962, sharply attacked commercial TV operations and recommended tighter legislative controls over them. British TV programing, it declared, was "vapid, puerile, cheaply sensational, sordid and unsavory," largely because of commercial TV. BBC standards were being lowered in an attempt to compete with ITA stations. The Pilkington Report also claimed that ITA companies were making unwarranted profits "from the use of a facility which is part of the public and not the private domain." To counteract this, the report recommended tighter revenue controls over commercial stations, a second channel for the BBC, and greater program control by ITA over its stations. The report accurately reflected the lingering Establishment feeling that commercial television was somehow or other un-British. It did not, however, reflect popular attitudes, nor did it show much awareness of the political influence commercial TV's operators wielded.[12]

As a result, the Conservative government was forced to tone down or eliminate some of the Pilkington recommendations in its own white paper on television, issued in December, 1962. A parliamentary bill, passed the following summer, authorized a second BBC channel, extended ITA's life for twelve years, and imposed a special government levy on television advertising revenue and on transmission facility rentals.

In exchange for ending the era of lush TV profits, the new bill benefited the commercial television companies by confirming their long-term credentials on the British scene. The twenty-two ITA stations, together with the BBC network of sixty-six stations, had replaced radio and the press as the most important British mass media. In addition to facing potential competition from a second commercial network, the ITA-licensed firms found themselves in a new competitive race with the BBC. Long known as "Auntie" because of its program emphasis on cultural uplift, the corporation set its dowager's hat at a rakish angle and announced that it intended to be "the most controversial network." Its first plunge into notoriety was "That Was The Week, That Was," a program which traded on irreverence for the Establishment. "TW3" was followed by "Not So Much a Program, More of a Way of Life," a show that stepped on so many toes it was shut down in 1965. The BBC also challenged the success of "Coronation Street" and other popular commercial TV dramas with its own soap-opera serials. One of these, "Steptoe and Son," was a resounding success despite its improbable cast of characters—two raggedy London junkyard men trying to avoid the bread line by such doomed projects as buying up a million second-hand false teeth. Another show, "Compact," concentrated on the sex lives of the editors of a women's magazine. The BBC was, however, less successful in winning large audiences for its new second channel. Inaugurated in April, 1964, as a UHF station, BBC-2 attracted only about 10 percent of the British audience each night in its first year.

At the end of 1964 a new element entered the British TV picture when the Labor party was returned to power after thirteen years in the political wilderness. The party's general opposition to the further spread of commercial television, coupled with its electoral promise to strengthen the educational and cultural content of British television, promised a new governmental look at TV's role in British life. A special working group was formed in the spring of 1965 to consider ways in which television could be better shaped to a socialist pattern. It was doubtful, however, that Labor would risk losing working-class support by tampering too seriously with the highly popular commercial TV system, despite the fact that the existence of such a system ran against the party's ideological grain.

The success of British commercial television has important repercussions at home and abroad. Domestically, it helped bring to power a new breed of mass media entrepreneurs wielding enormous influence over public opinion. They included such men as Granada Television's Sidney Bernstein, Associated Television's Lew Grade, and Roy Thomson, the Canadian-born press magnate whose Scottish Television station is home base for TV operations in a dozen countries throughout the world. Whether commercial television has raised or lowered British cultural standards is a debatable point; there is no question about the medium's impact in accelerating the pace of social change in Britain during the past fifteen years.[13]

Internationally, the British decision to adopt commercial television helped shift the balance in world-wide television away from strict government management of the medium to a new emphasis on commercial operations under varying forms of government supervision. Very few countries copied the British system directly; in general the British example was used to justify the introduction of commercialism in national TV operations.

One country directly affected by the British decision was Canada. Until 1960, almost all Canadian radio and TV stations were controlled by the government-chartered Canadian Broadcasting Corporation. The CBC differs from the BBC in that over half of its radio and TV network affiliates are privately owned commercial stations. Despite this strong commercial emphasis, about 70 percent of the CBC's operating expenses are covered by annual government grants. CBC affiliates are divided into two networks, one each for English and French language programs. In 1959 the government agreed to relax its restrictions against more than one competitive station in each Canadian city. This decision led to the formation of an eight-station English-language network, CTV, which went on the air in 1961. By 1965 the new network had eleven stations, compared with the CBC's sixty stations, thirteen of which were part of its French network.

Another area in which Canadian broadcasting followed a British lead was in restricting the amount of U.S. programs on its networks. In order to blunt criticisms that television was "Americanizing" the nation's culture, British stations voluntarily agreed to restrict American program imports to 14 percent of their schedule. Despite this restriction, U.S. programs have always been a popular element in prime-time evening schedules of British stations. The Canadian government sought to assure a dominant role for local programing by requiring that 55 percent of TV program schedules be Canadian in origin. Despite this restriction a 1965 survey of Canadian TV schedules indicated that, during prime evening viewing hours, less than a third of the pro-team offerings were Canadian. The rest were largely American imports.[14] In September, 1965, the Fowler Committee, appointed by the government to study Canadian broadcasting, issued a report recommending revision of the country's broadcast regulatory system. The new system, the report noted, should have power to correct the serious imbalance of trivial entertainment shows from the United States on prime-time Canadian television.

Another Commonwealth country, Australia, has also adopted the British mixture of commercial and noncommercial television. The primary difference between the two countries in this field is that while the BBC offers strong competition to its commercial rivals, Australia's state-chartered network attracts a small minority of viewers. Relying heavily on imported American shows, the country's thirty-four commercial stations virtually monopolize the medium.

Outside of France and the Scandinavian countries, most Western European countries have adopted some form of single state-supervised network in which commercial advertising is permitted. This format, with local variations, was developed successfully in Italy, Finland, Ireland, Austria, Switzerland, and Portugal. (The only two countries on the continent with wholly private television operations are Luxembourg and Monaco.) An indication of the commercial pressures involved in this evolution can be seen in the case of Switzerland. In 1957, when the Swiss government was debating how to develop its experimental TV system, a local commercial combine offered to pay the new television service up to three million francs a year for a half-hour's advertising time each day. The Swiss Association of Newspaper Publishers and other interests reportedly made a counter offer of two million francs a year for ten years if the proposed TV service would not take advertising during that time. The newspaper proprietors were understandably worried about TV's effect on their own advertising revenues.[15] After years of debate the issue was finally resolved in 1965 with the introduction of full-fledged commercial advertising on the state network.

West German television is unique among European systems in its reliance on self-regulating regional stations operating independently of central government supervision. This policy had its origins in a 1945 Allied occupation order requiring all broadcasting activities in the defeated nation to be organized on a regional basis. The order was designed to prevent the rise of a centralized broadcast service similar to the one Hitler had used so effectively as a propaganda instrument before the war. German television got started on the wrong foot—Hitler's. Although Nazi broadcasting was limited primarily to radio, Hitler was fascinated by television's propaganda possibilities. He encouraged early German television efforts, which involved thrice-weekly experimental broadcasts by 1935. The German dictator had grandiose plans for mass distribution of home receivers and for public "viewing rooms" where the populace could watch government propaganda programs on wall-sized screens. A start toward developing such a system was made in the late 1930's but wartime pressures on the German electronics industry later forced the cancellation of all television projects.

Although the Allied occupation edict on regional broadcasting was ignored in the Soviet Zone, it set the pattern for postwar radio and television in the rest of Germany. First priority was given to the development of regional radio organizations, based largely on new FM techniques. When television's turn came in the early 1950's, it was also developed at the *land* level. (A German *land* is the rough equivalent of an American state.) The first West German television station, Nordwest Deutscher Rundfunk (NWDR), went on the air on Christmas Day, 1952. Within two years television stations were broadcasting in all parts of the Federal Republic of Germany.

The new regional TV stations were set up under regulations intended to give all segments of German public opinion some voice in their operations. The chief supervisory organ for each station is a broadcasting council (*Rundfunkrat* or *Hauptausschuss*) which sets general policy on administration, fiscal affairs, and program operations. The council members generally include representatives of political parties, labor and business groups, and cultural, educational, religious, and professional groups. They select the station's administrative board (*Verwaltungsrat*) which supervises current administrative operations. This group usually selects the station manager (*Intendant*) who operates the station's day-to-day activities. This unique triparitite control arrangement provides a framework for what is possibly the best example to date of a national television system responsive to its viewer's full needs. There are, as we shall see below, defects in the system but they do not obscure the fact that West German television has successfully steered a middle course between the excesses of unbridled commercialism and stifling government controls.

In the absence of federal broadcasting regulations, German broadcasters set up a national consortium to handle relations between individual stations, particularly in network programing. Known as ARD from its German name (Arbeitsgemeinschaft der offentlich-rechtlichen Rundfunkanstalten der Bundesrepublik Deutschland), the new organization's structure reflected the wariness of German broadcasters in surrendering any of their local independence to a national body. ARD is a nonprofitmaking facilitative group without permanent headquarters. Its secretariat is rotated among member stations on an annual basis. By 1960 ARD had as members nine regional television organizations collectively making up the First German Television Network. ARD stations were originally financed by a monthly license fee charged to each television set owner. In 1956 these funds were supplemented for the first time by commercial advertising receipts.

In 1959 the regional character of West German television was threatened by the attempt of Chancellor Konrad Adenauer's government to regulate broadcasting at the national level. The bill submitted to the Parliament also provided for a second federally chartered network. Although *land* representatives would have had some voice in the operations of the new network, they objected to what they regarded as Bonn interference in a *land* function.

When Parliament turned down the bill, the Adenauer government attempted to negotiate a separate agreement with the local states. With the failure of this scheme, the government set up a private limited liability corporation with Chancellor Adenauer as sole stockholder. The new organization, "Free Television," made plans to operate a second German TV network. This effort was declared unconstitutional by the federal court in February,

1961, after an estimated nine million dollars had been spent by the company. In the ensuing debate on the disposition of Free Television's facilities the *land* governments decided to set up a new network in competition with ARD. The Second German Television (ZDF—Zweites Deutsches Fernsehn) network was given an administrative framework which paralleled to a large degree the tripartite controls governing ARD stations. Like the first network it is financed by a combination of license fee receipts and commercial advertising.[16]

The new network began regular broadcast operations on the UHF band in April, 1963. Its early years were marked by heavy financial deficits, compounded by the need to liquidate the losses incurred by the ill-fated Adenauer "Free Television" project. However, ZDF quickly took its place in the German television pattern. Meanwhile, the rival ARD stations proceeded with plans to introduce so-called third programs concentrating on cultural and educational productions.

In 1965 the number of television sets in West Germany passed the ten million mark, strengthening TV's claim to be the most accessible and most influential of all German media. However, the unique lesson of German television has been its general success in serving its audiences without undue pressure from political or economic sources. Commercial pressures on programing are a negligible factor because TV advertising is completely separated from the rest of the program schedule: the commercials are all crammed into a single twenty-minute period each night except Sundays. Political pressures are blunted by the autonomy of each station and the checks-and-balances factors built into its administrative structure. Decisions on the scope and content of German TV programing are largely in the hands of professionals. The result is a television schedule that provides, over and above the usual diet of sports and light entertainment, an unusually high percentage of programs designed to serve the upper levels of its audience's tastes. At times this has involved controversial programs which were, politically and commercially, "bad box office." West German TV has, for instance, taken the lead among all national media in dramatically depicting the Hitler regime and, in particular, the fate of German Jews under

Nazi rule. At another level, German television is a leading patron of modern drama not only of Germany but from throughout the Western world. It is safe to say that the ARD network has presented more plays by the best contemporary U.S. playwrights in recent years than any American network.

West German television is not without its defects. To an outsider, its programing often seems cold and impersonal, with perhaps too much emphasis on unadorned, long-winded talk. Domestic commentators cite these and other alleged faults in their attempts to discount German TV's public-service record. The most telling of these criticisms in recent years has centered around a series of incidents involving alleged political interference in the program operations of West German television stations. In most instances, the cases involved attempts to censor news and commentaries, particularly the popular "political cabaret" satire shows.[17] Despite the safeguards erected against such pressures, West German television is not completely free from pressure groups seeking to manipulate the medium for their own purposes.

Such obstacles are inevitable for a medium as influential as the West Germans have made their television. It is possibly the most sophisticated expression of TV's potential in the world today. On the one hand, it has generally avoided the Auntie-knows-best tendencies of government television as well as the frantic search for lowest-common-denominator programing which characterizes much of commercial broadcasting's search for big audiences. The significance of this is not whether the managers of West German TV have always been right in their program judgements but that they have considerable leeway to carry out their own ideas about television's role in German life. Thus West German TV comes closer than any of its counterparts throughout the world to being a cultural force, presenting a full range of ideas and events to its audiences, not simply a narrow spectrum selling a politician or a bar of soap.

A number of other European countries have benefited from the German approach to television. Notable among these has been

Italy, where television has been extremely popular since its introduction in 1956. Although there were fewer than six million television sets in Italy in 1965, average nightly listening audiences ran as high as thirty million persons because of the habit of placing sets in bars, coffeehouses, town squares, and other public places. Italian television and radio is operated by RAI, a private joint-stock company owned largely by the Italian government. RAI operates two television channels, one aimed at popular audiences, the other at a more intellectual level. The popular channel features a full range of what has come to be the international pattern of television—quiz shows, films, American serials, women's and children's programs. The second channel presents an uninhibitedly high-brow schedule—a nightly three-hour presentation of recitals, operas, dramatic productions, and documentaries. (One of the illusion-destroying facts about Italian television, however, is that operatic programs are not particularly popular on either channel.) Italian televiewers pay a stiff license fee—the equivalent of twenty dollars a year—for the privilege of owning a television set. These revenues are supplemented for RAI by commercial advertising, most of which is lumped together in a short nightly segment called "Carosello" ("Carrousel"). It is a tribute to people's willingness to be persuaded that "Carosello" is consistently the most popular feature on Italian television.

Television's greatest expansion outside the North Atlantic area has taken place in Japan. With almost twenty million receivers serving an audience of ninety million persons, Japanese television is second only to American TV in size and influence. In large part, the medium's spectacular growth was a natural development for the largest consumer-oriented economy in the Eastern world. Another factor which sets Japanese television apart is its relationship to the strong national urge for enlightenment and self-improvement. Although the Japanese television viewer turns to his set for entertainment—complete with singing commercials—in much the same way as his Western counterpart, he also has a particular respect for the ability of his television set to educate him. His attitude is partly traceable to traditional attitudes toward learning and partly to the extraordinary push which Japan has made in the mass education field during the past fifteen years.[18] Significantly, Japan has developed its educational television system to a far greater extent than any other country in the world.

The Japanese had developed a television capability before World War II in order to provide coverage of the 1940 Olympic Games scheduled to be held in Tokyo. The games were called off because of the European war and so was the television project as Japan stepped up her own militarist course. During the late 1940's a group of Japanese businessmen headed by newspaper publisher Matsutaro Shoriki petitioned American occupation authorities for permission to resume television on a commercial basis. The request was turned down on the grounds that television was inappropriate at a time when the Japanese economy was being guided through a period of austerity. However, in June, 1950, American authorities set a new pattern for postwar broadcasting in the country by approving a regulation which ended the traditional broadcast monopoly. The ruling permitted commercial stations to compete for the first time against the government-chartered Nippon Hosai Kyokai (NHK) system. When U.S. occupation rule ended in 1952, the Shoriki group took its television plans to the new government. In July, 1952, the group was authorized to operate Japan's first commercial TV station. Although NHK had started a small television operation of its own earlier, NHK officials did not plan for a rapid expansion in the medium. At the time there were only three thousand sets in operation in the Tokyo area.[19]

The Shoriki group's Nippon Television Network (NTV) decided to deal with this lack of television sets and viewers by creating an audience as quickly as possible. When it began regular broadcasts in August, 1953, it made all of Tokyo television-conscious by setting up large-screen receivers in hundreds of public places throughout the city. Although a year later there were only 16,000 sets in the Tokyo area, literally millions of people had become accustomed to the new medium through NTV's outdoor receivers. Their appetites were whetted by what they saw, particularly the professional baseball games televised from Korakuen Stadium, Tokyo's equivalent of Yankee Stadium.[20] Television soon moved from Toyko public squares into millions of Japanese homes all over the country. By the end of 1960 over 7,000,000 sets were in operation, served by 128 stations. Through the sixties television rode the crest of a booming consumer economy; it was also encouraged by liberal government broadcasting regulations, an electronics industry capable of turning out inexpensive sets, and, last but not least, the intangible Japanese urge for self-enlightenment. There are as many ETV stations in Japan as there are regular stations in any single Western European country.

The only national network in Japan consists of the fifty-eight stations operated by NHK, the state-chartered broadcasting company. NHK's administrative structure and operating procedures are roughly comparable to those of the BBC. Like the BBC, its revenues are derived from an annual tax levied on all radio and television receivers. It also shares the BBC attributes of being prestigious and highly conscious of its independent status and its public enlightenment responsibilities. Typically, NHK operates a research institute which provides it with a more accurate continuing profile of its audiences than is available to any other television system in the world.

Japanese commercial television, comprising forty-six stations, is centered around four Tokyo "key stations" and, to a lesser extent, several other Osaka stations. Commercial companies are not permitted to own more than one station. As a result, commercial network operations involve a complex series of affiliations between the big-city key stations and smaller provincial outlets. It is not unusual for the smaller stations to be affiliated with several Tokyo key stations throughout the day. In this way they share in the lucrative revenues from network advertising. In 1965 commercial stations shared over 30 percent of the billion-dollar Japanese advertising market, second only to the 37 percent share going to newspapers. Their program emphasis is on light entertainment shows, many of them adaptations of such American TV perennials as quiz shows, amateur contests, soap operas, and cooking classes. American serials such as "Perry Mason" and "Disneyland" are extremely popular; at one point in 1962 "Dr. Ben Casey" was the highest-rated program in audience polls. However, the most popular programs are locally produced, with sports usually high on the list. Japanese fans get a full schedule of wrestling, boxing, volleyball, and, of course, *besu-boru*.[21]

Japanese television established its full credentials as a major power on the international media scene during the 1964 summer Olympics in Tokyo. NHK assigned six thousand of its thirty-five thousand employees to the task of covering the games for its own network as well as providing facilitative services to foreign television crews. The network demonstrated its technical virtuosity by inaugurating an automated studio which operated several unmanned cameras by remote control. It also used for the first time a TV camera with a half-inch vidicon tube, all of it in a case no bigger than a still camera. NHK's imaginative coverage of the Olympics, seen via communications satellite and films in dozens of countries, was a preview of the day when Japanese television would be playing a larger role in international TV exchanges. The Japanese government underscored this point in 1965 when it announced plans for launching a Japanese communications satellite.[22]

The initial decade of television's remarkable expansion in Europe and Japan had at least three important lessons for the future of television. The first of these was the rapidity with which traditional government broadcasting policies were modified to accommodate the new medium. With few exceptions the trend has been for governments to surrender important prerogatives in this field. In a few cases local commercial interests have been granted direct control of television broadcasting outlets, with only nominal government supervision. In most instances, however, governments have relied on some blend of government control over a commercially oriented television operation. Even in those cases where the government exercises direct control, a subtle erosion of its authority becomes apparent as powerful economic forces seek to bend broadcasting policies to the benefit of their advertising investment.

The second lesson of television's growth in Europe and Japan has been that television quickly becomes available to all segments of society. This was the American experience in the late forties and early fifties, but there was at least some reason to doubt that it would occur overseas. By 1960 these doubts were dispelled; the most striking proof came from a 1959 Japanese survey which indicated that almost 70 percent of that country's TV set owners earned less than a thousand dollars a year and that 15 percent earned less than five hundred dollars. Throughout Europe as well, TV was no respecter of class or income levels.

This fact, in turn, reflected the most important lesson television has taught. This is the manner in which it reflected postwar desires of a new middle class and of those who aspired to middle-class status. The new medium not only mirrored these desires; it also magnified them through its ability to visualize them attractively. The trend toward permitting commercial advertising gave added emphasis to television's sight-and-sound vision of a new middle-class world.

Each of these lessons had important implications for the medium's expansion beyond Europe and Asia into the so-called underdeveloped areas. By 1960 this expansion was well under way; hundreds of television stations were operating in dozens of Latin American, African, and Asian countries. We will examine next how this development took place, how much of it resulted from American and European influences, and what it has meant for these countries.

3

East of Suez, South
of the Rio Grande

It is evening in Bangkok, and darkness has begun to settle among the tall palm trees along the canals. The small canal boats, paddled by women in colorful *panung* dresses, make way for the long commuter launches coming from the center of the city. In the launches men in white shirts, girls in Western cotton dresses, and Buddhist monks in saffron robes hold up umbrellas against the light rain. From among the stilt-legged houses along the canal come the evening's noises—a baby's cries, the moan of a water buffalo, the rattle of cooking pots, and the steady staccato of gunfire.

No one is alarmed by the gunfire. Almost every house along the canal is topped by a television antenna leading down to a set in the common room where a half-dozen wide-eyed children are watching the bad men meet their fate in an American cowboy serial. Later, when the children are chased off to bed, their elders will gather before the set to view a schedule of wrestling, quiz shows, American adventure stories, and news programs. If it is a typical evening, almost half of Bangkok's 1.8 million citizens will have looked at television presented by the city's two stations before the day closes.

Bangkok's addiction to television is an outsized example of television's rapid expansion in the so-called underdeveloped areas of the world. By all the textbook rules of economic development, television is a luxury that most Asian, African, and Latin American countries would be better off without at their present stage of development. However, the textbook rules do not always apply. Not only has television become a significant media factor in dozens of underdeveloped countries, but there is a growing body of evidence to suggest that, although it started off as a luxury, it may develop as a revolutionary force for upgrading educational and informational standards. However, the promise of future developmental benefits should not obscure the fact that present-day television in Asia, Africa, and Latin America is largely an entertainment medium. As in Western countries, it is the medium's compelling attractiveness as a leisure-time force, rather than its direct educative potential, that has set the pace of its growth.

Television has expanded quickly throughout the underdeveloped world. Ten years ago it was restricted to a few Latin American countries, primarily Argentina, Brazil, Mexico, and Cuba. By 1965, nearly every country in the world, except for a few African enclaves, either had television or had announced intentions to get it. Some of these plans often seemed more symbolic than serious: it is easy to be cynical about the reported intentions of a handkerchief-sized African republic to build a television network. The cynicism is mitigated by the fact that more than a dozen African countries already have operating television systems. A significant hold-out against television on the African continent is the most industrialized country on the continent, South Africa.

Most Latin American countries have had television since the late 1950's. In the Middle East the pace has been slower but by 1965 every country in the area had television either in operation or in direct prospect. Television's growth has been slowest in South Asia, due in large part to political instability in the former French territories in Indo-China and to the delays in introducing television in the area's two largest countries, India and Pakistan. By way of statistical summary, television is already operating in more than sixty of the eighty free countries of Asia, Africa, and Latin America; of the rest, fifteen can reasonably be expected to have operating systems by 1970. The remaining handful of countries, for internal reasons of one sort or another, will remain outside the pale of the media revolution for some time.

Although radio and the press continue their lively expansion, their over-all influence is being modified profoundly with the introduction of television. Radio in particular will continue to expand rapidly in Asia and Africa, due in large part to the introduction of cheap, simple transistorized sets. However, every indication points to television as the medium to which most people in these areas will increasingly devote their time and attention in the next years, to the exclusion of the older media. Television will be introduced to audiences who have been virtually untouched by the more traditional mass media. Here is the ultimate in its influence: where it is the instrument for bringing the modern world—from the news to "I Love Lucy"—to villagers who had previously relied on the wisdom of village elders. Less dramatic but more extensive is the impact of television on urban audiences, where it provides a nightly potpourri of frivolity and seriousness.

One constant theme that runs through the various national reasons for developing television is the prestige factor. Television is high on the list of "proofs" of modernism in Asia, Africa, and Latin America. Just as automobiles were a more common household necessity than bathtubs at one stage of American history, so television is expanding in nations where human needs call for new priorities. The mythology of modern times will not be denied, and it applies to television's development in countries which might better spend the money on hospitals or water systems. Its influence as a factor in keeping up with the Joneses can be seen in such situations as those in the slums of Buenos Aires where most of the ramshackle houses have antennas sprouting from their roofs. The poignant fact is that many of these antenna-tipped houses have no television sets inside.[1]

A spur to television's expansion in underdeveloped areas has been the demand for it by European communities in these areas. This accounts for the inauguration of television in former colonial areas such as Morocco, Kenya, and Rhodesia. It also explains television's development in such cities as Beirut and Hong Kong where there are large colonies of well-to-do Westerners. In most of these instances, however, the audience pattern is shifting from reliance on the local "European" population to a broader base in which a native listenership is predominant. This can be seen most clearly in the case of Hong Kong, where television developed as a commercial wired service, *i.e.*, transmissions were provided, for a fee, to individual homes on a closed-circuit system. At first, the audience was drawn largely from British and other European communities. By 1962, however, the balance had swung to Chinese families. The change inevitably led to programing shifts—less reliance on programs from American and British sources, with corresponding increases in Chinese programs in the Cantonese dialect. Similar changes are taking place in other "European" stations throughout Asia and Africa. However, European audiences played an important role during the 1950's in introducing television to these areas and hastening its development in nearby countries.

Commercial considerations have also been important in the spread of television. Whatever the prestige yearnings for television may have been during the 1950's, they were unrealistic until someone determined how to turn these dreams into the local equivalent of dollars. The chronology of television's growth in underdeveloped areas has been established almost exclusively by the combination of prestige and caste. This growth took place in three stages. The first, from 1950 to 1960, involved those countries—mostly in Latin America—where local business interests successfully gambled on television's capabilities as a money-making proposition. They faced the difficulty of high initial investment without hope of large immediate returns. Although this is not a combination which generally attracts the freewheeling investors in these countries, the willingness of some groups to invest in television on a long-term basis paid off handsomely. This pattern, pioneered in Latin America, was repeated sucessfully in other parts of the world, notably in the Philippines, Lebanon, Iran, and Nigeria.

By 1960, the pattern of local investment in television began to change, and the second stage of television's expansion began. This was keyed primarily to smaller countries where local business capital was unwilling or uninterested in television as a commercial enterprise. Their investment role was eagerly taken up by outside interests, notably from the U.S., Britain, and Japan. Although the operating techniques of the three countries were often different, their motivations were almost identical. In each case, they represented firms from industrially advanced countries where television had stabilized at a fairly high level and where commercial television companies faced the problem of a slowdown in the rapid rate of expansion which had characterized their operations in the 1950's. The only area of expansion for their operations was overseas, and they began moving into this field with an aggressive scramble that has eliminated most of the blank areas on the map of world television. The result has been to force the pace of development in areas where, in less competitive circumstances, television would have been merely a hope for the undefined future. In general, Japanese interests have concentrated on Southeast Asia, the British have moved into Africa, while American companies have been aggressive all over the world, with a special interest in Latin America.

The third stage of television's expansion in underdeveloped areas involves those countries which continue to adopt a wait-and-see attitude regarding the new medium. Their unwillingness to turn over their television operations to commercial operators, either local or foreign, makes the introduction of television less likely, except on an experimental "pilot" basis, for several years. India has been the primary example of a country where this attitude prevailed, although by 1965 the Indian viewpoint was changing. To get a closer perspective on the status of TV throughout the underdeveloped countries, it will be useful to trace its progress in specific places.

Latin America was the first testing ground for the development of television outside the industrialized North Atlantic countries. Within a short time in 1950 and 1951, television stations in four countries—Mexico, Brazil, Cuba, and Argentina—went on the air. Each of the new stations was operated by commercial interests with no governmental connections except in the case of Argentina. The first Latin American station was Mexico City's XH-TV, which began broadcasting August 31, 1950, as one of the business enterprises of financier Romulo O'Farrill. Although its audience was small, XH-TV was successful enough to attract two competitors within a year. The result was overcompetition which came close to bankrupting all three enterprises before they decided to merge in 1955 to form the nucleus of Mexico's national commercial network, Telesistima Mexicano. Within two years all the stations were out of the red, and Mexican television began to expand rapidly. By 1965, Telesistima Mexicano had two microwave networks covering 80 percent of the country's population.

The same pattern of commercial television was repeated, with variations, during the early years in Brazil, Cuba, and Argentina. In each case, television's initial success led to a scramble for commercial television outlets which threatened to bankrupt everyone concerned. This was particularly true in Cuba where, even in pre-Castro days, television coverage was one of the most intensive in the world. (Cuba was the first country in the world where television was available to the entire population.) By the time Castro had seized power in 1958, the little island had twenty-four television stations, six of them in Havana.[2] The entrepreneurial genius behind Cuban TV was a Havana businessman, Goar Mestre, who developed the island's largest network. Although Mestre relied heavily, as did all of his competitors, on filmed programs imported from the United States, he realized that the key to audience—and, therefore, commercial—success was live entertainment programs, featuring local artists. His stations exploited this concept with a flair that gave pre-Castro television a special niche in the history of international television. All this changed with the 1958 Fidelista takeover. The Cuban dictator was to demonstrate another aspect of television's possibilities, *i.e.*, as a tool for imposing totalitarian rule on a nation.[3] (Castroite TV is described in fuller detail in Chapter 6.)

Meanwhile, the television stations which had been established in the early 1950's in Brazil, Argentina, and Venezuela were demonstrating both the possibilities and pitfalls of the medium's development in semi-industrialized countries. In each case, TV's popularity was affirmed almost immediately. The problem was to make it an economic success by increasing the audience to the point where it became a significant advertising medium. This in turn meant increasing the number of sets available among groups below the thin upper-income crust. In the United States and in Europe this happened fairly quickly after the initial introduction of television services, primarily because the middle classes were affluent enough to invest in television sets.

The process moved more slowly in the Latin American countries where television was first introduced. The problem was complicated by the fact that, throughout the 1950's, all television equipment had to be imported, thus creating a "luxury drain" on foreign exchange balances. The expansion of television was often slow, but it never was in danger of being stopped. Brazil, which had begun commercial telecasting in São Paulo in September, 1950, had 10 transmitters in operation serving 850,000 sets by the end of the decade, together with the beginnings of a nationwide microwave relay network. Television in Venezuela had the advantage of serving a highly concentrated population in the Caracas-Maracaibo area. After a relatively slow start in the early 1950's, transmitters in this area were serving receivers in half the households of Caracas and Maracaibo by 1965.

Among the larger Latin American countries, development of television was slowest in Argentina which as late as 1960 had only one station—Radio Belgrano-TV—in Buenos Aires. Although the station began broadcasting in 1951 ostensibly as a private operation, it was under heavy government pressure from the Peron dictatorship which not only subsidized the station but operated its transmitter from the Ministry of Public Works.[4] Political instability in the post-Peron period inhibited any large-scale expansion of television until after 1960 when three private stations began operations in Buenos Aires. A much-postponed schedule for inaugurating television services outside the capital city was also put into effect. The result was a latter-day spurt in television's influence: by 1963 over a million sets were in operation in Buenos Aires, giving that city one of the highest percentages of coverage in the world at the time. A striking instance of Argentinian addiction to television occurred in 1962 when the government decided to shut down all television operations in Buenos Aires because of an electric power shortage. The proposal was withdrawn when the public, encouraged by the TV stations, compaigned to take its power cuts in other forms—including the darkening of the city's streets at night—so that television could continue.[5]

The latter-day resurgence of Argentinian television can be credited to two factors: the investment of American capital, and the appearance on the scene of Goar Mestre, the man who controlled a good share of Cuban television before he was forced to flee from Castro in 1958. Less than three years after he had arrived in Buenos Aires, he was the undisputed leader of the burgeoning Argentinian television industry.

His formula in Argentina was similar to the one he used in Cuba—strong management control together with a programing operation that emphasized "live" local shows. When his Proartel (Producciones Argentinas de Television) organization began operating its key Buenos Aires station, Channel 13, in 1960, Argentine television programing was dominated by American filmed imports. By the end of 1962, Channel 13 was programing eight hours of live programs daily and taking the lion's share of the audience. (Only one American serial film, "Route 66," remained in the Argentinian "Top Ten" at that time.) By 1963 Proartel expanded into the international field through the sale of Spanish-language program features. A year later, Mestre moved into Venezuelan TV with the opening of a new station in Caracas. Mestre financed his fast-moving operation with the remnants of his own Cuban fortune, combined with local as well as American capital.[6] The Columbia Broadcasting System was a founder-stockholder in Proartel in 1960. Two years later, Time Inc., the publisher of *Time* and *Life,* joined CBS as a minority stockholder. Both firms also participated in financing Mestre's Venezuela project. In bringing in American capital and mass communications known-how, Mestre was following not only his own fiscal instincts but also the lead set by the two other commercial television operations in Buenos Aires. Both the American Broadcasting Company and the National Broadcasting Company had invested in local stations.[7] The pattern of American investment in Latin American stations was to continue spreading TV throughout the continent.

By 1965, little more than ten years after television had begun in Latin America, it was a well-established medium in the larger countries. The bumptious optimism and the false starts of the early years had given way to better management and stronger programing efforts. Television was moving out of the capital cities and was expanding rapidly in provincial areas. By the beginning of 1965, Mexico had twenty-four programing stations in operation, Brazil had thirty-three, Venezuela had six, and late-starting Argentina had eleven. The parallel development to this was, of course, the rise in the number of receivers in operation; television was no longer a rich man's luxury. Both Mexico and Brazil had reached the million mark in receivers by the end of 1961; in Brazil, the number of receivers had increased by half a million in the same year. This growth was being hastened by the opening of production facilities for receivers throughout the continent; by 1965 sets were being produced locally in Argentina, Brazil, and Mexico.

By 1965 there were television operations in every Latin American country except Bolivia and Paraguay.[8] Most operations are under private, commercial arrangements. The major exceptions are Colombia and Chile. The Colombian television network, which began operations in 1954, is a state broadcasting system. Chilean television has been hampered by the country's financial difficulties and the government's classification of the medium as a "luxury." Meanwhile, experimental educational television is being transmitted under the auspices of Chilean universities in Santiago and Valparaiso. Commercial television operations have flourished in such countries as Ecuador, El Salvador, Guatemala, Costa Rica, Panama, Nicaragua, Uruguay, Honduras, Haiti, and the Dominican Republic.

During the 1950's, only two other developing countries, both in Asia—the Philippines and Iran—adopted the Latin American pattern of privately owned commercial television operations.

Television was started in the Philippines in 1953 when Manila's DZAQ-TV went on the air. The station was controlled by the politically and economically powerful Lopez brothers, Eugenio and Fernando, who had parlayed a postwar combination of sugar plantations, radio stations, and cement mills into one of the country's biggest business empires. The Lopez interests later added a second station, DZXL-TV, to their radio-TV chain. Between 1960 and 1962 four other television outlets were inaugurated in Manila in competition with the Lopez stations. This expansion involved political as well as economic factors. There was little reason to have six stations serving fewer than seventy-five thousand sets.

However, television had become an important counter in the political game played by high-level interests in the Philippines. This was particularly true after the unsuccessful second-term bid in 1961 of President Carlos Garcia, who had been backed by the Lopez brothers. With the development of competitive television in Manila, the groundwork was laid for the medium's expansion throughout the country. Although the number of receiving sets in the country was little more than one hundred thousand by 1965, Philippine entrepreneurs were planning to add eight more stations to supplement the thirteen already in operation. Whether the country can continue to sustain such an extensive transmitting operation depends largely on increasing the number of receiving sets by selling cheaper locally produced receivers.

The pattern of television in other parts of Southeast Asia is motley. Two of the largest countries—Thailand and Malaysia—have fully functioning television systems. Indonesia is slowly developing the medium, largely as a propaganda outlet for the Sukarno regime. Elsewhere, television has been slow in taking hold.

Thailand was the first mainland Asian country to have a television system. In 1952 the Thai government authorized an experimental station at Bangkok's Chulalongkorn University which was expanded into full operation as Thai-TV two years later. Although run as a nominally civilian venture, the new station had a strong measure of government supervision. By 1960 a second channel, operated by the Thai army, began transmissions. With both stations relying on advertising revenues they quickly became highly competitive. Over and above the perennial local program favorite—boxing matches—both channels rely heavily on American filmed serials to attract audiences in Bangkok and in areas north and south of the capital where relay stations transmit their programs over a network that serves an audience of over one million viewers. In 1964 plans were announced for a nationwide microwave link which would make television available to 90 percent of the country's population within three years.

Malaysian television went on the air in 1963 with stations in Singapore and in the capital city of Kuala Lumpur. Although the stations served fewer than fifty thousand receivers by 1965, the Malaysian government has plans for extending TV facilities to all states of the Federation. Both the station in Kuala Lumpur and the one in newly independent Singapore rely heavily on American film serials which make up about 60 percent of their program schedule. However, there is an increasingly heavy budget of local programs, including the beginnings of an attempt to utilize television for both child and adult educational purposes. The Malaysian government has indicated that it sees television as a unifying force in a country of many cultures and languages. The language problem is handled by broadcasting programs in one language with subtitles in another and simultaneous commentary on a separate radio frequency in a third.[9]

Indonesian television was inaugurated during the Asian Games in Djakarta in August, 1962. Although it had gotten off to a slow start, TV in Indonesia has begun to pick up momentum since 1964 as a result of the interest President Sukarno has shown in the medium. A fifty-thousand-watt Japanese transmitter was put into operation in Djakarta in 1965; the key apparatus in Indonesian television, however, is the mobile unit, which covers almost all of Sukarno's public appearances. There is little doubt that television would quickly become a major medium in the country if the government's elaborate plans for a national network were not held up by chaotic economic conditions. Many of the fifty thousand sets in the country reportedly have been smuggled in from Singapore and other nearby port cities. However, several

Indonesian companies have also begun to assemble sets locally from imported Japanese parts.

Television has been in a retarded state of development in Burma and in the countries which were formed from French Indo-China. The Burmese have shown almost no interest in introducing TV. A similar situation prevails in Laos and Cambodia, although the latter country had a brief fling with the medium in 1963 when a Japanese firm put up an experimental station in Phnom Penh. The Japanese reportedly backed away from their attempt to sell a television system to the Cambodians after going through months of governmental indecision and other frustrations.

The question of introducing television into South Viet Nam has centered largely around the medium's possible value in the war effort there. Proponents of the medium's use have cited its value as a communications weapon for the central government in Saigon to establish better contact with its citizens in provincial areas. Those skeptical of the proposal emphasize the difficulties the Saigon government has had in setting up a radio network throughout the country; they also cite the problems involved in distributing and maintaining television sets in outlying areas. In the past, American officials in Saigon and Washington have reacted warily to proposals for extensive U.S. assistance in developing a TV system in Viet Nam.[10] Late in 1965 the Vietnamese government indicated it was prepared to build a television network with outside help. One of the factors which may have influenced the Saigon leaders was the fact that Communist North Viet Nam had announced that it was obtaining a television transmitter from Hungary.[11]

The Republic of China on Taiwan enjoys the highest standard of living of any country in Asia, excluding Japan. Television has been part of this pattern since October, 1962, when the island's first channel began transmissions. Operated as a commercial venture under government license, Taiwan Television Enterprises lost money during its first two years of operation, but by the end of 1965 it attracted sufficient viewers and advertisers to overcome this handicap. As with most other stations in the area, a large percentage of its programing consists of American film serials.

Korean television has been in operation considerably longer than the Taiwan station but it has been bedeviled by the gap between its high operating costs and the nation's low living standards. The American armed forces have operated a network since 1957 which has had a large Korean "look-in" audience from the start. A local effort to develop the medium antedates the American network; in 1956 a commercial station went on the air only to be curtailed almost immediately by a fire that destroyed its studios. It was able to resume full-scale programing several years later, this time in competition with a government-operated station. Although television is popular among Koreans, the country had fewer than 50,000 sets in 1965 after ten years of TV operations. There was little hope that the medium would expand significantly in future years, with a receiver costing about $350 in local currency—the equivalent of a year's pay for a Seoul taxi driver.[12]

Only one other Asian country, Iran, followed the pattern of locally financed commercial television during the 1950's. In 1958 Tehran financier Habib Sabet was given government permission to open the first TV station in western Asia. The Tehran station was blessed by good timing; the Iranian economy was booming in the wake of the 1954 settlement of the oil-nationalization dispute with Great Britain. Television became one of the symbols of the new affluence. Although most TV sets were limited largely to the well-to-do, the medium was highly popular in working-class cafés where sets were usually perched on a platform high above the heads of the assembled tea drinkers.

By 1959 television in less-developed areas had reached the limits of its expansion as a locally financed commercial medium. Any further growth would require outside help, in money or in technical assistance or both. In some cases local entrepreneurs were reluctant to become involved in the strange new business of television; in other cases local financial and technical resources for developing a TV system simply did not exist. Whatever the reason, the pace of television's development in Asia and Africa since 1959 has been set largely by the willingness of foreign firms to help.

This help was not long in arriving. By 1960, the commercial television industries in the United States, Great Britain, and Japan had reached the point where the prospect of investing in foreign television was becoming increasingly attractive. In each case the home market was close to saturation as far as new investments were concerned. The logical place for investing funds and managerial talent was abroad. For the British and Americans, partnership arrangements with new television operations abroad also had the advantage of guaranteeing them an additional outlet for their own television program products. In a sense, they faced a situation similar to that of the motion-picture industry after the war. Caught between rising production costs and a constricting home market, Hollywood film companies and their British counterparts looked increasingly to overseas markets for revenues. (By the early 1950's, over half of Hollywood's gross income came from overseas operations.) The film industry's earlier search for international markets was duplicated in the late 1950's by the young television industry.

Television's development in free world countries after 1960 has, in large part, been determined by this situation. In three years beginning with 1960, American, British, and Japanese investors had put funds and credits into the television operations of over two dozen countries throughout Asia, Africa, and Latin America. In most cases they were investing in operations being started from the beginning. In a few instances, however, they were putting fresh capital into existing operations.

This was a new field for U.S. and European companies, one in which there was relatively little past experience. As we have seen, several American companies had invested in Latin American stations during the 1950's. The other precedent was a French attempt to develop a commercial network in Morocco in 1954 with stations in Casablanca and Rabat. This project failed, largely because the stations were designed primarily to serve a relatively small European community and not the Arab majority.[13] The American, British, and Japanese television entrepreneurs, with their experience in television as a mass-audience medium, would be careful not to make this particular mistake.

In the free-swinging market for new investments, there was little attempt by the Americans, British, and Japanese to remain in traditional markets. In general, the Americans had first claim on Latin America, the British on former colonial possessions in Africa and South Asia, and the Japanese on the Far East. In fact, however, the three groups ranged far and wide, competing with each other and with the French, Germans, and Italians who were beginning to interest themselves in the overseas television market.[14] There has been, curiously, little attempt by Communist governments to involve themselves in providing financial or technical assistance for television stations in developing countries, despite the possible political and propaganda advantages such assistance might have. Several instances of such assistance have been reported, notably an East German offer to the Indonesian government in October, 1961.[15] It is relevant to note that, by and large, Western governments have also shied away from providing direct technical assistance or other economic aid for television in so-called underdeveloped countries.

The Americans, British, and Japanese have organized their new international television activities in characteristically different ways. The Japanese have been concerned primarily with opening new export markets for their electronics industry. They emphasize the "package deal" for installing television in newly developing countries, centered around easy-credit purchase of studio and transmitting equipment and, in some instances, coupling this with an offer to build Japanese TV receivers locally. The package often includes an offer to provide technical and programing assistance for the new television system. The Japanese have supplemented these efforts by organizing regional broadcasting organizations in Asia. They have been the major element in the development of the Asian Broadcasting Union, a regional organization made up of eleven countries in Asia and the Middle East. In 1962 a group of Japanese electronics firms announced an ingenious proposal for an "Asiavision" TV network that would stretch from Tokyo to Karachi. While their plan undoubtedly included a desire to promote regional unity, it also encompassed the probability that the proposed network would rely heavily upon Japanese fiscal and technical resources.

The British, too, have had a commercial eye out for the export market in their various television proposals in Asia and Africa. Unlike the Japanese, however, they have coupled this interest with a willingness to make direct investments in local television operations. An early leader in this field was London's Rediffusion, Ltd., which had been operating radio stations in British colonies before television came on to the scene. However, the overseas activities of Rediffusion and other commercial British broadcasting firms are dwarfed by those of Canadian-born press tycoon Roy Thomson—or, to give him his newly-acquired title, Lord Thomson of Fleet. The "Fleet" refers to Fleet Street, citadel of British journalism which Roy Thomson invaded in 1959 after a successful career in Canadian media. His flair for upsetting hoary British press practices to meet the country's new middle-class affluence has since been expanded to include press, radio, and television ventures in over twenty countries throughout the world.[16]

The Thomson Organization, Ltd., describes itself, not unreasonably, as "a significant part of the social and economic life" of Great Britain. It and other Thomson affiliates control a total of 135 newspapers and magazines in Britain and abroad, together with a wide variety of projects in such fields as book publishing, teaching machines, computerized typesetting, and secretarial training. Its television operations, centered about the Thomson-owned Scottish Television commercial station in Glasgow, are conducted overseas by Thomson Television International, Ltd. (TTI). Although it has been active for less than a half-dozen years, TTI is perhaps the most significant single Western influence on television in the developing nations of Asia and Africa. It has already helped develop radio and television broadcasting operations in 14 countries throughout the area. By 1970, if its present rate of operations continues, TTI broadcast ventures will affect a potential audience of over 500 million people.

In his public pronouncements about TTI's activities, Thomson shrewdly emphasizes its service to developing nations. Without TTI, he has declared, "a number of the newly-formed nations of the world would have been obliged to turn for assistance to the Communist bloc, who do not share our view that the provision of such technical services should not be regarded as a lever for interference in the political affairs of the countries concerned."[17] This is quite true, as is the fact of TTI's success in attracting profitable business by offering developing countries a full range of technical and program services tailored to local needs. The exact level of TTI's profitability is buried in the over-all profit-and-loss statistics issued by its parent company. It is probable, however, that at the present time TTI is turning in a considerably smaller profit than other Thomson enterprises but that its fiscal potential will grow at a faster pace as television expands throughout Asia and Africa. In the meantime, Roy Thomson has been a major factor in giving Great Britain a place of prominence in the high-stakes international television game.

The other aggressive factor in this game is, of course, the U.S. television industry. Led by the three large national networks, American interests are actively associated with local television in over thirty countries throughout the world. The greatest concentration of these interests is to be found in Latin America, followed by Africa, the Middle East, and Asia. They cover a wide spectrum of activities from providing technical and program services to direct partnership in station control. American firms have had their share of failures in these ventures, due in large part to overenthusiastic early estimates of television's growth potential, combined with poor management practices on the local level. These have been temporary setbacks, however; the overriding fact is that the American television industry has taken an important lead in establishing management and other operational liaisons with its broadcasting counterparts on all continents.

The range of these activities is an impressive one. At the network level, the National Broadcasting Company has concentrated its efforts in providing management and programing services to new stations in over a dozen underdeveloped countries. In 1965 it also had a direct minority investment in thirteen overseas stations in eight countries. The Columbia network has followed a similar pattern. The American Broadcasting Company has been aggressive in organizing television stations in over twenty countries as a programing and advertising cooperative known as "Worldvision." ABC has also been active in buying management shares of TV stations throughout Latin America, the Far East, and the Middle East. These companies, together with a half-dozen smaller firms specializing as international TV consultants, give the United States a long lead as the major foreign influence on the medium in the underdeveloped world. It is useful to take a closer look at the way in which this pattern of foreign influence affected the medium's growth in Asia and Africa after 1959.

Nigeria was the first African country where a combination of foreign and local capital was successfully used to inaugurate a commercial television system. The Nigerian taste for television was whetted in 1956 when closed-circuit television was installed to permit more people to watch the visit of Britain's Queen Elizabeth to the country, then a British colony preparing for independence.[18] Nigeria's television began in October, 1959, in Western Nigeria, one of the country's self-governing regions prior to the formation of a unified Nigeria on a federated basis in 1960. The station, WN-TV ("First in Africa"), was controlled by the Western Nigeria Radiovision Company, with half its stock owned by the regional government and the other half by Overseas Rediffusion Company, Ltd., an affiliate of London's Associated Rediffusion, Ltd.

Nigeria may have seemed to be an unlikely place to begin television in Africa; in fact, it was the most likely. One of the problems television faces in Africa is the lack of big cities to provide an audience base. Nigeria has some of the continent's largest cities—Lagos, Kano, Kaduna, and Ibadan. Prestige factors also played a role in the decision: the Nigerians were well aware that, with independence in 1960, their country would be the most populous in Africa. Their leaders were also intrigued by TV's potential role in raising educational standards in their new nation.

During a visit to the United States, one of them declared: "Your radio and television are mainly intended to uplift and amuse. In Africa today, our big job is to instruct our people in such basics as health, sanitation and nutrition. We don't really need 'Pagliacci' when they are dying of pellagra."[19] However, this enlightened view of the potential of television was tempered by the problem of financing mass-education TV programs.[20]

Television developed primarily as an entertainment medium, with mildly instructional overtones, in Nigeria. Its success in Western Nigeria prompted the eastern and northern regional governments to inaugurate television, financed in part by British interests. After the country became independent in December, 1960, the federal government set up the Federal Television Service and contracted with the National Broadcasting Company of New York to provide management and program services for its key station in Lagos.

By 1965, Nigeria had eight programing and relay stations broadcasting in four cities and serving a total of twenty-five thousand receivers. This was by all odds the most extensive television operation in Africa. Although the programing emphasis on these stations was heavily American, the Nigerians were making a conscious effort to develop their own indigenous forms of television programing. In doing so, they had to compete with the slickness and technical competence of the filmed American shows which dominated the program schedule. Despite this, during television's early years, a number of significant attempts were made to utilize television for the purpose of telling Nigerians about their new nation and its problems and prospects. Typical of these efforts was a documentary series presented by Enugu's Station EN-TV in 1960. Entitled "Customs and Traditions," the series' subjects ranged from a documentary on the changes that improved transportation had made in Nigeria to an exposition of the importance of being efficient in business.

The leader in developing indigenous programs was Lagos' Channel 10, the federal government station. By 1963, 40 percent of its schedule was "local and live," ranging from variety entertainment to special shows for women and children. Working with American program technicians from NBC-New York, the station developed its news and public affairs staff to the point where it was able to market some of its filmed material abroad.[21]

Although the credit for this goes largely to the Nigerian management of the station, it was also a tribute to the work done by NBC-New York's advisers, and in particular their flexibility in guiding their Nigerian colleagues to develop programs which were not carbon copies of American productions but lively reflections of the Nigerians' own flair for telling a story or reporting a news event. NBC's work in Nigeria is perhaps the best example to date of how American commercial television expertise can adapt itself to the needs of underdeveloped countries. The impact of this was expressed by a Nigerian broadcasting official: "Some people were suspicious of the NBC technicians at first, particularly fearing that their purpose was to turn the station into an outlet for American films. In fact, the opposite was true. With their help, Channel 10 has been putting out more local programs than Channel 3, its competitor."[22]

Nigeria's success in inaugurating television set off a lively chain reaction in the rest of Africa during 1960 and 1961. Despite this general enthusiasm, only one other country—the British-controlled Federation of Rhodesia and Nyasaland—had definite plans for television at the time. In the spring of 1960, the Federation's Federal Broadcasting Corporation, a BBC-type operation, signed a fifteen-year agreement with British, American, and local business interests authorizing them to operate a commercial television service. The first station went on the air in Salisbury, the capital city, in November, 1960, and, within a year, two smaller stations were operating in Bulawayo and Kitwe.[23] The service was intended primarily for Rhodesia's ruling white minority, although it attracted from the beginning a significant African "beer hall" audience. Programing on the stations was heavily weighted in favor of American and British filmed material, with local coverage limited largely to news coverage and sports.

However, the new Rhodesian station took a significant step in inaugurating the first scheduled educational telecasting services in Africa. In turning over Rhodesian television to commercial interests, the government specifically reserved the right to utilize part of these television services for educational purposes. During the 1961/62 school year, an experimental schedule of educational telecasting, totaling three hours a week, was broadcast to secondary school classrooms in the Salisbury area. As with regular television programs, the service was intended primarily for the white European community, although a token number of seventeen sets were placed in African high schools.[24]

The Rhodesian decision to direct its programing efforts to a "European" audience set it apart from the main stream of African television development. In 1964 the white minority government nationalized the station as part of its local apartheid program.[25]

Throughout the rest of the continent, television's audience in over a dozen newly independent countries is African. After Nigeria's initial success with the medium, other African nations announced their intention to introduce TV. Ghana took an early lead by authorizing a survey of TV prospects, conducted by Canadian engineers, in 1959. Acting on the Canadian recommendations, the Ghanaian government called for bids for the construction of a fourteen-station network in 1961. The project moved slowly, hampered by fiscal and technical difficulties. Technical assistance was provided by the Canadian Broadcasting Corporation and by the Irish Republic's TV system.[26] Largely because of the leftist orientation of its leadership, Ghana has one of the few noncommercial, government-operated TV systems in independent Africa. Its first station in Accra opened in July, 1965, with considerable fanfare and then settled down to an intermittent programing routine of news, lectures, cultural events, and occasional appearances by President Kwame Nkrumah.

For most of the other new African nations, however, commercial operations are the key to TV development. And, in a significant number of cases, these commercial operations involve the ubiquitous Mr. Roy Thomson who had demonstrated a shrewd knack for providing African governments with attractive answers to their two biggest TV problems—money and program material. Almost all the African states which had rushed forward with promises of television did so with high-minded assurances that what they wanted was some sort of network which would instruct their citizens in the new ways of political independence and economic progress. These intentions soon evaporated under the cold economic facts involved in setting up and operating a non-profit TV system. The Africans quickly concluded that if television was to come, they would have to settle for the commercial, not the educational, model.

Many soon found themselves talking business with Mr. Thomson's negotiators from London. By 1964 the Thomson group had proposed or formed broadcasting enterprises in Ethiopia, Kenya, Sierra Leone, Southern Rhodesia, the Ivory Coast, the Sudan, and Mauritius.[27] In each case the Thomson group arranged a package deal involving the planning, financing, and operation of local television stations. The usual Thomson management and fiscal formula is to form a consortium made up of local financial interests together with Thomson's and other outside funds.[28] In return for its management services the Thomson group usually arranged for the right to serve these stations with filmed programs. By 1963 about two-thirds of the films supplied by the organization to its overseas affiliates were supplied from British sources; the rest were American programs. The Thomson organization also handles the selling of advertising time on its affiliated stations. By the end of 1962 the organization had established advertising-selling operations in Paris, Dusseldorf, Geneva, and other European cities to service, among its other interests, television stations in Africa and other parts of the world.

A specialized form of foreign assistance to African stations is provided by the French government in countries which once formed a part of France's extensive colonial holdings. In an effort to maintain the traditional political and cultural influence it has had in West Africa, France provides its former colonies with extensive technical and program assistance for their radio and television stations. This is done through a quasi-official government organization, l'Office du Coopération Radiophonique.[29]

American commercial involvement in African television has been relatively limited outside of Nigeria. Two American firms, NBC and Twentieth Century-Fox, were minority investors in the consortium which established a television service in Nairobi in November, 1951, when Kenya was still a British colony preparing for independence. In July, 1964, the new Kenyan government ended foreign participation in local broadcasting by nationalizing radio and television.[30] In 1964 an NBC affiliate, NBC Enterprises, was providing contract technical services for the development of television in Sierra Leone.[31] At a more modest level several smaller U.S. firms have successfully worked with new African nations in developing TV systems. Two American engineering organizations were largely responsible for planning and building a national system for Uganda in East Africa.

This American-designed network in Uganda is unique in the manner in which it deals with a key African communications problem—the multiplicity of languages within each country. Uganda television is part of an integrated national telecommunications system with a multiplex capability that permits each of the four major tribal zones to listen to TV in the local language while viewing the same image.[32]

Only one country in Africa is actively resisting the introduction of television. This is South Africa, where a white minority government views the medium as a major political threat to its racial policies. In 1964 a group of South African industrialists, led by Harry F. Oppenheimer, chairman of the powerful Anglo-American Corporation, were reportedly making plans for a local TV system. The report resulted in an official government denial by Dr. Albert Hertzog, Minister of Posts and Telegraph. Dr. Hertzog's statement was a hyperbolic and largely unintended tribute to television's influence:

> The overseas money power has used television as such a deadly weapon to undermine the morale of the white man and even to destroy great empires that Mr. Oppenheimer and his friends will do anything to use it here. They are certain that with this mighty weapon and with South African television largely dependent on British and American films, they will also succeed in a short time in encompassing the destruction of white South Africa.[33]

Despite the government's strong statements about television there are persistent reports from South Africa that local business firms are continuing to make preparations for producing and marketing television equipment within the country. Licensing arrangements reportedly have been signed with British and French firms for local assembly and distribution of TV sets if and when the government relaxes its ban on the medium.

In 1965 television in Africa (not including the Arab countries of North Africa) had expanded to over thirty transmitters operating in fourteen countries. These stations served fewer than three hundred thousand sets, somewhat smaller than the number in Baltimore, Maryland. However, the influence of these stations is considerable—both in their present impact and in their potential role in the not-too-distant days when television will be a common experience for urban Africans. The sudden upsurge of television in Africa during the early 1960's, much of it artificially induced by outside commercial pressures, has obscured any real consideration of the medium's implications for African countries. Is it to be primarily a highly effective advertising device for selling consumer goods to newly affluent urbanized Africans, or will it have a larger role to play as an educator and guide in handling difficult problems of political independence and social modernization? What role can television play in channeling African loyalties from a tribal base to a more complex, less personal national identity? For the time being these questions have largely been pushed aside by the sheer novelty of television itself. Inevitably the novelty will wear off and these larger questions will have to be answered by African leaders and their British and American advisers.[34]

Television has developed unevenly in the Middle East, largely as a result of the area's endemic political instability. The medium was first introduced into the region by British electronics firms who sponsored a closed-circuit system at a 1955 trade fair in Baghdad. The first program telecast was an ice show, complete with clowns and pretty girls, which had been imported for the occasion. A highlight of the inaugural show was the attempt of one of the attending local notables to run out on to the ice to get a closer look at the lightly clad chorus line. He slipped and went skidding across the icy stage, burnoose flying, missing his target. Iraqi television soon settled down to less spectacular program events. With the aid of British and American technicians, the government began regular transmissions two years later. The station was in operation only a short time when the ruling monarchy was overthrown and an anti-Western revolutionary government installed. Television was turned into a propaganda outlet for the new regime, a development which was given an ironic twist in 1963 when the revolutionary government was overthrown and the bullet-riddled bodies of its leaders were displayed on Baghdad TV as proof that they were indeed deposed. Since that time, however, Iraqi television has regained much of its former promise as an educational and entertainment medium.[35]

Most Near Eastern television projects have followed the Iraqi pattern of relying on Western assistance for their development. Lebanon's two television stations have each been financed and managed by consortiums of local and Western interests. The first attempt to introduce TV took place in 1956 when the Ford Foundation, working with Beirut's École des Arts et Métiers, tried to set up an educational station. The project foundered and the country turned to commercial sources for its television needs. The first commercial station, operated by the Compagnie Libanaise de Télévision (CLT), began operations in 1959. Its management affairs are controlled by Beirut interests who also rely on assistance from ORTF, the French government's broadcasting organization. The ORTF contribution is part of a long-standing interest by the French government in maintaining its cultural influence in Lebanon. The local managers of the other Beirut station, opened in 1962, have fiscal and management arrangements with British and American interests. One of these is the Roy Thomson organization; another is the American Broadcasting Company. For several years, Time-Life Broadcasting, the radio-TV division of Time Inc., owned a minority interest in CLT.

American technical and programing know-how have been important factors in the development of the medium in Saudi Arabia. Television has been long regarded as an unwanted infidel device by the country's conservative religious leadership. In 1962, Crown Prince (later King) Faisal moved to amend this prohibition. He reportedly had been impressed by the medium's effectiveness several years earlier, while recovering from an operation at a Boston hospital. Television was not, however, new to his country: a station has been operated by the Arabian-American Oil Company (ARAMCO) for its employees since the late 1950's.

The King requested assistance from the U.S. government which later made a corps of engineers unit available to construct two small stations in Jiddah and in Riyadh, the capital.[36] However, the basic responsibility for developing a planned thirteen-station national network has been given by the Saudi government to NBC International of New York.

The first station was scheduled to begin operation on April 1, 1965, but the day came and went without any transmissions, reportedly because of the continuing opposition of conservative religious leaders. The King was said to have pointed out to them that the Koran, sacred book of the Muslim religion, did not specifically ban television and therefore the medium should be allowed. The *ulema* (religious leaders) apparently were not placated by this argument.[37] It is probable that television will soon get under way in Saudi Arabia, however, giving the King and his advisers a potentially important communications tool for their program of social and political modernization for the country.[38]

American, British, and other Western interests are involved in television's development in a half-dozen other Middle Eastern countries. Kuwaiti television, one of the most technically advanced systems in the area, is largely the work of American engineers. The Roy Thomson organization has a major interest in the medium's development in the South Arabian Federation. Television on Cyprus was inaugurated by British commercial interests in the late 1950's while that country was still a crown colony. The French have a major interest in the medium's growth in Algeria, Tunisia, and Morocco. Israeli television, limited largely to educational broadcasting, is the result of a gift of a transmitter and other facilities from the Rothschild banking family. (A detailed account of Israeli television is given in Chapter 10.)

The largest TV system in the area, in the United Arab Republic, is in part the result of Western assistance. In December, 1959, the Nasser regime signed an agreement with the U.S. government which made available the equivalent of 12.6 million dollars in American-held Egyptian currency to pay for the local costs of building an Egyptian TV network. The agreement was, and still is, the only instance in which the American government has provided large-scale financial assistance for a foreign television system.

The Egyptians began telecasts from Cairo in 1960. Alexandria and other cities in the Nile delta region were linked with the Cairo station during the next two years. Television was also inaugurated in Damascus, then the capital city of the United Arab Republic's "northern region" after Egypt and Syria had agreed to political union. In the fall of 1961, when a *coup d'état* returned the northern region to its original status as independent Syria, Damascus television was reduced to makeshift operations because of the withdrawal of Egyptian technicians.[39] Since then Syrian TV has been gradually built up with additional stations in Homs and Tartous. Meanwhile, in Egypt television was enjoying a boom limited only by the shortage of sets. Its popularity became more marked after the original Cairo channel, featuring Arabic programing, was supplemented in 1961 by a second channel with a schedule that relied more heavily on American and other Western materials. The second channel quickly became the more popular of the two, a situation which led to criticism of the possible negative effects of so much Western influence on the concepts of "Arab socialism" and positive neutralism in international affairs—two major ideological themes of the UAR's President, Gamal Abdel Nasser. The Nasser regime's decision to give major emphasis to television as an instrument of both political propaganda and social modernization is one of the more fascinating episodes in the early history of international television. It is described in more detail in Chapter 6.

Several other countries in the area have delayed the introduction of television, usually because of domestic controversy on how it should be done. In 1965, the Greek, Jordanian, and Turkish governments each announced plans for developing the medium, ending a long period of indecision on the subject in each country.

The two major international television holdouts were India and Pakistan. With their combined populations of almost six hundred million persons, the omission was a significant one. The Pakistan government gave general support to the idea of a television service in its western and eastern regions in the late 1950's but it did little to implement the policy. A false start toward introducing the medium was made in the autumn of 1962 when two Western firms, Time-Life Broadcasting of New York and the Dutch electronics firm, Philips, erected a small TV facility at the annual Pakistani industrial fair in Karachi. With several hundred sets distributed throughout the fair grounds and in other parts of Karachi, the TV demonstration was a riotous success. (It caused, in fact, a near riot one evening when Pakistani viewers at the fair angrily swarmed over the facility because the transmissions had been ended for the day.) The facility was closed down shortly after the fair ended, despite attempts to keep it operating.[40]

This initial venture into television had an influence in stepping up the pace of TV developments in Pakistan. In November, 1963, the government announced plans for a National Television Corporation whose stock would be 51 percent government-owned with the rest sold to private interests. It proposed that the competition between private groups wishing to participate in local television would be determined by having such groups set up, at their own expense, pilot stations in the six largest Pakistani cities for a three-month trial period. The first station under this arrangement was opened in October, 1964, in Lahore, with Japan's Nippon Electric Company as the commercial participant. A second station was opened several months later in Dacca, the capital of East Pakistan. Other private competitors, including the Roy Thomson organization, reportedly were negotiating in 1965 for similar participation arrangements.[41]

The Indian government was considerably more reluctant to get deeply involved in television. The subject was debated inside and outside the government as early as 1954. The discussion at the time was dominated, particularly within government circles, by the idea that any television broadcasting arrangements would have to come under strict government control, untainted by commercial considerations. Television, when and if it did come, would be operated by All-India Radio, the national broadcasting network.[42]

From the beginning, however, there was pressure in favor of a private television operation. Commercial stations, offering programs (and advertising) to the upper-class elite in such metropolitan centers as Bombay, Calcutta, and New Delhi, would have undoubtedly been successful even a decade ago when such stations were first proposed. In ruling against them, the government argued that the importation of transmitters and receiving equipment would cause a heavy drain on the nation's foreign-exchange reserves. However, the decision against commercial television was also affected by the government's belief—shared by a large segment of India's intellectuals—that commercial television was not merely an unnecessary luxury but a threat to Indian culture, a belief reinforced by continual reports in Indian newspapers of the medium's alleged excesses in the United States and Europe.

"The vulgarity of commercial television in the United States is too well known to need detailed comment," a leading Indian newspaper stated in 1962 in a typical dismissal of the entire problem. "Frivolity is all the country is going to get if television in India is going to pay its way."[43] One of the hurdles that television will have to overcome in the world's largest free world country is the self-righteous belief of the intellectual elite that the medium somehow or other is inherently wicked.[44]

Having relegated the question of commercial broadcasting to the indefinite future, the Indian government in the late 1950's opened a small experimental station in New Delhi to test the possibilities of educational television. The project was sponsored by Indian education officials, working with the United Nations Economic and Social Council (UNESCO) on an adult-education project and with the Ford Foundation on a school broadcasting project. The foundation was anxious at the time to examine the possibilities of educational television in underdeveloped countries, following its experience in helping launch school television projects in the United States. Ford agreed to finance part of the Delhi school project; several hundred schools in the Delhi State educational system participated in the four-year experiment which ended in 1964.

However useful the Delhi educational TV project was, it demonstrated only one phase of the medium's potential role in Indian life. By 1965 the Indian government had before it a number of proposals for both governmental and private telecasting. In May, 1964, a government spokesman informed the Indian Parliament that the government was considering a proposal submitted by the Roy Thomson organization.[45] Although this, and other, indications pointed toward some form of commercial operations, other Indian officials continued to stress the theme of government-sponsored educational television. In November, 1964, Mrs. Indira Ghandi, the information minister, declared that TV would be good for India only if it were used to expand educational opportunities rather than as an entertainment medium.[46]

In June, 1965, the government took a small but significant step in the direction of a state-controlled pattern for the medium that would include both educational and entertainment programing when it accepted a West German government offer of expanded television studio facilities in New Delhi. The new studios, supplementing those used for the UNESCO and Ford Foundation projects, reportedly would be equipped to handle both school broadcasting and general entertainment shows when they were finished in September, 1966.[47]

Whatever the final pattern of Indian television, however, it will have an important influence on the medium's development in other countries of Asia and Africa. Although puritanical in their attitudes on the perils of commercial television, the Indians have been in the lead in trying to work out a sensible pattern for television's use as a force for social and political modernization. The fact that they have not succeeded yet is less a criticism of their attempt than it is a reminder of just how little attention has been paid to this aspect of the medium's potential in the newly developing countries.

4

Television's Global
Networks

At the BBC's new London studios there is a small room with a futuristic sign on its door. The sign reads: International Control Room. Here BBC engineers can exchange programs with over two dozen other television systems in Europe and North America. Soon, with the development of world-wide communications satellite facilities, they will be able to provide BBC viewers with programs for fifty countries. Within a decade this will extend to a hundred or more countries.

The BBC's international control room is a working symbol of the next major development in world television—the formation of regional and intercontinental networks. Such links are an old story in Europe where the pacesetting Eurovision network has been in operation for over a decade. Intervision, a Soviet-sponsored network, links eight East European countries. Fiscal, political, and geographical barriers have decreed a slower pace for similar networks in other parts of the world. Despite these difficulties, regional networks will play a key role in television's development in Latin America, the Middle East, and the Far East. In each of these areas, the first steps toward forming electronic links between national television systems have already been taken. Africa has, understandably, lagged behind in plans for regional telecasting, but even here the managers of that continent's thirteen national television systems talk confidently of TV links among themselves and with the rest of the world.

In any event, it is already clear that by the early 1970's regional and intercontinental network links will be available to a billion or more viewers in over sixty countries throughout the globe. The prospects of simultaneous sight-and-sound transmissions on such an unprecedented scale has political, economic, and cultural implications for all countries, and for American world leadership in particular. What we say about ourselves on these new links, and what is said about us by others, can seriously influence the image the world has of our national character and our international role. A closer look at the present development of these networks and their future prospects is therefore in order.

American interests in this field will, of course, be served if international network programing develops as an instrument serving a democratic world order. This will mean avoiding the fate that overtook international radio during the twenties and thirties. A number of well-meant attempts to develop radio as a constructive world force faltered in their own good intentions. The United States, tied to isolationist mythologies, did little to encourage these movements. As a result, international radio evolved primarily as a propaganda instrument, its tone set largely by Fascist and Communist regimes. It was not until World War II that the democracies demonstrated the potentialities of radio as an instrument of international information and persuasion. By and large, however, radio missed its opportunity as a communications medium that could unite rather than divide nations and men.

There is, fortunately, a good chance that television may avoid this course. In part, this will be due to the medium's technical characteristics. With some exceptions, television does not lend itself to direct international broadcasting. The reason for this, of course, is its short transmittal range. International television transmissions are effective only when they can be retransmitted through the facilities of cooperating foreign stations. The result, so far, has been to minimize in international television the strident propagandistic tone which characterizes so much of short-wave broadcasting. This does not mean that international telecasting will not have propaganda overtones. These will still be present, in a more subtle form. The change will be one of emphasis, with greater attention paid to straight programing which will be bland enough to be acceptable to television authorities in other countries without losing its impact on mass foreign audiences.

Within these confines, international television exchanges have already proved their effectiveness as an informational and entertainment medium. In large part, this is due to television's inherent ability to attract and hold its audiences through its sense of immediacy. International TV relays are, for the most part, "live" transmissions of actual events. The drama of simultaneous sight-and-sound eavesdropping on major news happenings, whether they involve the death of a pope or a soccer game, has proved itself a powerful magnet, attracting large audiences whenever it happens. It is this factor, more than any other, which will make regional and intercontinental television transmissions an increasingly common occurrence in future years.

The earliest TV transmissions to cross national frontiers came from the United States. In the late 1940's, television stations in U.S. cities bordering Mexico and Canada began attracting large audiences across the border. By the early 1950's, the process became reciprocal as Canadian and Mexican television entrepreneurs began building stations with an eye on nearby U.S. audiences.

This across-the-border TV eavesdropping is now common in other parts of the world. In Europe, the largest audiences of the commercial stations in Luxembourg and Monte Carlo are nearby French, German, Belgian, and Italian viewers. Belgian and German programs have larger audiences in parts of the Netherlands than does the state-controlled Dutch station. In the Mediterranean area, the low-lying littoral provides excellent transmission conditions for long-distance telecasting. Viewers in Greece and in North Africa tuned into Italian television for years before television became a reality in their own countries. Cairo television is readily available to viewers in Lebanon, Israel, and Jordan.

In a number of cases, this factor of geographical proximity has been used to beam programs directly across borders for political purposes. The best-known example of this is in Germany where the West and East Germans conduct an elaborate, expensive form of electronic warfare aimed at attracting each other's television audiences.[1] A similar, smaller example of directed Communist television programs was reported in 1963 when a Soviet station in the Arctic instituted programs in Norwegian design to attract audiences in northern Norway. A similar effort has been reported in Korea where North Korean Communist authorities have directed part of their programing efforts toward nearby South Korean viewers.

These across-the-border telecasting operations, whether random or intentional, are a small part of the new international character of television. The major emphasis is on binational, regional, and intercontinental agreements to connect television systems at all levels.

The first formal exchange of television programs on an international scale took place on August 27, 1950, between Great Britain and France. With British equipment, the inaugural program was sent from Calais to Dover. A major problem at the time was the incompatibility of British and French equipment, due largely to differences in television tube line counts. BBC and Radiodiffusion Télévision Française engineers successfully developed converter systems to a point where in July, 1952, formal bilateral exchanges of programs between the two countries were inaugurated. It is doubtful that even the most enthusiastic supporters of the exchange realized that they were taking the first practical step toward forming a link which, in little more than ten years, would reach from the Urals through Europe and across the Atlantic to California.

The initial Franco-British television exchanges were not simply an exercise in technical virtuosity or hands-across-the-Channel camaraderie. They were part of a pattern, planned several years earlier, for strengthening European cooperation in the television and radio fields. The result was the Eurovision international network whose parent organization was, and still is, the European Broadcasting Union, a precocious stepchild of the post-war sphere-of-influence split between Eastern and Western Europe. EBU's origins were in the International Broadcasting

Union (IBU), a prewar attempt to encourage international co-operation in the radio field. The IBU's somewhat hesitant efforts were drowned out during the thirties by the increasingly national-istic uses to which radio was put, particularly in the field of international short-wave broadcasts. At a 1946 conference in Brussels, it was replaced by a new group, Organisation Interna-tionale de Radiodiffusion (OIR), whose membership included most European countries on both sides of the Iron Curtain. Since television was a future aspiration for most countries at the time, OIR devoted its efforts primarily to radio activities. However, by 1948, the new organization was considering a proposal by Marcel Bezençon of Radio Lausanne for a "program clearing-house" to facilitate exchanges of television productions between national networks throughout the continent.

This and similar plans were delayed, however, until the larger issue of East-West tensions within the OIR could be resolved. It had become increasingly apparent that the Soviet Union and its satellites intended to use the organization primarily for propa-ganda activities. The British Broadcasting Corporation (which was not a member of OIR) took the initiative in proposing the formation of a new West European radio-television organization. The result was the formation of the European Broadcasting Union in February, 1950, with twenty-one regular and associate mem-bers. EBU took over the OIR's administrative offices in Geneva and its technical center in Brussels. OIR, now completely under Communist domination, was moved to Prague where it quickly became an all-out Communist transmission belt, coordinating radio and television exchanges between "socialist" countries.[2]

Freed of Communist harassment, the new European Broad-casting Union moved quickly to set up a coordinating mechanism for handling a range of problems, including technical research, legal questions, and program exchange. In this latter field, televi-sion was beginning to dominate the broadcasting scene by 1950. The Bezençon plan for a "program clearinghouse" was revived, with the provision that the EBU assume over-all responsibility for exchanges of both live and filmed programs throughout Europe. In his proposal, M. Bezençon stated that the question of such television exchanges needed to be faced and that only a central organization such as the EBU could deal with the problem effectively. Such exchanges, he argued, would benefit larger countries interested in distributing programs for prestige reasons, and also smaller countries which would need foreign programs since they could not bear the cost of locally produced programs.

A modified version of the Bezençon plan was sent to all EBU member organizations late in 1950 for comments. Only ten of the twenty-one members responded—a rough measure of the extent of television's development at the time. Most of those who replied simply approved the proposal without further comment. Two organizations, the BBC and the French televison services, offered extensive—and somewhat contradictory—statements. The British strongly approved the idea and offered suggestions on solving the legal, organizational, and technical problems involved. The French reply suggested a cautionary approach, citing the complexity of problems involved. It proposed that international contacts be limited to bilateral exchanges for the time being. This attitude was reflected within the EBU itself. In a separate report, the organization's newly formed legal committee noted that there were few precedents in international or national law for the activities proposed in the Bezençon plan.

This caution delayed but did not stop plans for a European television network. In May, 1951, the EBU administrative council authorized a study leading to the establishment of an experimental program exchange system. Meanwhile, the initial Franco-British successes in bilateral exchanges, coupled with the rapid development of television plans in other European countries, gave added impetus to the idea of an inter-European network. The event which more than any other brought the network close to reality was the coronation of Britain's Queen Elizabeth II in June, 1953. While legal and technical experts wrangled over the difficulties involved in international TV transmissions, the French, Dutch, Danish, and German television systems began negotiating with the BBC for sound-and-picture coverage of the coronation ceremonies. A dozen television transmitters on the continent relayed the event to millions of viewers. The colorful pomp and circumstance of the London ceremonies gave Europeans an intriguing preview of how television would bring the outside world into their homes.

In the year following the coronation, the EBU made steady progress in clearing up the technical and legal problems of its budding international network. A technical conference held in London in September, 1953, had advanced plans for linking up hitherto technically incompatible European national networks.[3] By the following summer, program planners and technical experts in eight countries were ready to carry out the first multilateral series of exchanges. The highlight of that first summer's programing was the world football championship match, viewed by over sixty million Europeans on a thirty-eight-hundred-mile network involving forty-four television stations. In four weeks, during June and July, eighteen programs totaling thirty-one hours were relayed over the network. It was an auspicious beginning for an experiment with the newly minted name of Eurovision.

Any doubts about the network's future were laid to rest during those summer days in 1954. In the decade that has passed since then, Eurovision has become a permanent part of the European scene. Although the network is distinctly European in concept and operations, it also has lessons for the rest of the world, including the United States. A closer took at the present scope of its operations is in order.

Eurovision is a massive test case of the opportunities, and the limitations, involved in developing regional and intercontinental networks. It is doubtful that any area of the world will come close to European accomplishments in this field for a long time. Europe had the advantages of a relatively small geographical area, high technical competence, cultural compatibility, and, above all, a strong impulse toward regional unity at many levels. Eurovision was nurtured in the dynamics of postwar European regional cooperation, and in turn it has contributed to this movement through a unique sight-and-sound ability to dramatize it.

Behind this effort lies the elaborate organizational mechanism of the European Broadcasting Union. In 1965 it had 28 active members and 32 associates, including the major American networks and the United States government. EBU's over-all governing body is its General Assembly. Its regular activities are governed by an administrative council and a secretariat operating from EBU headquarters in Geneva. Under the administrative committee are three functional groups concerned respectively with programing, legal, and technical affairs. These in turn are supported by an array of "working parties" which probe into such specialized subjects as educational television and film exchanges. The EBU also publishes its own magazine, *EBU Review,* the most authoritative source of information on international television activities not only in Europe but throughout the rest of the world.[4] In all, EBU has a staff of 110 employees, working on an annual budget of 1.5 million dollars drawn from prorated contributions by its active and associate members.

Eurovision's ground rules are basically simple ones. The most important operating principle is that EBU is a clearinghouse for providing programs that its member organizations want. The organization's success is rooted in the fact that it has never required its member stations to accept a program. Its neutrality in this matter is its continuing strength. The result has been that EBU presides over what is undoubtedly the most elaborate program-planning operation in the mass communications field. It involves a complex schedule of relay arrangements in many cases involving only two countries but in others as many as two dozen. The great majority of interchanges involve a half-dozen countries or less. Only rarely is the full Eurovision network used for a simultaneous program transmission. In most cases, EBU's role is that of a routine middleman. In large-scale exchanges, however, it becomes more involved in program planning. Thus EBU's programing committee began planning for the coverage of the 1966 world football championship in Great Britain two years before the event.

During its first full year of operations, EBU handled fewer than fifty program originations. By 1963, it served as clearinghouse for over six hundred programs, involving over thirty-one hundred "exchange participations," *i.e.,* the number of times its member organizations took a Eurovision program. Thus, the average number of "participations" in a Eurovision program is six television systems.

The other guiding principle of Eurovision operations is that each of its member organizations assumes the technical equipment and financial costs of Eurovision programs originated from its services. There has been pressure in recent years to have these costs shared by organizations receiving the programs. This proposal has been defeated most recently in an EBU program committee meeting in Lausanne in April, 1964.

The end result of this organizational activity is to permit over 150 million viewers in 17 countries to watch programs beamed by 2,000 transmitters that take them beyond the physical and psychological confines of their own cities and country to the wider world beyond. The range of Eurovision programing they see is a varied one. There is no doubt, however, about which type of program is most popular. It is sports, and particularly soccer. The partisanship that Americans demonstrate toward their favorite teams in baseball and football pales before the frenzied interest that most of the rest of the world shows in soccer. The Olympic Games aside, the one truly "world's championship" sporting event is the annual contest for an award most Americans have never heard of—the cup symbolic of victory in the World Football Championships. Whatever noble thoughts its organizers might have had about Eurovision as a regional cultural force, the fact is that the new network was given its initial boost when it broadcast the 1954 world soccer contest. Here was something that all its viewers, actual and potential, could understand, without any significant interference from political, linguistic, or other barriers.

The field of sports has dominated the Eurovision programing pattern from the beginning. During the network's first six years, sports accounted for more than half of all its transmissions. Since 1960, this ratio has dropped to a fairly consistent pattern of between 40 and 50 percent of total transmission time. Aside from the always-popular soccer games, the Eurovision sports schedule includes such varied events as Wimbledon tennis, boxing, wrestling, sports car racing, and track and field events. Huge audiences watched the Olympic winter games at Cortina, Italy, in 1960 and at Innsbruck, Austria, in 1964. Not to be outdone by these international events, Eurovision has organized its own regional contests, a Eurovision swimming competition first held in Sweden in 1961.

Sports broadcasting gave Eurovision its initial impetus as

a mass regional medium, and it has been a major factor in sustaining this large audience. In recent years, the trend in Eurovision's programing pattern has been away from sports and toward more diversified types of programs. Sports accounted for 70 percent of the network's programs in 1956; their share of the program pie dropped to under 50 percent by 1960. The most significant factor in this change has been the increasing emphasis on news coverage. In 1964 over half the network's transmissions involved either "live" coverage of major news events or the network's daily transmission of more routine news.

Simultaneous coverage of major European events has been an important Eurovision function since its experimental success with the British coronation in 1953. The network has since built a well-deserved reputation for the imaginative coverage it has given to regional news events. Its cameras have given viewers a unique, incomparable view of the men and events which have brought Western Europe closer to regional unity in the past twenty years than at any time in modern history. It has done this without ever resorting to consciously directed propaganda programing advocating European union. The network's approach has been the more effective one of reporting, without editorializing, the sights and sounds of postwar Europe. The only guideline for Eurovision news coverage from the very beginning has been the event's newsworthiness, as determined by each individual member. With this standard, Eurovision has covered the deaths of popes, the marriages of kings, NATO military exercises, the formation and progress of the Common Market, United Nations' disarmament meetings in Geneva, the funeral of Toscanini, and such natural disasters as mine cave-ins, floods, and avalanches.

The network's imaginative approach to much of its news coverage has strengthened its popularity. Thus, when the International Geophysical Year opened in 1957, Eurovision by-passed the idea of having scientists give dull talks about international cooperation. Instead, it placed its cameras high up on Switzerland's Jungfrau and deep under the Mediterranean to dramatize for its viewers the IGY's scope and purpose. In 1962, Eurovision cooperated with U.S. authorities in bringing to Europeans the first transatlantic television transmissions relayed by the Telstar satellite. During the following year, European stations originated 101 programs to the United States and received 40.[5] More spectacular was the Soviet Union's August, 1962, achievement in providing, through the Eurovision network, live transmissions from an orbiting manned space capsule.

Although Eurovision's ground rules for the coverage of news events emphasize newsworthiness, there are numerous political factors involved in what is shown—and what is not shown—via Eurovision. Each country can agree to, or veto, a request by its Eurovision colleagues for coverage of a particular event within its borders. Although most of the network's members have a good record of cooperation, there is a natural tendency to emphasize events which show their country in a favorable light. In a few cases, this tendency moves into the realm of conscious policy. The largest originator of Eurovision news coverage is the French state network. If there are political parties in opposition to General de Gaulle which hold political rallies or are involved in other newsworthy events, Eurovision's audience will have to learn about them from other sources. The emphasis in French television's news output to the regional network is heavily weighted on coverage of General de Gaulle's activities.[6] General de Gaulle and his provocative views do not, however, go unchallenged on Eurovision. When the French government vetoed the admission of Great Britain into the Common Market in 1962, the British Prime Minister, Harold Macmillan, was able to bring a forceful presentation of the British case before a large Eurovision audience in rebuttal.

American politics and its leaders have become more familiar to Europeans through Eurovision. The enormous European popularity enjoyed by Dwight Eisenhower and John F. Kennedy was enhanced by live network coverage of their presidential visits to Europe. Television played an important role in strengthening the Kennedy image in Europe during his first presidential visit there in 1961, shortly after his inauguration. Any European hesitations about the youthful new leader and his pretty wife vanished in the air of assured style and quiet competence which both Kennedys showed as they moved through cheering crowds in Paris and Vienna. Television confirmed, as no other medium could, the image of John F. Kennedy as the symbol of American vigor and confidence.

The abrupt end of the President's life had an enormous emotional impact on Europeans, and again television played a central role. In the days following his assassination, Eurovision covered events in Washington through the most extensive news transmissions in its history. Two hundred million people witnessed the President's funeral through satellite relay transmissions sent by Eurovision to all its own member networks and to the East European Intervision network. Eurovision arranged ten other multilateral transmissions from the United States and two full-scale sequential news transmissions during those somber days.

Complementing this "live" coverage of major news events are Eurovision's day-to-day activities in covering the normal flow of news. Almost from the network's inception, Eurovision officials had talked of plans for systematic daily exchanges of news between member stations. Without such an exchange, individual national networks must rely on shipments of newsfilm which are delayed by the time it takes to process the film and to ship it. The need was for a system to relay news events, "live" or on film, through Eurovision facilities on a scheduled daily basis, in time for local nightly news programs. The Eurovision system, which has been in full operation since 1962, is an imaginative precursor of the day when there will be world-wide facilities for exchanging television news coverage.

EBU began its first serious investigation of daily news exchange possibilities in 1957. The advantages of such a system were obvious—and so were the disadvantages. Among the latter were the technical difficulties involved in coordinating a daily visual news exchange between a dozen or more networks. The second roadblock was fiscal: would the proposed system be sufficiently utilized to justify the high transmission costs involved? It took Eurovision officials almost five years to work out answers to these two problems.

In March, 1957, a conference of European TV news editors recommended that the EBU explore the possibilities of a daily news interchange. The EBU's preliminary investigation indicated that the technical problems were manageable; the greater problem was the reluctance of smaller networks to commit themselves to the added financial burdens involved. (It is useful to recall that, at the time, television itself was relatively new in most European countries, and particularly in the smaller ones.) Despite these difficulties, two experimental series of daily transmissions were carried out in October, 1958, among the British, French, Dutch, Belgian, and Italian networks. The second experiment coincided with the death of Pope Pius XII; the ability of the experimenting stations to provide daily scheduled coverage of events in Rome gave valuable support for the idea of a permanent daily news transmission. During the following year, another round cf news exchange experiments had eight Eurovision national networks as participants. It was not until 1962, however, that daily exchanges of visual news material became a permanent feature of the Eurovision network.

Behind these transmissions is a complex technical and programing plan. The focal point of the programing operations is in the office of the Eurovision news coordinator in Geneva. During the day, he draws up a news transmissions schedule after consulting with news editors of Eurovision stations. The editors tell him what news material they are prepared to feed into the network and what material they are prepared to take "off the line." Once a firm schedule for news is set up, the news coordinator clears his schedule through Eurovision's general program coordinator at EBU headquarters in Geneva and with the staff of the EBU Technical Center in Brussels. At 5 P.M., the Technical Center sets into motion the complex transmitting pattern which feeds a visual news exchange over thousands of miles of Eurovision relay lines from Helsinki to Rome. Stations feed material into the line according to the day's prearranged schedule. Others pick up material, broadcasting it "live" in some cases but in most instances taping it for use on news shows later in the evening.

Eurovision's daily news exchanges have overcome the early hesitations that many of the network's member stations had about their utility. In 1964, 29 national television systems made 7,878 pickups of Eurovision news transmissions. These pickups involved 1,134 originations from 21 national networks, or an average of about 4 a day.[7]

Over 90 percent of Eurovision transmissions involve either news or sports. It is probable that this pattern will also hold for any regional or intercontinental television network arrangements in other areas of the world. Both news and sports are, for the most part, readily understandable; the picture tells the story. A network can, if it wants to, add its own commentary. The individual Eurovision stations have over the years developed a split-second system for adding local language commentaries to foreign news and sports shows through the use of simultaneous translators or by supplying their own commentators at the scene of the event. However, language is a major barrier outside the news and sports fields.

This lesson was learned by the Danish, Norwegian, Swedish, and Finnish networks several years ago. The four networks are linked by what might be called a subregional network. Known as Nordvision, the four-nation network provides exchanges of purely Scandinavian interest, although each member also makes heavy use of regular Eurovision transmissions. In 1960 Nordvision decided to break out of its news-and-sports format by transmitting a variety show every Saturday night. The show originated from a different country each week, on a rotating basis. Language was considered a minor barrier since Danish, Swedish, and Norwegian are linguistic partners, and Swedish is widely understood in Finland. However, language differences proved to be the undoing of the experiment. Most viewers were not prepared to watch a show in which the commentary, and even the jokes, were in another language. The series was soon suspended.

Eurovision has attempted to solve this problem by relying heavily on "spectaculars" in its network entertainment shows. A typical Eurovision entertainment program is an open-air performance of *Aida* from Italy, complete with horses, camels, and a cast of hundreds. The network's variety shows generally feature well-known international stars. Ballet and ballroom dancing are popular items on the Eurovision schedule. Although the network seldom transmits plays in their original language versions, it has its own intermittent drama series, known as "The Largest Theater in the World." The title is not entirely an exercise in hyperbole. An estimated audience of fifty million persons saw the play,

"Heart to Heart," by British author Terence Rattigan. The Rattigan play, and others in the series, are commissioned by Eurovision
to be shown in several language versions by the network's member
stations as nearly simultaneously as possible. (In practice, this
has turned out to cover a period of about one week.) Eurovision's
dramatic series, together with its other entertainment shows,
will always represent a small portion of the network's total schedule. They have, however, established themselves as a permanent
part of the European television scene.

An increasingly important EBU activity is encouragement
of television film exchanges among its members. This has been
done largely within the framework of MIFED, the most important television film trade show, held twice yearly in Milan.
In 1963, EBU joined with MIFED in sponsoring a special series
of showings of European television programs to representatives
of its member stations attending the fair. The union's purpose
was to encourage greater sales of films between its members.
The initial results have been encouraging enough to make EBU's
participation in MIFED one of its permanent activities.

Behind Eurovision's daily transmissions lies an impressive
technical organization which has mastered most of the problems
involved in long-distance television broadcasting. Its primary
task is to move audio and visual material in a dozen languages
over a 25,000-mile network of over 2,000 stations. It has to sort
out four separate and incompatible transmission standards so
that any program on any one station in the network can be fed
to another station. This virtuoso trick is carried out almost daily
without a hitch. EBU's technical experts in Brussels are now
looking at other problems facing the network.

One of these involves color transmissions throughout the network. The technical feasibility of long-distance color transmissions in Europe was demonstrated in 1962 when a color-TV
experiment was successfully carried out between Italy, Switzerland, and West Germany.[8] The problem of a regional color-TV
network is no longer technical; it is political and economic. In
the early 1960's, European national networks had four separate
color-TV systems from which to select a uniform regional color
system. One was the well-tested American system developed by

RCA; the others were French, British, and German systems. The winner of this technical sweepstakes was assured a highly lucrative lead in the potentially important market for color television transmission and reception equipment throughout Europe and other parts of the world. The selection of a universal system soon settled down to a largely political struggle in which each of the major parties involved lobbied for its own system. For several years, no one system received enough support to win. In February, 1964, a ten-day London conference of the International Radio Consultative Committee (CCIR) ended in an impasse on the issue. The deadlock was scheduled to be broken at an April, 1965, meeting in Vienna. However, in a move that had strong political overtones, the Soviet Union and its allies voted to support the French system while other nations backed the RCA method.

Another technical achievement in which Eurovision stations have an important stake is communications satellite transmissions. Since 1963 European governments have exchanged views on the desirability of a European-sponsored satellite system to supplement the American satellite network. These consultations are not, however, carried out under EBU auspices, although the union would undoubtedly play an important role in the television activities of any future European communications satellite system. In the meantime, EBU technical experts are gaining important experience in such transmissions through their cooperative activities in exchanging programs by satellite with American networks.[9]

This cooperation is rooted in the continuing close relations the U.S. government and commercial networks have had with the EBU for over a decade. The United States is an EBU associate member through its official agent, the United States Information Agency (USIA). In addition, each of the major American networks is an associate member. In 1963, EBU officials took the unusual step of holding a meeting in New York, their first meeting in a country which is not an active member of the union. Held at the invitation of the American government, the conference gave EBU leaders an opportunity for a firsthand look at U.S. communications satellite operations.[10]

Eurovision's success in regional transmissions led the Communist nations to attempt a similar venture within their own borders. The result was Intervision which is—technically, at least—Eurovision's opposite number in Eastern Europe and the Soviet Union. The technical achievements of Intervision are, in fact, considerable. It is geographically the most widespread single land network, stretching from East Berlin to the Urals, with the prospect of being extended to Vladivostok on the Pacific Ocean within a few years. This latter achievement would involve a linear distance of over nine thousand miles. Intervision does not, however, service as many individual stations or as large an audience as its Western European counterpart.

The most important distinction between Intervision and Eurovision is, of course, their purposes. Intervision is intended primarily to be a transmission belt for the propaganda of the Soviet Union and its European allies. It is international television in the service of Marxism-Leninism.

Intervision was founded in February, 1960, by the state television organizations of Czechoslovakia, Hungary, East Germany, and Poland. A year later the Soviet Union joined the system, followed by Bulgaria and Rumania.[11] Organizationally, Intervision is an activity of OIRT, the Communist radio-television organization which free world nations deserted in 1950 to form the European Broadcasting Union. Since that time, OIRT has provided a clearinghouse for radio and television activities of Communist bloc countries as well as those with leftist or neutralist leanings.[12]

Intervision's organizational setup is a frank imitation of the one adopted by Eurovision. It includes the Intervision Council, a program coordination center, and a technical coordination center, all in Prague.[13] Since early in 1964, all of the network's active members have been linked directly by cable and microwave connections. This linkage was, however, slow in developing. The first links between "socialist" countries took place in 1960 when Moscow and Warsaw were connected. The Soviet Union, however, seemed more interested in securing links with Eurovision than with smaller countries in the Communist bloc. A roundabout link with Western Europe was achieved in 1961 through a relay between Leningrad and Helsinki. Later a more direct route from Warsaw to East Berlin was completed.

Intervision programing efforts are considerably smaller in both scope and imagination than those of its Eurovision counterpart. There is a fairly active interchange of sports programs, but the mainstay of the programing schedule involves events which the Communist leadership considers politically important. This includes coverage of May Day parades, national day-of-liberation celebrations, ribbon-cutting ceremonies involving socialist achievements, and the like. Whatever its political strengths, Marxism-Leninism does not make good television material. Added to this is the significant fact that ties between countries in the "socialist commonwealth" are no longer as tightly bound either by the dominance of the Soviet Union or by their own need for mutual cooperation.

This has had its effect in stunting Intervision's influence. It is a trend that is difficult to identify clearly. There is little doubt about the actuality of the trend, however. Its most important indicator is the relatively small number of programs exchanged on the network. A Polish summary of Intervision's activities claims that in 1963 about "500 to 600 items" would be exchanged. This compares with the Eurovision total of over 3,000 for the same period. More significantly, the Polish report declares that in one three-month period, Polish television would take only 36 programs of the 111 offered by the network. This is a low level of socialist unity which, in an earlier and more repressive Stalinist era, would not have been permitted.[14] There are some indications that other East European networks have cut back their use of Intervision facilities. In 1961, Czech TV devoted 5 percent of its programing to Intervision; the following year this had dropped to 4 percent.

The strongest trend in Iron Curtain television seems to be the desire of East European countries to step up their contacts with West European television. There are, in fact, strong indications that the prospects for such contacts have always been a strong consideration in Intervision's growth. The Soviet Union took the lead in exploiting the possibility of live television contact with the West. Circumstances permitted it to couple this significant achievement with another one. On April 14, 1961, the first live relay took place between Moscow and London via Helsinki; the event it recorded was the tumultuous Moscow reception accorded Major Yuri Gagarin, the first Soviet astronaut. The program was retransmitted by the BBC to other Eurovision stations throughout the continent. It was a stunning technical and political achievement for the Russians, and they proceeded to follow it up with other relay programs. A few weeks later, Europeans saw a spectacular May Day parade in Red Square. In August, a special transmission was made between Moscow and Rome at the time of Italian Premier Amintore Fanfani's visit to the Soviet Union.

Since that time an intermittent series of exchanges between the two television networks has taken place. Premier Nikita Khrushchev took advantage of the link to put his ideas directly to the vast Eurovision audience; in one such program in April, 1964, the former Soviet leader set out his side of his dispute with the Chinese Communists in a speech that was carried by sixteen national networks on both sides of the Iron Curtain.[15]

Only minor technical difficulties are involved in connecting the two networks. An Intervision program can move through East German TV studios to Eurovision's regional network center in a matter of seconds. For several years after the first 1961 exchanges, the two networks operated on a pragmatic basis, sharing program expenses on an agreed-upon scale. At its Nineteenth General Assembly, in September, 1963, OIRT proposed that more permanent arrangements for greater cooperation between the two networks be developed. The obstacle to any such arrangements is likely to be a political one. Eurovision members have already indicated that they will insist on a formula of more or less equal reciprocity in any formal agreement on exchanges, together with guarantees against blatant propaganda exploitation of any exchanges.

In this policy, they are aware of Communist policies which emphasize the desirability of parading their achievements to the outside world while keeping a tight reign on information coming into their own countries. Eurovision was involved in a ludicrous incident in 1964 which underscored this point. The occasion was the television relay of a soccer game from Great Britain to, among other countries, the Soviet Union. The British national team played an all-star team which included Ferenc Puskas, a world-famous Hungarian player who had defected to the West after the Budapest uprising in 1956. His defection, however, had never been reported in the Soviet press. He was, therefore, officially a "non-person" as far as Soviet television was concerned. Although he played a brilliant game—all of which was recorded on the visual part of the transmission—his name was never once mentioned by the Soviet commentator describing the event.[16]

There is no doubt that Europe, both East and West, has a long lead in regional network television. Geography, politics, and financial considerations are all formidable obstacles to the development of similar networks in other parts of the world. Despite these barriers, however, such regional links will become a reality on every continent within the next decade.

If current plans develop, Asia will have a regional network by 1970. This planning effort is being carried out largely under Japanese leadership. Japanese television broadcasters and equipment manufacturers are fully aware of the long-range financial benefits of their participation in television's development in the Far East. Supporting this is the Japanese government's desire to re-establish its political and economic influence in Southeast Asia—influences which are still checked by local memories of Japanese military occupation during World War II. Television offers the Japanese a uniquely effective medium for further strengthening their role as a political and economic power in the Far East.

Japanese efforts to play a leading role in Far Eastern radio and television date from the formation of the Asian Broadcasters Conference in 1957. The conference was, to a large degree, a Japanese creation. All of its early meetings, in 1957, 1958, and 1960, were held in Toyko, where delegates were appropriately impressed by the fact that Japan has the most advanced radio and television systems in Asia. At its 1962 meeting in Kuala Lumpur, the conference voted to establish itself as the Asian

Broadcasting Union. The new union came into formal being in July, 1964. It is modeled, in form and spirit, on the European Broadcasting Union. Headquartered in Tokyo, its membership includes the broadcasting systems of most major nations in the Far East, South Asia, and the Middle East.[17]

Although it is still in its formative stages, the new Asia Broadcasting Union will undoubtedly be quickly involved in a plan for regional television networks during the next few years. The initial impetus for such a plan is, of course, Japanese. In 1961, a group of Japanese equipment manufacturers and broadcasters formed a corporation known as Asiavision to explore the possibilities of directly linking the Japanese television network with other Far Eastern systems. Asiavision began as a wholly-owned subsidiary of Fuji-TV, one of the large commercial Japanese networks. Its board of directors included officials of major electronics firms. Basically it was a commercial combine, designed to explore the prospects of expanding television equipment and broadcasting sales throughout Southeast Asia.[18]

According to its original prospectus, the Asiavision link would run from Japan to Okinawa and the Philippines, crossing over to the Asian mainland via Saigon, and then on to Laos, Cambodia, Thailand, Burma, Pakistan, and India. Korean television would also be included in the network. The technical problems involved in such a link are formidable but not insoluble. Japanese engineers have plans to span the overwater segment between southern Japan and Okinawa by microwave circuits. The other overwater distances are comparable in the technical hurdles they present. More formidable, technically, is the fact that several countries, notably Cambodia, Laos, and Burma, do not have television systems. These gaps preclude any direct regional telecasting for years to come. In its early stages, Asiavision will have to restrict itself to exchanges of taped and filmed program material.

Japanese broadcasters have already had a taste of some of the political difficulties involved in their attempts to play a leading role in Asian television. Japanese offers to assist in the development of television in the Philippines have been treated warily, despite the fact that a number of stations there have been hard pressed financially in recent years. Another example of such cautiousness took place in Formosa in 1962. Fuji-TV, sponsor of Asia-vision, had signed an agreement with the Chinese government in Formosa to build a television system on commercial terms generally regarded as favorable to both sides. Among other concessions, the Japanese planned to advertise Japanese products on Taiwan television and to provide a fixed amount of Japanese programing. In April, 1962, the Chinese parliament passed a resolution which in effect vetoed these provisions in the contract. The issue became a political one between the Japanese and Chinese foreign offices. It was settled eventually, but not without leaving a legacy of doubt about the speed with which an Asian television network might be formed.

There is no doubt that such a regional network will become a reality eventually, or that the Japanese will play a leading role in its formation. However, it is probable that the network will develop slowly, first through the exchange of filmed and taped programs, and then through limited binational microwave connections which will one day be extended to other countries in the region, probably under the auspices of the Asian Broadcasting Union.[19]

Similar political and economic difficulties have inhibited realistic planning for regional telecasting in the Middle East and Africa. The idea of a network linking Arab television systems has been discussed since television was introduced into the area in the late fifties. However, political differences within the Arab bloc have militated against any practical implementation of what would undoubtedly be an important step toward dramatizing Arab unity. The strongest force behind a regional network, if it should materialize, would be the UAR's Gamal Abdel Nasser, who has already developed Egyptian television into the best of its kind in the region. Paradoxically, the first practical move toward an Arab network has been made by an American firm, the American Broadcasting Company. In October, 1963, ABC International announced the formation of an "Arab Middle Eastern Network" consisting of TV stations in Syria, Lebanon, Kuwait,

Iraq, and Jordan. The "network" is primarily a program and advertising sales arrangement, linked to ABC International's affiliations with these stations. There is, however, some significance to the fact that the network's organizing meeting in Beirut drew almost five hundred businessmen, advertisers, government officials, and station representatives.[20]

The prospects for regional television links are perhaps dimmest in Africa. It will probably be a decade before African countries move beyond bilateral program exchange arrangements to a multinational regional network.

The most practical planning in regional television outside of Europe has taken place in Latin America. Three Central American countries are already linked directly in a small-scale version of a larger regional network that will eventually stretch from the Mexican-U.S. border south seven thousand miles to the tip of South America. The first "live" program exchanges between Latin American countries took place in 1961 when Argentinian television carried news reports of the Organization of American States conference at Punta del Este in neighboring Uruguay. A year earlier, telecommunications experts from Latin American nations, meeting in Mexico City, agreed in principle to the idea of planning a continental network.

Since that time, the international network idea has been kept alive largely by the Mexicans. It was not, however, until the Central American network began operations in 1964 that any practical moves were made to realize the plan. The network is known as CATVN—Central American Television Network. (The participants are Nicaragua, Costa Rica, Guatemala, Panama, Honduras, and El Salvador.) It was originally set up in 1960, largely under the guidance of the international division of the American Broadcasting Company of New York. As with its "Arab network" efforts in the Middle East, ABC International organized CATVN primarily as a commercial advertising and program sales organization.

It would, however, be incorrect to dismiss CATVN as a sales

promotion gimmick. In fact, the nations involved have growing political and economic ties that make a television link part of a logical pattern of regional interdependence. In 1963, five of the six CATVN countries—all except Panama—formed a Central American Free Trade Area, somewhat on the model of the European Common Market. Trade barriers were eliminated on more than half the commerce between the member countries, with further reductions scheduled in 1965. A regional bank has been established as another effort to raise economic levels well above the current per capita income of 250 dollars a year. Whether it is reporting a sports event or a regional political conference, television has a role to play in the new efforts of Central American nations to strengthen each other politically and economically.

Plans are currently underway to extend "live" interconnections between CATVN's members. The success of this "subregional network" will undoubtedly have an important influence in encouraging other Latin American nations to move forward with their much-discussed plans for a network spanning the entire continent.

The next step beyond regional television networks is, of course, intercontinental television linking all areas of the world. Most speculation about world-wide television broadcasts has emphasized the role of space communications satellites (comsats). However, comsats may, in fact, play a relatively minor role in such a system. It may be more practical, financially and technically, to base the system on interlocking regional networks connected by land cable or microwave systems. TV networks in Europe, Africa, and Asia could be linked in this manner. One comsat over the Atlantic or Pacific could connect the Western Hemisphere with this Eurasian system. (The two American continents would be joined either by microwave relays or a comsat system operating on a north-south axis.) The potential role of regional networks in a global system was demonstrated at the time of President Kennedy's death. Only two communications satellites—one each over the Atlantic and Pacific—were needed in an international network that involved twenty-six countries on four continents and a viewing audience of over three hundred million persons.

There will, however, be few similar events that will enlist such world-wide interest as to justify global coverage. Most television exchanges between regional networks will involve areas with common cultural or political interests. Thus, U.S. television will probably concentrate most heavily on program exchanges with Europe and Latin America. The two regional networks in divided Europe will undoubtedly develop a more active exchange schedule.

A number of proposals for a world television network organization have been put forward in recent years. Most of these have come from American sources. In 1962, several U.S. television officials proposed that American and European broadcasters take the lead in this field. However, none of the proposals have been acted upon.[21] It will probably be several years before any active planning for world television network arrangements is begun. The chief reason, of course, is that technical achievement of such a network, through comsat and surface connections, is five to eight years in the future. In the interim, however, there will be a steady increase in the number of bilateral regional television exchanges, notably in the North Atlantic area. For the rest of the world, the question of intercontinental television may depend largely on the pace of regional network developments.

In summary, regional television networks will become a reality in all parts of the world within the next decade. The model for such arrangements will be the ten-year-old European network which has demonstrated both the opportunities and the pitfalls involved in international telecasting. A world-wide television system will be formed by the combination of communications satellites and interlocked regional networks.

The United States has, of course, an important stake in these developments. Increasingly, television is taking over Hollywood's role as the chief purveyor of the American image abroad. The America that foreign viewers see on their living room screens is already a major factor in the shaping of their attitudes toward us. Equally important is the part that international television can play in defining and clarifying, as no other medium can, the realities of the rest of the world beyond their own borders. Using this gift in ways that strengthen the prospects for a democratic world order will be increasingly important for American leadership in the future.

5

TV Politics, International Style

Television is so overwhelmingly an entertainment medium that it is easy to slight its other attributes. None of these secondary characteristics is more fascinating than its role as a political soapbox. TV has brought about the greatest sight-and-sound contact between leaders and the people since the days of ancient Greece. This confrontation has political implications as significant as those that got their start in the Athenian agora over twenty centuries ago.

The pacesetting example of this new electronic politics occurred in the United States. TV politics had its origins in an event that took place on a hot summer night in 1948. Harry Truman, the man scheduled to lose a presidential election, told the delegates to the Democratic national convention in Philadelphia that he was going to win. His twang-voiced spunk roused the convention delegates. More significantly, it transmitted itself subtly to the millions of Americans who were watching their first televised convention on their ten-inch screens. Television did not have a major effect in determining the 1948 Truman victory, but its coverage of the campaign established the medium's political credentials.

Almost every major U.S. political event since that time has been influenced, directly or indirectly, by television. The medium has changed the form and substance of election campaigns, and much of what happens in between campaigns. The roll call of

103

such events, from the 1953–54 McCarthy investigations to the civil rights movement, is a capsule history of U.S. politics in the past fifteen years.

The civil rights issue is the most dramatic example of TV's political impact. As newsman James Reston has pointed out: "It is the almost instantaneous television reporting of the struggle . . . that has transformed what would have been a local event a generation ago into a national issue overnight. Even the segregationists who have been attacking the photographers and spraying black paint on their TV lenses understand the point."[1] For most Americans, their understanding of the civil rights issue is formed in large part by what they have seen on their television screens. It is an issue in which television has played a subtle but significant role as teacher and guide, setting a tone of consensus and stability for a particularly sensitive social development.

The medium's ability to mirror national consensus was strikingly demonstrated in the troubled days following the assassination of President Kennedy. The mood of the country was one of deep disturbance because of the violence and senselessness of the act. It was a time when divisive suspicions could have seriously threatened national unity. In large part, this was averted by the firm manner in which President Johnson moved to restore popular confidence. For most Americans, this mood was conveyed by television. A revealing study of people's reactions to the assassination confirmed that television had been the major factor in defining their attitudes toward the tragedy and, in particular, allaying their feelings of hysteria and panic. The study found that television's return to normal programing activities after four days' coverage of the President's death "set an orderly limit to the period of mourning," in effect, informing the public that it was time to get back to normal tasks.[2]

The U.S. political experience with television is, in many respects, a unique reflection of a vast, wealthy, democratic, and pluralistic society. However instructive our experience, it is not readily exportable. Other nations are going to have to work out their own approaches to TV's political role. Even at this early stage in the development of the medium, these approaches are extremely varied. They reflect, in large part, long-standing local patterns for carrying out public business. Thus, British television handles its television politics with a careful, even fastidious, concern for preserving old traditions of free discussion and fair play. British TV stations are probably the only ones in the world which give "equal time" to a political party, the Scottish Nationalist party, which advocates the secession of part of the country from central government control. At another extreme there is the crude use of television as a political weapon. One such instance occurred during the 1962 national revolt in Iraq when the bullet-riddled bodies of deposed Premier Abdul Karim Kassem and his associates were dragged into a Baghdad television studio and shown on the air as proof that his regime had been overthrown. Television can be a weapon of political democracy or autocracy. The United States needs to understand both uses if it is to measure correctly the medium's role abroad.

The key political question about television in any country is, simply, who controls the medium. As we have seen in earlier chapters, the pattern of television control abroad is a mixed one. The only clear-cut cases occur in totalitarian countries, notably those under Communist rule. Here television, like all the other media, is a consciously directed instrument of state control. Once we have put aside these obvious cases, however, the pattern becomes less clear. If television had followed the example of radio in most free world countries, it would have developed as a noncommercial state monopoly. In many cases, however, this did not happen. Beginning in 1954, when a separate commercial network was authorized in Great Britain to compete with the state-chartered BBC, the tide ran strongly in favor of loosening direct government controls over television. In 1965, fewer than twenty free world nations had strict noncommercial government television. The other seventy-five had settled on some form of commercial venture, under varying degrees of government control. In its early stages, at least, the trend of world television has been away from government controls and toward commercial operations.

As we have seen, the reasons that led governments to modify their public monopoly rights over TV were varied. Economics played a key role: television was an expensive proposition. There were private economic interests—usually allied with those in political power—ready to take over the medium. The other important reason was that many governments simply underestimated television's potential influence: they regarded it as an entertainment toy, a form of home movies with little or no political significance. Whatever the reasons for their decision, governments now find themselves dealing with a powerful, expanding medium to which the old rules do not apply. In country after country, television is well on its way to becoming the most influential medium —not simply as a home entertainment gadget, but as a political force with which to reckon.

The political elite in these countries may have been somewhat cavalier in their earlier attitudes toward television. They did not, however, surrender their rights over the medium. The fact that it was not developed as a strict state broadcasting monopoly in many countries reflects primarily changes in the postwar composition and interests of the local Establishment. Generally, the pattern was that the political elite redistributed some parts of its state monopoly powers over TV to other segments of the Establishment. It did not, in any case, give up the principle that television's purpose was to serve the Establishment's over-all interests. There is no country in the world where television systems operate in political opposition to the government.

It is within this framework that television's political impact has to be measured. In a few cases it is used as a direct, even totalitarian, weapon of Establishment control. In most other countries, however, television is subject to all the normal give-and-take of daily politics. The Establishment may be in control, but it has to consider many other pressures. These include the opposition political parties, the conflicting interests of the press and other powerful media, the censorship efforts of a large assortment of self-appointed guardians of public morals, and the whole amorphous area of public whims and fancies. Television is a powerful ally of the Establishment, but it does not bestow its benefits easily. As a political force, it is new, untested, and not to be ignored.

The hard evidence of its force is still somewhat scattered, but the evidence that exists is striking indeed. For example:

—In a Swedish poll of media influences on voters in the 1962 national elections there, television ranked first (58 percent), far ahead of the press (27 percent), private discussion (18 percent), and radio (8 percent).[3]

—A 1962 Japanese survey showed that 46 percent of the respondents named television as their first news source. Twelve percent cited radio.[4]

—British polls have confirmed for years the importance of television as a major source of news and opinion. During the 1959 national elections, two British sociologists found that of all the media and sources of political persuasion, only television added significantly to the voters' knowledge of issues and personalities.[5]

—In a Roper Poll taken after the 1960 U.S. presidential election, 57 percent of the voters polled said their decision was influenced by the Kennedy-Nixon television debates. An additional 6 percent said the debates not only influenced but decided their voting. Of this critical group—representing 4,000,000 voters—Kennedy got the support of 72 percent. The significance of this figure is highlighted by the fact that Kennedy won the election by only 112,000 votes.[6]

These and other surveys confirmed TV's growing importance as a political force. They provided, however, few clues on how the medium should be used for best political effect. There were no old comforting traditions or shiny new formulas for a guide. For most of the world, however, the outsized example both of TV's influence and its practical application has been the United States. No other country comes close to the way the U.S. has restructured political practices around television requirements, from the organization of conventions to the split-second reporting of election results. It may be years or decades before other nations can—or may want to—match the level of U.S. television's political ubiquity. In the meantime, they will be copying individual American techniques and adding distinctive touches of their own.

The most influential of U.S. television techniques has been the idea of direct televised debate by opposing candidates that was pioneered in the 1960 presidential campaign. The Kennedy-Nixon debates were shown widely on overseas television. They had

the immediate effect of making a large foreign audience aware
for the first time of the personality and the policies of the young
and largely unknown Senator from Massachusetts. The televised
debates also created an overseas demand for similar appearances
by local politicians. Such debates were carried out in a surprising
and precedent-shattering number of cases.

Japanese television was the first to take up the challenge. In
the week of Kennedy's victory, Japanese viewers watched a
frank imitation of the U.S. debates as the incumbent Liberal
Democratic Premier Hayato Ikeda debated with his Socialist and
Democratic opponents. To complete the analogy, Ikeda announced that his party platform was based on the New Frontier.[7]
Later, during national elections in Venezuela, the two leading
presidential candidates debated on national television for three
straight hours.[8] The 1962 provincial elections in Canada were
marked by television debates in the Kennedy-Nixon mold. In
at least one case, however, the debate got so unruly that Canadian
authorities later settled for the technique of having candidates
quizzed by local newsmen. This and other variations on direct
debating have also been tried on European television. A notable
holdout in such televised confrontations has been British television. During the 1964 parliamentary elections several commercial
stations tried without success to get the leading Labor and Tory
candidates to participate in face-to-face debate.[9]

Whatever form is used, there is no doubt that television has
been an important factor in getting politicians to state their
case directly to the full electorate. It has brought about changes
both in electoral techniques and in voter attitudes. The following
analysis of television's impact on the 1963 Italian elections could
be applied with minor changes to most Western nations at the
time:

> The election campaign is quite unlike any preceding contest in
> Italy. Television has almost completely ousted other methods of
> propaganda. The politicians find that they need to develop a fire-
> side manner in place of the old public-square rhetoric or the
> esoteric parliamentary jargon. Moreover, prosperity (not to men-
> tion, perhaps, a growing experience in democracy?) have greatly
> changed the public's attitude. Italians seem to have lost some

of their taste for vocal political argument. Each voter is puzzling it out for himself (or so he thinks) in front of his own television set.[10]

For most political leaders abroad, there is no longer any question about television's present or potential influence. The question they need answered is how to regulate this new force in ways that serve their purposes. They are already being made aware that television's political impact extends beyond election campaigns into everyday affairs. And they are learning that television is fair political game for all kinds of pressure groups.

Heading the list of such groups in free world countries is the Establishment's political opposition. Alleged deficiencies in the local television system can be a useful vote-catching issue for parties out of power. In Australia, the Labor party, out of power since 1949, has maintained a steady drumbeat of criticism against the ruling Liberal administration for allegedly neglecting Australian cultural interests in local television. A favorite Labor proposal is an import quota on American and other foreign television films which dominate Australian TV programing. The charge that the government condones the Americanization of local television is, in fact, a popular one for opposition parties around the world. It has been used in such countries as Great Britain, Japan, West Germany, Brazil, Mexico, Canada, and Sweden.

The government's handling of television affairs has often been a lively issue in Canadian politics. In June, 1964, the opposition Conservatives brought charges of censorship against the Liberals when the government-chartered Canadian Broadcasting Corporation announced that it would not televise a film about Prime Minister Lester Pearson. The film, made in realistic documentary style, presented Mr. Pearson as a man of vigor and decision but also one who could be bored by a long-winded visitor and who was capable of swearing on occasion. Although the Liberal government denied charges that it had influenced the cancellation of the film, the opposition pressed censorship charges. A few months later, the Conservatives called for a review of

CBC programing practices when the network presented a documentary on hate groups in which the American Nazi, George Lincoln Rockwell, expressed anti-Semitic and anti-Negro remarks.

Although the Conservative opposition in Canada was pressing for stricter control of television, opposition parties in other countries often argue for less government control over the medium. In 1964, the opposition Christian Democratic party in El Salvador severely attacked the government for proposing to apply more stringent regulations on local television programs.

Opposition party policies on television in South Africa are unique in that they oppose the government's policy of banning any kind of television in the country. The government, dominated by Afrikander white nationalists, sees television as a "subversive" force, "an insidious influence that destroyed mighty empires" and one which threatens the destruction of white rule in South Africa. Television films showing mingling of the races, government officials have declared, would lead to crime, rape, and political holocaust.[11] Opposition support for the introduction of television has been unsuccessful, although in 1965 there were signs that the government was under strong pressure to reconsider its policy.

Perhaps the most ingenious solution to the problem of political attacks on television has been worked out by the Dutch. The Netherlands' state television system has been operated as a consortium by the five major political parties. Each party's TV organization is responsible for each day's network programing on a strict rotational basis. By making television a joint political monopoly the Dutch government has been able to keep tighter control over the medium in past years than have most other European governments. Its naval and police forces moved swiftly in late 1964 to seize a "pirate" commercial TV station located on a "Texas tower" off the Dutch coast. However, the pressure for commercial broadcasting was strong enough to force the resignation of an otherwise well-entrenched coalition government in February, 1965.

Another pressure on government control over television comes from regional interests within a country. In Britain both the BBC and the commercial Independent Television Authority have been criticized by Scottish groups who claim that programs originating from London present an unfair image of Scotland. Protesting against a 1963 BBC documentary on Glasgow, the lord provost of that city accused "bearded weirdies" from the BBC of staging sensationalized scenes which allegedly presented an unbalanced picture of the city. A year later, Glaswegian sensitivities were again aroused when a commentator on the commercial ABC network suggested that no one in his right mind would want to live in Glasgow.[12] Regional sensitivities also affect television behind the Iron Curtain. In 1964, a Western observer reported that in Bratislava, the most important Slovak city in Czechoslovakia, there was considerable resentment against the canceling of local Slovak shows by national authorities in favor of programs transmitted from Prague.[13] Regional interests have also played an important role in the development of television systems within countries. Regional rivalries within Nigeria, to cite one case, were undoubtedly responsible for the swift development of television in that country under local auspices in each of the three major regions of the country.

Another political complication for television in over twenty countries is the language problem. Most of these countries have two or more official languages, and local nationalist and regional groups have been wary of attempts of their linguistic opponents to dominate local television. The problem was a fairly simple one in the days of radio when it was relatively inexpensive to have two or more transmissions, each devoted to a separate language. This solution is considerably more expensive for television.

Nevertheless, in countries where language feelings run high, this solution has been put into effect. The best example is Belgium which has two separate television systems, one each for French and Flemish. Considerable amounts of time, money, and patience are devoted to the problem of assuring "equal time" to each of the networks in an effort to maintain the country's precarious linguistic peace. Belgian television became involved in the language problem long before it ever went on the air. In 1948, when the government first began studying television possibilities, it found that linguistic considerations were closely tied in with the question of technical standards. Spokesmen for Flemish-speaking groups requested that a 625-line standard be adopted so that set owners could tune in on the neighboring Dutch television stations, operating in a language similar to Flemish. French-speaking elements in Belgium requested the French government's 819-line standard. The Belgian government sought an international solution to the problem by requesting the Permanent Commission to the Brussels Treaty (predecessor to NATO) to set a common European technical standard. It was probably the first time that television had become the subject of international negotiation. The Permanent Commission failed to find an acceptable solution, and so the Belgian government finally adopted the television pattern based on two language networks.[14]

Language has also been a factor in the South African government's refusal to permit television in that country. The Afrikaans-speaking majority among the white minority is keenly aware that its attempts to encourage the use of Afrikaans will not be helped by a television system which will have to rely heavily on English-language filmed imports to fill its program schedule.

Another example of linguistic pressures on television's development is visible in Britain where a small but vocal group of Welsh nationalists have forced the British Broadcasting Corporation and the regional commercial station (TWW—Television West and Wales) to supply a large number of all-Welsh programs.[15] Another country with complex language requirements for its television service is Malaysia. Its major TV station in Kuala Lumpur transmits programs in four languages—English, Chinese, Malay, and Tamil.

Perhaps the most unusual solution to television's problem in a bilingual society occurred in 1960 when the new nation of Cyprus was set up. In order to assure that the local radio and television systems used a proper ratio of Turkish and Greek in their transmissions, an agreement on this point was written into the nation's basic laws at the time.

Another television system which has solved its bilingual problems by utilizing two channels is Hong Kong's. The commercially operated closed-circuit system in that British colony now has separate channels for English and Chinese. Before opening this two-channel operation, however, Hong Kong television ran both English and Chinese programs on one channel, with the ratio between the two shifting in favor of Chinese as the number of its Chinese subscribers increased.

Bilingualism in television broadcasting is one of the points at issue in the political and cultural controversy over the role of French in Canada. French Canadians have argued for greater recognition of their language and culture in Canadian television. Their suspicions of alleged discrimination against such recognition were heightened in 1963 when the government turned down a recommendation of the Board of Broadcasting Governors—the Canadian equivalent of the Federal Communications Commission —for a French-language station in the capital city, Ottawa. (There are a number of French stations in other cities.) The strongly pro-French leadership of Quebec province has threatened periodically in recent years to set up its own provincial radio and television network if its linguistic demands were not satisfied. In July, 1964, the Canadian Royal Commission on Bilingualism and Biculturalism was authorized to make an over-all study into the problems of television and other mass media in a two-culture society.

In large areas of Africa and part of Asia, language problems of television are being solved, temporarily at least, by use of two foreign languages, French and English. The linguistic situation is particularly complicated in sub-Sahara Africa which has eight hundred languages, of which only two—Swahili and Hausa —can be understood by more than a small fraction of the population. Only one African nation, Tanganyika, adopted a native language, Swahili, as its official tongue when it became independent. The other new African countries chose English or French. In a few instances, they have also included a local language. The complication, of course, is that English and French are understood by only a small segment of the population. Presently television programing throughout Africa is often limited to English or French, depending on local preference. Eventually, these restrictions will have to be resolved through more extensive use of local dialects if television is to serve effectively as a communications medium reaching all the people.

The same problem will be faced in such countries as India and Pakistan where English has been the only linguistic link between different areas. Regional television systems in the subcontinent can effectively reach most people through the use of perhaps six major languages. It seems probable, however, that English will be the major language for network broadcasting in these countries for many years to come. There are political and cultural implications in this fact for the United States because of its effect on strengthening the role of English as a major *lingua franca* in these countries.

Another politically potent local pressure on television is religion. Local churchmen, acting in their role as guardians of public morals, have added television to their list of concerns. In some cases, their doubts about the medium have significantly influenced decisions about its development. The long delay in introducing television into Israel was due in part to the opposition of orthodox religious elements. The same is true in Chile where the conservative wing of the Catholic hierarchy has been opposed to wide-scale television operations as a threat to the moral standards of the country. Ultra conservative Muslim religious leaders blocked any consideration of national television in Saudi Arabia for many years. In 1964, when King Faisal authorized television as part of his modernization program, he reportedly first arrived at an understanding on television morality with local religious leaders. One provision reported at the time was an agreement not to show the female form on Saudi TV for the first six months of its operation.

Italian television, introduced by the Christian Democratic Party, was strongly influenced by Vatican commentaries on its programing, particularly in its early years. Catholic organizations have been active in monitoring television moral content in a number of countries. In 1962, the Mexican Legion of Decency extended its activities to reviewing TV productions.[16]

Lutheran church groups in two Scandinavian countries have taken the lead in questioning the handling of moral problems on local TV. In 1964, Danish Lutherans protested a televised biology program which demonstrated to Danish teenagers the use of contraceptives and which suggested that they seek further information at their city sex guidance clinics. Although the program advised against premature sex relations, the Lutheran group demanded that the program be canceled for "teaching school children and teenagers to violate God's Commandments—and how to see to it that there are no consequences."[17] A month later, leaders of the state Swedish Lutheran church announced that the church planned to review its teachings on sex as a result of the campaign for more sexual freedom pressed by television and other media.[18]

In several countries, television viewers have organized to press their complaints. A striking case of this action occurred in 1964 when a half-million Austrian viewers petitioned Parliament to look into alleged abuses in the national television system.[19] Australian viewers have organized themselves into a "National TV Congress" to improve the quality of television in that country. In Britain, a "Women of Britain Clean TV Campaign" was formed in 1964 to boycott alleged trashy programs. A major theme of such groups is the baleful effects of television on children. The range of these alleged effects is impressive. A 1963 Japanese Ministry of Education survey declared that the incidence of neurosis among three-year-olds had nearly quadrupled since television was introduced. The reason given was insomnia caused by late-night television programs. A Glasgow health service report blamed an increase of rounded shoulder posture defects on schoolchildren's imitation of the slouching walk of television cowboys.[20] Other accusations, familiar to Americans, are that television discourages reading, interferes with schoolwork, and causes bad eyesight. The most popular theme, however, involves the influence television has on the morals of the young. The medium finds few defenders on this point anywhere; the weight of the pressure is heavily on the side of those who regard television as a menace.

More specialized private groups keep a watchful eye on television to see that their interests are not harmed. The pressure on television stations and their managers not to offend anyone is as strong abroad as it is in the United States. To protect themselves, they have developed a maze of rules and regulations covering sensitive subjects.

Most free world television systems have elaborate regulations for the medium's political use. The most meticulous of these arrangements is found in Great Britain where the parties and the networks have developed complex formulas for political broadcasting.[21] British practices are generally followed in Australia, Canada, and other Commonwealth countries. Japanese television also adheres generally to an "equal time" formula for political broadcasting. One Japanese innovation is the provision that the networks can decide whether a government request for broadcast time is for partisan party purposes or for national interests. If it is the former, the government has to pay commercial rates for its program. A 1963 Brazilian decree made the transmissions of official government programs obligatory for all stations. Italian television's political regulations are monitored by a parliamentary committee which includes all the major parties. Time allocations are liberal, running as high as three hours a week for each of these parties during election campaigns.

Another important regulatory area involves children's programs. Many television systems abroad are required to program special children's shows in the afternoon, in part to offset the influence of adult shows seen by the children at night. Some networks make special efforts to identify programs as "for-adults-only" shows. French television does this with a little white dot in the corner of the screen. A 1964 directive from the Canadian Board of Broadcasting Governors prohibited any discussion of such subjects as prostitution, lesbianism, and homosexuality before 10:30 P.M. when, presumably, Canadian children are asleep. The effectiveness of banning children's viewing of certain TV shows was questioned in a 1963 Finnish study of children's program preferences. All of the shows banned for children on Finnish TV had been seen by half the 4,903 youngsters surveyed, aged nine to eleven; every child had seen at least one proscribed program.[22]

Television advertising abroad is hedged in by a variety of

restrictions. German TV advertisers are discouraged from using superlatives. A company cannot say that its widget is the best widget in the world; it has to be content with the statement that its widget is a very good widget. Irish television regulations include a provision against commercials which encourage children to enter strange places or to converse with strangers. British regulations insist that any advertiser offering a "free gift" must show it in relation to a familiar object so that its actual size can be judged. Swiss television prohibits commercials on Sundays or public holidays. In New Zealand, commercial advertising is carried only on alternate days. Italian, German, and other European systems limit television commercials to less than half an hour a night, all shown at the same time.

These restrictions probably have been useful in blunting much local criticism of TV abroad. However, it is already apparent that overseas television, like its U.S. counterpart, will be a continuing target for a wide assortment of local pressure groups. The danger, of course, is that television programing will be pushed into a kind of bland uniformity in which experimentation and controversy are by-passed. American television can provide a full quota of case studies on this subject. However, as in the United States, there are bright spots abroad. Typical of these is the attitude of the BBC's television director, Kenneth Adams, who announced several years ago that he was not going to let "the outcry of ladies from Birmingham and Glasgow" prevent the BBC from discussing sex, violence, and other controversial subjects.

Despite Mr. Adams' blunt words, neither he nor his other television colleagues abroad can escape the censoring eye of public pressure. The ladies from Birmingham will have their say, and so will their parliamentary representatives. In 1964 an all-party "advisory group" on broadcasting was formed in the British House of Commons to guard against what was described as too much violence and other faults in British television.[23] The BBC said at the time that it would refuse to recognize the group on the ground that it already had adequate channels of communication with Parliament. Labor party members of the group later decided to withdraw their sponsorship.

One of television's most subtle political effects has been the changes it has forced on other media. In the past decade, TV has elbowed its way to prominence largely at the expense of the press, radio, and films. In doing this it has upset powerful, long-standing influences of these media on the local Establishment and on the public at large. It has challenged the older media in the areas of popular appeal, economic stability, and political influence in ways that are shifting the whole pattern of mass communications throughout the world. Almost every country where television has been introduced has witnessed a power struggle between the various media as they scramble for places in the new electronic order. Inevitably, local governments have been involved.

Hardest hit by television's rise has been the film industry. For most people abroad, as in this country, the purchase of a new television set meant, among other changes, that they went to movies less often. Foreign film producers watched, with considerable trepidation, the effect of mass television on the U.S. film industry during the early 1950's. Hollywood fought a rear guard action against the new medium, notably by withholding its vast stock of old feature films. But it capitulated within a few years. The old films were released, and Hollywood became the largest single producer of new television serials for both the domestic and foreign TV markets.

Foreign film makers, however, could not do this. In most cases, they were in no position to threaten a boycott since local television managers could get suitable products to fill their schedules from the United States. The local producers were also unequipped, financially and professionally, to produce television serials which could compete with the slick, popular American products. Meanwhile their regular business was falling off, often at an alarming rate. Their audiences were declining in number and, what was worse, so were the outlets for their films. Hardest hit were the British producers. Between 1960 and 1963, over 600 film theaters closed in Britain.[24] A 1963 estimate of European film audiences showed how 1962 total admission figures differed from those of a few years earlier:

Germany—458 million, down from 818 million (1956)
Belgium—61 million, down from 110 million (1956)
France—325 million, down from 435 million (1957)
Italy—728 million, down from 819 million (1955)
Netherlands—48 million, down from 70 million (1956)
Spain—230 million, down from 328 million (1959)
Austria—90 million, down from 122 million (1958)[25]

The reason for this decline was not, of course, only television. The general rise in living standards and particularly the new influence of automobile ownership were also important factors. Film producers and theater owners could do nothing about car production, but they could have an influence on television through political, economic, and legal pressures. They had certain advantages over their Hollywood colleagues in this area. In the first place, television abroad is much more closely controlled or regulated by the government than television in the United States. Secondly, there is a long political tradition in many countries of subsidization and protection of the local film industry. In its fight against television, the film industry abroad has drawn heavily on both these advantages.

In West Germany, the industry has lobbied effectively to get a special "film aid plan" committee set up by Parliament. The committee has successfully sponsored a number of bills designed to give the German film industry some protection from television. One bill required German TV stations to pay a special fee of ten thousand dollars for every feature film they broadcast.[26] German film producers have asked for stricter safeguards against TV network competition, however. They have proposed legislation requiring the networks to turn over all their program production facilities to private concerns, i.e., the film producers.[27] Italian film producers have concentrated their legislative efforts largely on efforts to get tax rebates and special subsidies for their productions in order to compensate for the decline in cinema audiences.

While subsidies are a factor in other countries, they do not solve the main problem, which is television's rapidly growing popularity. Film producers and distributors have tried a variety of means to make TV less competitive with their product. In

1963, Spanish film exhibitors tried, without success, to force the government-run network to broadcast bullfights and soccer games only during hours which were not competitive with film-going.[28] Swiss film distributors were successful in a 1964 attempt to limit the showing of television in so-called "tele-cafés," bars, and restaurants where television is a major attraction.[29] A year earlier, French film exhibitors sought government curbs on the seventeen thousand sets located in bars and cafés in the Paris area. The French exhibitors have also attacked the showing of old feature films on local TV. In 1965, the National Federation of Movie Theaters sued the government for twenty million dollars in damages, saying that the state television network competed unfairly with film theaters by renting feature films at very low prices.[30]

The most extreme example of television's effect on a local film industry occurred in Finland several years ago. In an effort to meet audience demands for feature films, the Finnish networks bought up practically every Finnish film ever made. Finnish cinema owners had already lost half their customers and were faced with the prospect of losing most of the rest. They retaliated first by expelling the country's leading film producer from their trade association for selling most of his old films to television. Later they were more successful when they appealed to the government to limit the effect of television's competition by lowering cinema admission taxes and raising television film-rental fees.

The British film industry was successful for almost fifteen years in keeping feature films off television. The producers and distributors maintained a united front through a group known as FIDO, the Film Industry Defense Organization. FIDO's bark was, however, worse than its bite. The boycott was a success, but the film industry's audiences and box-office earnings kept getting smaller. Obviously the absence of televised feature films was not going to drive the populace from their parlors into the cinemas. By 1964, there were strong pressures to unleash FIDO so that the film industry could get the economic advantages of selling off its older products to television. In August, 1964, Hollywood producer Samuel Goldwyn defied his British distributors by selling thirty of his old films to the commercial Associated Television. There was an immediate rush to make similar deals, and by the end of the year, FIDO had voted itself out of existence.

There are increasing signs that the overseas film industry will follow Hollywood's example in dealing with television, namely to cash in on it rather than waste time fighting it. Most of the major foreign film production organizations in Europe and Japan are involved in television production. In 1964, Werner Hess, general manager of the major German network outlet in Frankfurt, could declare with considerable justification that "the television industry is the salvation of the German film industry." German film producers could (and did) grumble over his statement, but their studio production schedules confirmed the truth of what he said.[31]

Radio overseas has suffered somewhat less than the film industry as a result of television. The rise of television has overlapped with a very strong expansion in the number of radio stations and receivers throughout the world. This expansion has been especially marked in the underdeveloped countries which have been flooded with inexpensive transistor receivers. The world radio audience is still rising. However, it is also apparent that as television reaches a population saturation point in each country, radio listening begins to fall off sharply. In many countries today, television is still not a serious rival for radio.

Television has been, however, generally regarded as a threat by the press overseas. This attitude was muted in the United States by the simple fact that American newspapers were so deeply involved in television. In 1964, one-third of U.S. television stations had newspaper or magazine ownership or affiliations. This situation existed in only a few countries abroad, notably in Australia, the Philippines, and several Latin American nations. In most other countries, representatives of the press regarded the introduction of television, initially at least, as a direct threat to their advertising revenues, newsgathering reputations, and political influence. As a result, foreign newspapers have usually taken the lead in opposing the introduction of commercial television (for instance, in France, India, Greece, and the Scandinavian countries) or in inhibiting its growth.

One of the bitterest fights between the press and television has taken place in West Germany. German newspapers have maintained a steady editorial barrage against what they claim are the monopolistic privileges enjoyed by television. A major theme of the campaign is the threat of television advertising to the newspapers' economic base.[32] The German newspaper campaign against television was particularly strident in its attempts to prevent the formation of a second German network which finally went on the air in 1963. The following year, the Federal Association of German Newspaper Publishers proposed that Parliament take over the commercial activities of the second network as one means of cutting back German TV's alleged competitive advantage.[33]

As with the film industry, there are indications that the press overseas has begun to take a more sanguine view of its electronic rival. This change has been particularly noticeable in Great Britain. During the debates over the introduction of commercial television in the early 1950's, the British press was almost solidly opposed to the idea because of the threat to advertising revenues. Since then the press has been attracted to commercial television's economic possibilities. Associated Television, one of the four main independent companies, is owned in part by the London *Daily Mirror*, the *Sunday Pictorial*, and three other newspapers. The weekly *News of the World* is part owner of the Welsh television station; press magnate Roy Thomson has television interests in Britain and more than a dozen other countries. At the end of 1964, the London *Daily Express*, one of the most vitriolic early opponents of commercial television, acquired a large bloc of stock in a commercial station.[34]

Japanese newspapers, once leery of television, have taken a new look at the medium in recent years. The country's largest and most respected newspaper enterprise, *Asahi Shimbun,* has important television interests. The press is expected to make a strong bid for allocations of UHF television channels which a special government commission began studying in 1964. Reflecting on this new attitude, the Tokyo daily *Yomiuri* declared: "The day, in fact, may not be too distant when newspaper companies will rely less on the printed word than the broadcast word for fulfilling their function in disseminating news to the people."[35]

With some exceptions, the press in industrialized countries has adjusted to the initial impact of television. This impact may prove to be somewhat more unsettling in less developed countries where the press does not have the advantage of a large readership or of stable revenues. The ability of sight and sound to win large audiences quickly may prove to be a more serious threat to the development of the press in these countries than almost any other factor.

Television's impact on the other media has also had a comparable effect on government budgets. In some cases, television represents a red-ink item on the national ledger; in other instances it is a new, promising source of revenue. In either instance, television affects national budgets in ways that can have strong political overtones. The new medium is, of course, a growing expense for those governments which have decided to finance its operations directly as a noncommercial state monopoly. In France, where this is the case, the Radiodiffusion Télévision Française deficit for the fiscal year ending in April, 1964, was 29 million dollars, up 5 million dollars from the previous year. The RTF's major revenue source, aside from direct government subsidy, is a license fee imposed on each radio and television set. Austrian television's deficit is about 12 million dollars a year, despite a similar license-fee arrangement. The BBC's annual television deficit has been chronic in recent years, reaching 1.3 million dollars in 1964.[36]

These state broadcasting systems have two ways out of their deficit financing. The first one, raising their license fees, is politically unpopular. The Norwegian government braved opposition criticism in 1963, raising its television license fees by 25 percent to an equivalent of $17.50 in a move to cover its state network deficit. The BBC has urged a similar course for several years, proposing that the government's $11.20 annual fee be raised to $16.80.

The other alternative for meeting television's high costs is to become commercial, either by turning the medium over to private interests or by permitting commercial advertising on state-operated stations. In varying forms, this is the course that most national governments have taken in the past decade. In most cases, they have been able to keep their television finances at the break-even point or better. There are, however, exceptions. The state-chartered Canadian Broadcasting Corporation accepts such a limited number of commercials that it has to be heavily underwritten by direct government grants. For the fiscal year ending April, 1965, CBC received 85.9 million dollars in grants, covering about two-thirds of its operating costs in all fields.[37]

For many other governments, however, television has proved to be a useful and growing source of revenue. RAI-TV, the Italian network, reported net revenues of eight million dollars from its commercial advertisements and license fees in 1963, up 17 percent over the previous year. License and tax revenues from both the state-chartered and commercial networks in Australia in the same year netted the government thirty-eight million dollars. At the end of 1964, the government set higher tax rates on commercial television stations, siphoning off some of their booming revenues into government coffers.

The Australian government's decision reflected a common error made by many other governments in underestimating the profitability of commercial television and its tax-producing potential. The most striking example of this took place in Great Britain. During their first decade of operations, commercial television revenues and profits zoomed far beyond any of the cautious projections made in the early 1950's. In 1962–63, these stations made a combined profit of twenty-two million pounds on revenues of sixty-four million pounds—a rather impressive profit return of one-third.[38]

In an expansive moment, British press and television tycoon Roy Thomson declared that a license to operate a TV station was like a license to print money. Part of the reason for this was the relatively low tax rate laid upon the industry in its early years. The British government took active steps in 1963 to close this gap when it renewed licenses for the commercial stations. Parliament established a special levy on advertising revenue beginning in August, 1964. The new tax bite was a stiff one, calculated to provide the government with an additional 210 million dollars during the first three years of the special levy. "There has rarely been a case in British economic history," wrote one observer, "when an industry has been so penalized for success."[39] However, despite these tax restrictions British commercial television was expected to continue to average a two-to-one ratio between receipts and profits.

The prospects for such large-scale tax revenues is considerably dimmer in most underdeveloped countries. Here the problem of television revenue often centers on the difficulties of spending precious foreign exchange for American and other foreign films to fill local TV schedules. The American television industry has inherited from the film industry the problem of getting foreign-exchange remittances for its overseas sales, particularly in the dollar-short nations of Asia, Africa, and Latin America.

Aside from these fiscal problems, many governments find that their domestic television systems are increasingly involved in international relations. Most countries in Europe, Asia, and Latin America belong to intergovernmental broadcasting organizations dealing with such subjects as regional program exchanges, broadcasting of legal problems, and the like. Another international television project which will eventually involve every country is the world-wide communications satellite network.

Foreign governments are also beginning to take official measures to improve their television image in other countries. In recent years TV has become an increasingly important factor in the international propaganda field. The United States was the first country to recognize the medium's value in official information and cultural programs abroad. The U.S. Information Agency began a small TV project as part of its radio Voice of America in 1953. The project suffered from administrative and fiscal difficulties in its first years, but by 1959 it had expanded to the point where it was detached from the Voice of America and set up as a separate USIA media service.[40] Although it is still the smallest of the agency's media operations, television has established itself as a permanent element in the U.S. overseas information program. In 1965 it was supplying program materials to two thousand stations in over eighty countries.

These programs range in subject matter from presidential policy speeches to a special series of English-teaching programs that have been telecast successfully in over forty countries. The agency produces this material either in its own Washington studios or by contract with commercial producers. USIA has also assigned television officers to American embassies who place domestically produced agency shows on local television as well as prepare local programs which strengthen U.S. policy objectives in the country concerned.

The information agency produces very few programs for world-wide distribution; the overwhelming bulk of its television efforts is tailored to individual countries and regions. An example of this is its "Panorama Panamericano," a weekly review of events that have taken place in the United States and elsewhere in the Americas. The show is a regular feature on over a hundred television stations throughout Latin America. USIA television is capable of moving as fast as its commercial counterparts in covering current events. Following the first dramatic "walk in space" by astronaut Edward White in June, 1965, the agency processed and distributed a documentary film of the achievement to television stations in eighty-five countries within days after White's Gemini spacecraft landed.

Congressional legislation governing USIA limits its overseas media operations to activities where it does not compete with those of private U.S. mass media firms abroad. This is not, however, a major constraint on the agency's television service, given the small proportion of commercial television exports dealing with public affairs matters together with the lively interest shown by most TV stations abroad in acquiring materials to fill their program schedules. USIA television programs are "propaganda" in the sense that they concentrate on themes designed to advance understanding of this country and its policies. However, propaganda is an art that can be done well or done poorly. The agency's ability to make good television products can be best measured by the willingness of foreign stations to transmit its programs: in 1963 these stations broadcast over thirteen thousand hours of agency-produced shows.

Other countries are now beginning to follow the American

television lead in their own foreign propaganda programs. The British government distributes television films to foreign stations through its Central Office of Information, the London counterpart to USIA, and the world-wide facilities of the British Information Services. France has concentrated its television activities in Latin America and in the new nations of West Africa formerly under French control. The government's overseas television arm, OCORA, supplies the latter countries with technical assistance as well as with program materials designed to strengthen their traditional ties to France. The West German government began official distribution of television programs in 1965 through Deutsche Welle, its overseas broadcasting organization.

André Malraux has said that if Lenin were alive today he would have made television the primary instrument of world revolutionary activities. Communist nations have been generally slow, however, in recognizing television's international propaganda potential. Soviet government exports of television materials have been limited largely to exchanges arranged through the Communist-dominated OIRT television organization in Prague. Among East European regimes, Czechoslovakia seems to be the leader in developing TV as a propaganda asset abroad. A 1964 Czech report on these activities said that the state television organization had provided foreign stations with 3,841 news items, 409 domumentary films on Czechoslovakia, and 513 TV films during a 12-month period.[41] The Chinese Communists have made a small but effective entry into world television markets by supplying newsreel clips to Western newsfilm organizations. In view of the difficulties of getting any kind of news material from mainland China, these news clips are usually given extensive placement despite their often blatant propaganda content.

Since the end of the war international film festivals have become a popular way for a country to display some of its cultural wares and perhaps to win some prizes. A 1964 UNESCO survey showed that there were no fewer than 164 film festivals being held during that year.[42] Television has only begun to arrange its own festivals (there were only 8 of them in 1964), but there is little doubt that such events will proliferate in the coming years. The oldest of these annual events is the Prix Italia, founded in

1957; the most prestigious one is held in Cannes as a companion event to the annual film festival. The Cannes TV festival, held annually since 1961, has the special benefit of being recognized by Eurovision through the awarding of an annual Grand Prix by the network. The United States, which has generally done well in international festivals, won this Eurovision prize in 1964 with David Wolper's magnificent documentary on the 1961 election campaign, "The Making of a President." However, American television has shown little interest in sponsoring its own festivals; for years the closest it came to a competitive festival is an annual New York event which selects the best TV commercials of the year. In 1965, however, the San Francisco Film Festival added a television competition to its activities.

Occasionally one country's television programing will become a subject for international disputes. Thus, in 1964, a British satirical program which poked fun at Kenyan Prime Minister Jomo Kenyatta found itself involved in a cross fire of charges about alleged insults to a friendly foreign power. Several years earlier, the South African government declared its intention to take punitive actions against an American firm, Bristol-Myers, because it had sponsored a CBS television show allegedly critical of South African racial policies. Governments have also used television regulations as a tool to express their displeasure with other governments. In 1963, a leftist regime in Brazil issued a decree prohibiting the showing of any television programs dealing with "police events of any nature, the Far West or sex"— a fairly direct description of most of the U.S. productions being shown on Brazilian television at the time.

This all adds up to a convincing picture of television's political effect. Even though the medium is still comparatively young, it is possible to identify some trends which define both the opportunities and the limitations on television's influence in this area.

The most interesting of these trends is the manner in which the local Establishment is readjusting its original cavalier attitudes toward the medium. In country after country, the local government accepted television at first primarily as an entertainment medium, a home cinema. Its managers made the same mistake that U.S. commercial broadcasters made in the 1940's by assuming that television would be restricted largely to an upper-income elite audience. The facts were otherwise: television's appeal covered the entire social and economic spectrum overseas as it did here. Economic factors have been a more limiting factor abroad in making TV available to lower-income audiences, but the difference is smaller than the self-styled experts predicted. The poor need better medical care or sanitary facilities before television, but these needs are often muffled by the din of the television sets in the *favela* slums of Rio and the back streets of Tehran.

Faced with this reality, the governing elite in most countries abroad has been revising its attitudes toward the medium. In most cases, this involves tightening up the regulations governing television and its use. The original regulations were often loosely written, tied to the government's belief in the medium as a limited entertainment outlet. As television has expanded, so has the regulatory grip. In part this has been done by the Establishment as a form of self-protection. In part the government has been goaded into stronger regulations by its political opposition or other groups.

The more significant trend, however, has been the attempt by some governments to reassert their direct influence over television. The most interesting such attempt has taken place in Great Britain. The government's 1954 decision to introduce a separate commercial television network was predicated on the idea that the new service would be a roughly equal counterpart for the state-chartered BBC. However, things did not work out that way. Their brash, Americanized program efforts quickly gave the commercial stations the lion's share of the British TV audience. The BBC was able eventually to recoup some of its losses, partly by imitating the commercial stations. But commercial TV was too popular to be effectively cut back in size or influence. Another approach was needed. The Establishment chose a venerable British political institution—the royal commission of inquiry—to meet the challenge. The Pilkington Commission's report, issued in 1962, was archly critical of low-brow commercialism in British TV. It recommended a series of stricter regulations for the commercial network. But its most significant recommendations dealt with the future pattern of British TV expansion. The commission proposed a freeze on the expansion of commercial TV and endorsed the idea of a second BBC channel as the best means of equalizing the imbalance in the influence of the commercial and state-chartered services. Parliament gave its legislative approval to both these proposals in the most recent Television Act.

The British government's move to give active preference to the BBC over commercial television through legislative controls may have some far-reaching effects on the pattern of television control abroad. It is useful to recall that the original 1953 British decision to introduce commercial television in competition with the BBC set the pace for commercial television arrangements in many other countries which had previously relied solely on state broadcasting. The 1964 decision to restrict the expansion of commercial television at the expense of the older state-chartered service could have a similar long-range influence by suggesting to other governments how they can reassert stronger control over local television.[43]

For the present, however, few governments have taken direct action to strengthen their control over local televison facilities. The Finnish state television network bought out the competing commercial network in a move that had more financial than political overtones. (The commercial network was losing money because of its inability to compete with the popularity of the state network.) Two other takeovers, both in Africa, provide a more reliable clue to what may be a new political development for overseas television.

The first example took place in 1964 in Southern Rhodesia, the last of the British East African possessions to be ruled by a white minority. As part of their effort to prevent increased African control of the government, the white ruling class decided to buy out the commercial television system. The government's announced purpose was to prevent television from being controlled by "enemies of the state," i.e., anyone who advocated a greater political role for the African majority. Early in 1965, Southern Rhodesian commercial television became a government monopoly enterprise.

At about the same time, the African leadership of neighboring Kenya decided to nationalize the local television system. The country's commercial system had been operating for little more than a year under a government charter by a consortium of Kenyan, British, and American financial interests. Of these two moves, the Kenyan decision is by far the more significant. There are few minority governments similar to that of Southern Rhodesia, which will attempt to perpetuate its power by tightening controls over television and other media. Kenya's decision to nationalize television, however, is one which is likely to be repeated in the coming years as sensitive new Asian and African nations take a harder look at local television systems controlled in whole or in part by Western interests.

The major world-wide trend is still heavily weighted toward television's development as a commercial medium, operating under varying forms of state regulation. The heavy budgetary costs of operating a television system outside a commercial framework is still a strong inhibiting factor for any governments contemplating a return to the old system of strict state control over all broadcasting facilities.

During the next decade, governments will be taking a longer look at the most revolutionary of television's political strengths— its ability to affect basic social patterns in which all political actions are rooted. Television sets up a new order of aspiration for its mass audiences, all of which is translated eventually into political pressures. Politicians in most industrialized countries are already aware of this facet of television's influence. Their political colleagues in the underdeveloped world have still to face the full force of a medium which will bring to their people, in sight and sound, a new world of expectations that cannot be realized, in many cases, for generations.

Here is where television takes on the form of a revolutionary instrument. The methods by which it is used and controlled will have implications not only for all countries overseas but also for the United States.

6

Three TV Stars: Castro, de Gaulle, Nasser

Television's role as a political force throughout the world is still being formulated. However, there is already sufficient evidence to settle the fears of those early prophets who saw the new medium as one which would strengthen world-wide trends toward impersonal, totalitarian controls.

The real effects have been somewhat different. As we have seen, television is a powerful influence, both presently and potentially, in political affairs. It confers an advantage on those who control it. There is, however, no special political mystique about television which assures that its managers can impose their influence through it. The available evidence tends to confirm its weaknesses rather than its strengths in this area. In most cases, TV's potential as a consciously used instrument of political and social control is compromised by the fact that the medium is too distracting, too ubiquitous, too much a home entertainment diversion. When the history of the medium is written, it may be said that Big Brother met his match in Lucille Ball, and lost.

It would, however, be foolish to dismiss television's Orwellian implications completely. The early history of world television includes several examples where strong-willed political leaders have demonstrated television's special attributes as an instrument of political influence and control. We will examine three such leaders: Cuba's Fidel Castro, France's Charles de Gaulle, and the United Arab Republic's Gamal Abdel Nasser. Each represents

132

a different level of political leadership, from Castro's quixotic totalitarianism through Nasser's somewhat more tolerant Arab Socialism to de Gaulle's development of personalized control within a basically democratic structure.

What they have in common are the attributes of charismatic leadership, serving as the central element in an intensely nationalistic situation. The role of such leaders in modern societies has been hotly debated since sociologist Max Weber first tried to define it in his classic study *The Theory of Social and Economic Organization*. However, most political scientists agree that an essential element is the ability of the leader and his followers to identify with each other. Each of the three leaders discussed here have gone about securing this element in a different way; our concern is the way in which each has recognized the role that television can play in strengthening his charismatic influence over his followers.

The most dramatic example is, of course, Fidel Castro. When the bearded guerrillas seized control of the Cuban government in 1959, Castro was an unknown to most Cubans, a creature of divergent mythologies built around him by his opponents and his followers. Cuba had witnessed revolutions before, but never one like Castro's. All the earlier revolts had involved exchanges of power at the top, with little or no attempt to win mass support. Fidel Castro changed this pattern by seeking popular support for his new government. It was this factor, and the subsequent betrayal of his early reformist program, which make his actions so significant for the United States and the other nations of the Americas.

Castro is the first modern revolutionary leader to use television as a major instrument of influence and control. During the first months of his regime, the bearded leader consolidated his hold on the country in a series of extraordinary TV appearances. The studios of Station CMAB-TV in Havana literally became the seat of government. For nights on end, Castro addressed the Cuban populace in speeches that ran the histrionic gambit from soft cajoling to hysterical ranting. He had the unique advantage of being the first dictator to take over a country with a fully developed television system. With twenty-four stations throughout the island, Cuba was the leading television country in Latin America at the time of the Fidelista revolution. There were fifty-six sets per thousand population in 1959; by 1963, this figure had risen to seventy-four per thousand.[1]

"Once it was possible to walk down any street in Havana and not miss a word of a speech by Castro since the television set in every house or commercial establishment was turned at full volume, as is the custom of Cubans," wrote one American observer in Cuba at the time.[2] Because of the Latin propensity for sharing TV sets with their neighbors, it is probable that Castro was in sight-and-sound contact with over 90 percent of the Cuban population during his early major television appearances.

In pre-Castro days, Cuban TV was a highly commercialized operation, controlled by businessmen who were aware of the political value of stressing light entertainment programs and of shying away from anything that might irritate the Batista regime. The medium was a bland melding of local talent shows and American serials. At the time of the Fidelista takeover, there were sixty-two American serials on Cuban TV, heavily weighted toward comedies and cowboys.

Castro changed all this, and more. One of his early actions was to nationalize key stations throughout the country; by September, 1960, all Cuban stations were part of the Independent Front of Free Stations (FIEL).[3] The previous emphasis on light entertainment programs was replaced by a schedule which stressed Castroite propaganda. Cuban viewers soon learned, however, that the printed schedule was just a formality, subject to change whenever the Cuban leader chose to appear on television. Whatever program was in progress was abruptly halted. A disembodied voice would break in to announce that Fidel Castro, maximum leader of the revolution, had arrived at a meeting; and suddenly the TV screen would fill with scenes of the frenzy accompanying the dictator's appearance before a workers' group or a youth rally.

In the early days of his regime, Castro made live television appearances almost daily, his performances calculated to appeal to the emotions of his viewers. One evening he publicly berated the Spanish Ambassador and informed him, via television, that he was no longer wanted in Cuba. On another occasion, Castro made a dramatic move toward consolidating his power by attacking, without warning, President Manual Urrutia Lleo on charges of treason and assorted crimes of malfeasance. The hapless President, aware that his life was in danger, fled to domiciliary exile through the back door of his palace while a mob howled in the front. Many of Castro's other major decisions were announced first during his marathon television appearances. These included the agrarian reform decrees, the imposition of the death penalty for terrorists and saboteurs, the declaration of a "socialist state," and the prisoners-for-tractors proposal to exchange hostages from the unsuccessful 1961 Bay of Pigs invasion for agricultural equipment. At one point, Castro used his television forum to announce his resignation; several weeks later, he again appeared before the cameras to announce that he would "sacrifice" himself and take up his job as Premier once again.

It quickly became clear to Cubans that their leader's television appearances were replacing elections and other democratic processes. From the start, the fiery Premier offered the rationalization that his "consultations" with the people at mass rallies or over television were advanced forms of democracy. It was, he argued, the democracy of the market place, permitting him to discuss his policies with the people and thereby to gain their approval. In this way, he by-passed the electoral process—and the danger of identifying the size of his opposition—by having elections decided by "acclamation" at televised mass rallies.

Later, Castro gave this procedure a more institutional cast by inaugurating "People's Assemblies." These assemblies were nothing more than mass rallies at which Castro asked the crowd— and a nation-wide audience of television onlookers—to approve his latest policy. These meetings were, particularly in the early days of the regime, virtuoso performances. One observer noted at the time:

> Facing a rally of hundreds of thousands of ardent supporters or an equally enthusiastic studio audience, Dr. Castro carefully holds

back any specific proposals that he plans to make. With the chanting of slogans, the rhythmical clapping of thousands of hands, his own histrionics of voice and gesture, he orchestrates a frenzy in the overstimulated crowds. Then, sensing the exact moment when they have become fully receptive to him, he springs his surprise—a threat or a promise or an announcement set before an audience conditioned to accept anything he may suggest.[4]

There was, of course, no chance for the presentation of a minority viewpoint on these decisions. The only significant rebuttal to Castro's policies took place in March, 1960, when Luis Conte Aguero, a well-known Cuban journalist and an early supporter of the Fidelista movement, went on television to denounce the increasingly dominant influence of Communists in the revolutionary government. He argued forcefully for the maintenance of Cuba's traditional friendship with the United States. Immediately following his broadcast, a government television commentator suggested that Conte Aguero be shot or else expelled from the country within twenty-four hours. Three days later the Maximum Leader himself went on the air to denounce Conte Aguero as a traitor. Conte Aguero then sought refuge in the Argentine Embassy in Havana and left Cuba shortly after. This isolated example of anti-Castro television activity resulted in the tightening up of the regime's control.[5]

Cuban television became a direct instrument of injustice in the early days of the Castro regime when it was used to televise the public trials of regime opponents before the so-called "revolutionary tribunals." Whatever the legal merits of the cases against the defendants, there is no doubt that mass hysteria against them prejudiced whatever chances they had for a fair trial.[6] There was no possibility for such legal niceties as a change of venue in the nation-wide atmosphere of hostility toward the accused prisoners, created largely by television.

A similar procedure took place after the abortive Bay of Pigs invasion in 1961. Survivors of the ill-fated venture were placed before the television cameras as examples of the Yankee imperialist threat. Since that time, Cuban TV has been used to display other captured anti-Castro activists who are usually described as agents for the U.S. Central Intelligence Agency.

This procedure seems to have two purposes. The first is to fan the standard anti-American sentiments among Castro's followers. The second is to warn his opponents of the perils of taking active steps against the regime. This warning is directed not only to anti-Castro elements within Cuba but also to the large Cuban exile colony in Florida. This can be done directly: atmospheric conditions often permit direct reception of Havana television in Miami and other Florida cities.[7] A group of captured exile infiltrators, interviewed on Cuban television in February, 1965, made a direct appeal to Florida-based exile groups to "reflect" before attempting to land in Cuba since conditions on the island were "different" from what they had been led to expect—a statement which was also probably intended as a counsel for greater caution to those who might follow.

These "spy shows" are special features in a program schedule that has become more heavily propagandistic as the regime becomes aware of the effect of a gap between its early reformist promises and the realities of Cuba's creaking economy. The main task of television and other elements of the Cuban propaganda apparatus is "to create a new consciousness about Socialist productions among the people," a key regime spokesman declared late in 1964.[8]

The result is a leaden program schedule, heavy on pro-Castro bombast and repetitious warnings about the enemies of the regime. A special half-hour series on Cuban history, prepared by the Ministry of Education, has rewritten past events to conform to the regime's line. A typical segment is entitled, "How Cuba Became a North American Colony." Heavy-handed documentary films record the travels and speeches of the Maximum Leader when he is out of range of FIEL's cameras. Visiting delegations from other "socialist" countries are almost always given their turn before the cameras, usually to repeat the dual-theme litany of fraternal greetings and attacks on the United States. With its former supply of free world television materials cut off, Cuban television has programed considerable amounts of television shows supplied by other Communist countries.

These programs are supplied usually under cultural agreements which the regime has negotiated with these countries in the Soviet sphere of influence, including a somewhat academic promise to exchange television materials with Outer Mongolia, announced by Radio Havana in May, 1962. In April, 1964, the Cubans announced that they had agreed to exchange radio, film, and television materials with the Chinese Communists.

Cuban viewers also get a heavy diet of Soviet and other Communist feature films. It is, however, older American films, left behind after commercial film distributors were forced out of business, that attract the large audiences. According to one British observer in 1964, Cuban television at the time was filled

> with what seemed to be an endless succession of vintage Hollywood films, of the kind I had supposed were preserved only for the weary weekends of England's BBC. The Director of the Cuban television service, who chances to be an old-guard Communist of much taste and erudition, told me with a sort of ironic resignation that the customers could not get enough of these archaic productions. In any case there was little else, and nightly the shades of Fred Astaire and Judy Garland gamboled eerily over the shaky screens. This seemed to produce no adverse reaction from the high command. Indeed, it was said that the favorite TV personality of Fidel, after Fidel, was Ginger Rogers. To Cuba, for so long the repository of all the pop art of the United States, the North American film culture had been fossilized in its 1960 period.[9]

Films, documentaries, and the appearances of enemy spies are, however, all secondary to the self-appointed star attraction, Fidel Castro. In 1960, he announced that he would limit his television appearances by speaking regularly on Friday nights. Television was too important a political tool for him to exercise such restraint for very long. The Friday night schedule was soon supplemented by other appearances. In July, 1960, the entire island buzzed with rumors about Castro's ill health after he had canceled an appearance at a large rally. A few hours later he ended this speculation by having a television camera installed in his hospital room, permitting him to make another dramatic address to the nation. After this incident, his television appearances became somewhat less frequent, but they were no less long-winded or emotional.

Commenting on this phenomenon, a Swiss observer has said:

I have seen the Bouglione Circus, Cinerama atrocities by Cecil B. De Mille, Arab festivals and Broadway parades but never have I witnessed a show to hold a candle to Fidel Castro's television marathon. (He warms up slowly) . . . but suddenly the storm breaks—the first drop appears on his neck, the green shirt blackens with sweat, his powerful torso begins to sway above the table . . . and for the next six hours I sit glued to my seat, fascinated, rooted to the spot like a mouse in front of a snake. And in all Cuba exactly the same thing is happening to over four million people. . . . What is government by television? A cheap newspaper gimmick? No, for with his non-stop TV show, Fidel Castro has actually created a new form of government that is just as original and will prove no less significant in its historic effects than the Greek invention of the ballot, better known under the name of Democracy. For six million Cubans, the sole expression of their government's will is the television speech. . . .[10]

This analysis was written in 1960, at the height of Castro's campaign to impose his will by television. However, the trend of events in Cuba since that time tend to discount premature claims of "government by television," of electronically mesmerizing a population into submission. Television has played an important role in consolidating the position of the Castro regime and, in particular, maintaining the enthusiasm of its supporters. It is still far from becoming an Orwellian nightmare. Regime enthusiasts may listen to television out of devotion to their leader, but the average Cuban turns on his set now primarily to find out what is next in store for him and his country. The problem of holding a television audience is compounded by the reported decline in the number of TV receivers throughout the country. Some sets have been imported from the Soviet bloc. Most TV sets are, however, pre-Castro American models for which spare parts are virtually unobtainable. As a result, sets are kept in working order primarily by cannibalization of other sets.[11]

The major reason why Fidel Castro is getting smaller audiences, however, is simply that his TV dramatics have become a bore. It would be wrong to underestimate the continuing role of TV as a propaganda weapon for the Castro regime. It would be equally incorrect to underestimate TV's harsh ability to disenchant its audience when the flickering screen shows fraud. The stubborn facts of economic decline and political repression cannot be explained away by televised rhetoric. It is perhaps significant that in recent years Cubans have seen considerably fewer televised performances by their Maximum Leader than at the beginning of the regime. The tone of his appearances has also changed. Whereas his earlier marathon speeches were omnibus productions, discussing all types of national and international affairs, they now concentrate more directly on the country's internal economic difficulties. They often include stinging attacks by Castro on the directors and administrators of agricultural and industrial enterprises, putting on them much of the blame for the sorry state of the country's economy. In an October, 1964, TV speech he warned against the practice of assigning the blame to the "imperialist blockade," declaring that "inexperience, incapacity, superficiality, and irresponsibility" in state officials are also factors. Otherwise his speeches are exhortations for harder work, particularly in assuring a good sugar harvest. Waving his arms (complete with two Rolex watches, as usual) Castro warns that without a good harvest, Cuba would not have even electric lights. The appeal often falls on deaf ears. "The only time we can be sure of electricity is when Castro speaks," a Havana housewife said in 1965. "They want us to see him on television."[12]

There was, perhaps, rough justice involved in the unconfirmed April, 1964, report that a group of anti-Castro Cubans in Havana planned to assassinate Fidel Castro by electrocuting him with a television microphone. The plotters planned to hook a high-voltage cable to the microphone scheduled to be used by the Premier at a student rally. The plan was allegedly betrayed by one of the participants, resulting in the execution of two and the jailing of fifteen others.[13]

Castro's use of television is a dramatic example of the medium's political potential in a totalitarian regime. In the Free World, the most striking example of TV as a political fence has taken place in General Charles de Gaulle's France. The General's exploitation of *les étranges lucarnes*–the queer little windows of the TV screen—has been a significant factor in rallying French opinion to his policies since he returned from his self-imposed rural exile to take over leadership of the country in 1958. Television has served him in much the same way as radio did in World War II. Then, as David Schoenbrun has noted, he became the symbol of France and the French people largely through broadcasts from outside their borders: "They never laid eyes on their leader until Liberation Day itself. General de Gaulle, the image of the great leader of the Free French, was a man invented by radio."[14]

French television was in a state of retarded infancy when de Gaulle came to power. A succession of postwar governments had failed to make any fundamental decisions on the role of the new medium in French life. Television, which is a government monopoly, was given a low priority in the national budget. Its program resources and physical plant were affected accordingly. In 1958, France was at the bottom of the list of Western European countries in the number of per capita television stations and home receivers. The new Gaullist leadership began to change this. The desultory planning for a nation-wide network was speeded up and greater attention paid to the program offerings of Radiodiffusion Télévision Française (RTF). TV was being shaped according to the requirements of the Gaullist vision of a nation destined for new grandeur and influence in Europe and throughout the rest of the world. As the medium expanded in size and influence, it also took on some of the austere, no-nonsense coloration of its Gaullist managers. French TV is conspicuously free of avant-garde unconventionality which forms such a significant part of the nation's theater, films, and literature.[15]

The central figure in this development was, of course, the General himself. Every major turning point in French politics since 1958 has been marked by his television appearances, in which he has alternately cajoled, scolded, praised, and informed a vast audience. The average Frenchman's image of his President is the austere *le grand Charles* looking at him through the living room TV screen. Seated at an elegant desk, the General sonorously calls for the support of his countrymen—addressing them grandiloquently as *Françaises! Français!*—in whatever new project he is engaged.

"As always," he said in one typical speech, "I neither could nor would do anything without your help. As always I shall soon ask you for it. Thus, as always, it is you who would decide." Commenting on this speech, one American observer noted the superb rhetorical effect it had, with the "*votre* and *vous* booming out each time like a stroke of a big bell calling the countryside."[16] However much this might be dismissed as bombast by de Gaulle's opponents, there is no doubt that it struck an emotional chord in most Frenchmen.

Perhaps the most dramatic of General de Gaulle's many television appeals for French unity occurred on a tense night in April, 1961, when a French Army coup in Algeria presented him with a serious challenge to his leadership. His television appeal to Frenchmen, forbidding them to cooperate with the coup leaders and calling for national unity, was a key move in rallying public opinion at a crucial moment.

The General's television appearances are not, however, limited to times of crisis. Television cameras are fixed hypnotically on all of his public activities. Such coverage is carefully planned in ways that are often strikingly dramatic, or theatrical, depending upon the political point of view of the French onlookers. The General's appearances on television are possibly more frequent than that of any other major political figure in the world. During one twelve-month period, he was reportedly featured on the single national channel no less than 376 times, including rebroadcasts.[17]

By contrast, the General's political opponents have been systematically limited in their television appearances. This practice is not a Gaullist innovation; it was also common to all of the coalition governments of the earlier Fourth Republic. There is, however, an important difference. In previous postwar governments, a succession of constantly changing ministers—particularly those in charge of television and other government-controlled media—tended to neutralize each other's influence in this respect. A Socialist might be followed by a Roman Catholic Popular

Republican, a Radical by a conservative. The other difference is that television was a negligible influence during most of the Fourth Republic because of the limited number of stations and home receivers. There has been no such confusion of method or purpose under the de Gaulle administration. Television reflects the regime's views, and it has done so consistently and without any significant opposition since 1958. The government's defense for such strict control of television is pegged largely to the need to by-pass the generally anti-Gaullist French press in making known the government's position on important issues.[18]

Whatever the Gaullists' defense, they have been thorough in limiting the airing of any contrary views on the national radio and television networks. "Equal time" broadcast arrangements, common in most other Western countries, are a negligible factor in French politics. Television played an important role in the 1962 Gaullist campaign for amending the Constitution to strengthen the presidency at the expense of the traditionally dominant legislature. For months before the national referendum on this issue, television and radio facilities were used to give a sympathetic explanation of the proposed changes. The major opposition parties were each given one ten-minute segment on national television to explain their views. The Gaullist proposals won handily in the ensuing referendum.

In February, 1964, the government announced similar restrictions for the first presidential elections under the new laws. Under the rules, the campaign was to last only two weeks, with the opposition parties permitted time on the national radio and TV networks only during this period.[19] Some indication of the treatment opposition candidates might expect was given during the previous month when the Socialist mayor of Marseilles, Gaston Defferre, announced his candidacy for the presidency at a large meeting. French television covered the announcement in a filmed report lasting a half minute. As one observer noted wryly, the camera, sweeping through the crowd, somehow managed to miss M. Defferre's face.[20]

French television has also been used to reflect General de Gaulle's international policies. The French television system has made greater use of Eurovision, the European international network, to highlight the policies and personality of its national leader than any other member system. In 1963, French TV originated 134 Eurovision network programs—almost twice as many as any other Eurovision member.[21] French domestic television also reflects the government's international concerns. During the winter of 1963/64, the rapprochement between France and Communist China was supported on French TV by a heavy dose of pro-Peking documentaries that left the impression that the Chinese Reds were a group of mild reformers. On the other side of the coin, in February, 1963, French television abruptly canceled a scheduled special interview with Soviet Premier Khrushchev marking the twentieth anniversary of the Battle of Stalingrad. Diplomatic observers concluded that the about-face was ordered to avoid embarrassing the West German government at a time when France was seeking German support for its European policies. The Russians retaliated by distributing extensively the text of the interview with the explanation that "words of truth cannot be stopped by order of the French authorities or those of their Bonn allies."[22]

A similar incident, involving the cancellation of a program for American and West European viewers, occurred in July, 1963. A transatlantic televised conversation between former President Eisenhower and three European leaders was arranged by the Columbia Broadcasting System to mark the first anniversary of the successful orbiting of an experimental Telstar communications satellite. The subject of this international dialogue, to be carried via satellite, was European-American relations. In a last-minute switch, the French television network withdrew from the arrangement, citing technical difficulties. The more plausible explanation, according to independent observers, was that the French spokesman on the program was Jean Monnet, the famed economic planner whose conception of a supranational Europe is opposed to General de Gaulle's "Europe of states."[23]

American observers of French television programing have often been disturbed by its sporadic overtones of anti-Americanism, over and above the normal level of reporting on U.S. faults and failings. According to these observers, French news and commentary on American involvement in Southeast Asia, to cite one example, has on occasion used, uncritically, films and other news materials from Communist sources which stress the theme of alleged U.S. aggression in this area.

A somewhat more picturesque example of critical attitudes toward the United States took place in 1964 when the French television network inaugurated a new series on the American West. French viewers had long been accustomed to American-produced cowboy programs; this series, however, was produced in France by the state television network. The series was entitled "The Indians," and it featured, by way of a French quirk, the cowboys as the villains and the redskins as the heroes. As the series continued, the uncomfortable truths of the Indians' exploitation by the palefaces began to look to some observers like a Gallic comment on American political attitudes.

Allegations of progovernment bias on French news broadcasts have been made, often with considerable justification, against all postwar French governments. The most flagrant example cited by critics was French radio and television coverage of the Algerian revolt in the 1950's. A leading French television personality, Pierre Lazaroff, has claimed that between 1956 and 1959, when the Algerian fighting was at its worst, French television did not devote a single program to the revolt.[24] There have been a series of flash strikes and walkouts in the French television service in recent years in protest against alleged censorship and other interference in news programing. During the 1962 referendum campaign, a group of TV announcer-reporters walked out just before the main evening news program, alleging heavy-handed government interference with the contents of the program. Later in the same year, network employees conducted a one-hour radio-TV "blackout" for similar reasons.[25]

For millions of Frenchmen, the solution to alleged bias on their own national network is to switch their sets to the highly popular stations in neighboring Luxembourg, Monaco, and the Saar. In recent years, a small but vocal minority has chosen to attack the problem head-on by lobbying for improvements in local coverage. In 1963, a private organization, *Union Nationale des Téléspectateurs,* was formed to lobby for improved program quality on French TV.[26] Other attempts have been made to amend French broadcasting laws in ways that would restrict government control. In 1963, Jean-Maurice Bugat, director of the French Television Study and Information Center, and other experts announced that they would press for broadcast time for individuals wishing to rebut charges or comments made against them on the state-controlled radio and television.[27] These and similar pressures were clearly a factor in the French government's 1964 decision to set up a new radio-television organization, l'Office de Radiodiffusion Télévision Française (ORTF). Direct policy control over broadcasting operations was shifted from the Ministry of Information to a council composed of government and public representatives. Most French critics of alleged Gaullist dominance in broadcasting affairs considered the change an improvement; they noted, however, that day-to-day control of the radio and television system was placed in the hands of a three-man directorate, appointed by the government and subject to replacement at will. The government is permitted "to broadcast any declaration of communication it deems necessary," although such an announcement has to be identified as an official one. In effect, French broadcasting has become a public utility after forty years.[28]

With its new administrative setup, French television has expanded, in terms of both its facilities and its audience. A second network, inaugurated in April 1964, has added a new competitive note within the country; meanwhile the entire broadcasting system has shown increasing awareness of the competition from border stations in neighboring countries. A more significant development is the increasing pressure to include commercial advertising on ORTF stations as a means for providing more money for programing.

These changes in French television have not affected the Gaullist view of television as a useful political weapon. There has, for instance, been little flexibility shown under the new arrangement in providing a greater television voice for the government's political opposition. General de Gaulle is still the nation's number one TV personality, if only because of the relatively colorless character of the men who oppose him.

Fidel Castro and General de Gaulle had each taken over a fully developed television system and turned it to his own purposes. Egypt's Gamal Abdel Nasser found a different situation when he and his fellow colonels overthrew the monarchy of King Farouk in the early morning hours of July 23, 1952. There was no television in Egypt at the time. The new regime took care to seize control of the Cairo radio station immediately. This was, however, a standard gambit in Middle Eastern military coups which did not indicate one way or another Colonel Nasser's propaganda capabilities. This side of his complex character was to emerge in the months that followed when the new government gave high priority to the expansion of the Egyptian broadcasting system, including television.[29]

At the time of the Nasser coup, Egypt had only two radio transmitters, broadcasting 22 hours a day. By 1960, Egyptian radio capabilities had been boosted to 11 transmission centers, broadcasting a total of 198 hours daily. A new short-wave service broadcast 130 hours a day in 19 languages. Having strengthened its radio capabilities, the newly named United Arab Republic (UAR) turned to television. Its early plans to install a TV system had been disrupted by the 1956 Suez crisis. By 1958 these plans were revived, and in 1960 the first television transmissions were made from Cairo on the eighth anniversary of the revolution.

The UAR's television system is undoubtedly the most extensive and probably the most effective of its kind in any of the newly developing countries of Asia and Africa. Almost from the beginning, Cairo television and its coaxial links reached most of the heavily-populated areas of the Nile River basin. In 1966, the completion of a microwave link with Aswan, three hundred miles south of the capital, will bring UAR television within range of most of the nation's populace. The number of sets in 1965 was an estimated half million, serving an audience of over three million persons. While this is largely an urban audience, the UAR government has made special efforts to make television sets available in rural areas for mass viewing. In 1965, the government announced that its television receiver factory had begun production of a battery-operated transistor set primarily for use in villages without electricity. At the same time, it declared that it would distribute two million of these sets to such villages during the first year of production.[30]

Egyptian television is a judiciously effective mixture of entertainment and government-directed "enlightenment." American cowboys, detectives, and comedians compete for attention with popular Arab singers and dramatic groups on Cairo's three channels. Unlike television in most developing countries, the UAR program pattern is heavily weighted in favor of local shows. A 1963 survey showed that 78 percent of its programs were produced within the country.[31] (In many other developing countries, the ratio would be almost reversed, with the bulk of programing consisting of American and other Western filmed serials.) From the salons of Cairo's exclusive Garden City district to water-front teahouses at Port Said, television is rapidly taking its place as Egypt's most important entertainment medium. The Nasser government's propaganda experts have usually been careful not to bore their audiences with too much official "enlightenment."

Nevertheless, Nasser-styled guidance is very much a part of UAR television. The medium is directly controlled by the Ministry of Culture and National Guidance, an oganization that has figured prominently in the Nasser regime from the start. The ministry has never made a secret of the propaganda role it expects radio and television broadcasting to play in the regime's plans. In a "new policy for programs" issued in 1960, the ministry listed its main broadcasting objectives as follows:

—United efforts for the success of Arab nationalism and to resist imperialism internally and externally in all its forms and shapes.

—Throw light on the glories of our Arab history, the stages of our struggles against the invaders, heroic feats and the life of our heroes, leaders and pioneers who stood in the face of the colonialist tyrants.

—Raise the standard of the arts.

—Inform the people of the great achievements of human civilization.

—Give prominence to the progress of the industrial drive in the country.

—Give due consideration to vocational and craft programs.

—Combat harmful habits and traditions handed down from past generations, dealing with social problems and call for closer adherence to spiritual and moral values.

—Give prominence to the role played by women in the progress of the family and society.

—Disseminate sports consciousness and the athletic spirit among the rising generation.

—Encourage new talents in the field of thought and creation.

—Create the group spirit between individuals and groups.

—Give due consideration to the celebration of national and religious feasts in such manner as to render a true picture of our traditions and glories.[32]

This would seem to add up to heavy-handed television. In fact, it generally does not. This is due in part to the UAR television system's willingness to recognize that the medium is essentially an entertainment outlet. It accepts the fact that televised propaganda and enlightenment efforts are best handled in relatively small doses. A corollary is the regime's general inclination not to lay President Nasser open to that most stifling of television perils—overexposure.

The Nasser enlightenment-by-TV campaign operates at two levels. The first is the use of the medium as an instrument of social education, linking the masses to government modernization programs in such fields as health, sanitation, home economics, and school television. Cairo's television schedule is heavily weighted in favor of how-to-do-it shows and other educational programs. The third channel has been reserved largely for such efforts, including a plan to provide instructional programing for the national school system. The United States has provided assistance to this effort since 1963 through the services of two Ohio State University audio-visual specialists, Dr. Keith Tyler and his wife. The Tylers have drawn up a five-year program for school television which is slowly being implemented.[33]

The second educational chore of UAR television is the more directly political one of extolling the achievements of the revolutionary regime and its dynamic leader. Working from Cairo's new radio-television center, film crews and mobile television units record the public activities of Gamal Abdel Nasser. His speeches, ribbon-cuttings and other appearances usually pre-empt all of Cairo TV's normal schedules. No factory or public work is inaugurated by him without the presence of television cameras and commentators giving appropriate credit to the regime for a new step along the path of Arab socialism. News programs are carefully prepared with an eye toward the government's current views in domestic and international affairs. The result is to make Nasser, his policies, and his accomplishments better known to the public than is the case with government leaders in any other Middle Eastern country.

In large part, this can be explained by the fact that Nasserite policies and achievements are the only political fare presented on UAR television. There are no provisions for permitting opposition viewpoints of any kind. Television's primary function is the maintenance of popular support for the regime; the government has amply endowed the medium with facilities and funds to carry out this objective. These are the conditions underlying the political role of the television system of the UAR. They do not, however, explain TV's general success as a persuasive medium in Egypt. Other totalitarian regimes throughout the world have attempted to bend television's peculiar characteristics to their domestic propaganda needs; few have been as successful as the Egyptians. The reason for this must be found in the *relative* restraint that the Nasser regime has shown in its television propaganda.

This restraint is not readily apparent to a Western observer of UAR television to whom its propaganda efforts may seem heavy-handed, repetitious, and larded with excessive rhetoric. In fact, Egyptian television tends to rely on a comparatively "soft sell" approach much of the time. The exceptions occur when the government is greatly concerned with advancing a tactical political policy—a new effort at Arab Socialism or a step-up in the anti-Israel campaign. Normally, however, the government's efforts at television enlightenment are kept within what are, by Arab standards, reasonable bounds. An example is the relative infrequency of appearance of Gamal Abdel Nasser on the television screen, particularly as compared with the heavy exposure accorded

Fidel Castro and Charles de Gaulle on their respective TV networks. Egyptian television covers all of its leader's major public appearances, but it seems to be under no compulsion to picture him or mention him at frequent intervals. The tone and pace of this approach is set by President Nasser himself. His television presentations, unlike those of Castro or de Gaulle, tend to avoid direct appeals to television audiences in favor of televised coverage of events in which he is the leading orator addressing a meeting to which the television audience is invited as onlookers. The interaction of Nasser's strident rhetoric and the frenzied responses of the crowd is a potent influence on the millions of viewers gazing at TV screens throughout the country. Appropriately, most of them watch the performance on a TV receiver whose trademark is "Nasser."

Despite these successes, television propaganda has its limitations in the UAR as elsewhere. The Nasser government had hoped to utilize the medium to secure popular support for the political union between Egypt and Syria in 1958. At the time, Syria had three television stations to Egypt's one. A major effort was made by UAR propaganda specialists to promote support for the merger through television. Heavy schedules of material were interchanged between TV stations in the Northern and Southern Regions, as Syria and Egypt were known at the time. One Cairo quiz program, "Ticket to Damascus," offered an all-expense tour of Syria as first prize. Despite these efforts, the Egyptian-Syrian union failed in 1961. Historical and regional differences were stronger than the ties of Arab unity—or the ability of television and other propaganda efforts to paper them over. There were, moreover, indications at the time that the Syrians resented the pre-emption of their regional television stations by a program schedule heavily weighted with Egyptian material.

Despite the failure of the Egyptian-Syrian union, the Nasser government is even more strongly committed to the theme of Arab nationalism and the corollary of Egyptian leadership of the movement. Increasingly, television is becoming a key element in relaying this message to mass audiences throughout the Arab world. Every Arab state except Yemen has television facilities serving rapidly expanding audiences; already TV is second only to radio in influence and popularity in many large cities throughout the area. Anticipating the day when TV will become the dominant mass medium, Cairo is laying the groundwork for establishing its primacy in Arab television. The Nasser government's ultimate goal seems to be the establishment of an Arab TV network, a subject constantly discussed at the many unity meetings held by Arab governments. The chances for implementing such a project are thwarted by the shifting pattern of intrigues and suspicions among the Arabs themselves.

A direct example of the difficulties involved occurred in May, 1962, when relations between the United Arab Republic and Jordan were strained. At the time, Jordan did not have television, but UAR television was readily being picked up by Jordanian receivers. The Jordanian government, apparently irritated at the local effect of UAR television attacks on its policies, ordered a 200 percent retroactive import tax on the hundreds of receivers already in the country and placed a 500 percent duty on all newly imported sets. Several months later, it banned the use of TV sets in cafés, clubs, and other public places.

Until political and economic conditions favor direct television links between Arab countries, the UAR is concentrating its efforts on bilateral TV arrangements with other Arab states. In 1963, for instance, the UAR concluded an agreement with Algeria to provide, among other services, an hour of Egyptian programs daily on Algerian TV. A 1964 agreement with Iraq made two hundred hours of UAR programs available to Baghdad TV. The UAR also agreed to train Iraqi engineering and programing technicians at Cairo's UAR Television Institute. The Institute, originally planned only for Egyptian trainees, was expanded in 1963 to include foreign students. The first class of foreign technicians included trainees from Algeria, Syria, Sudan, and Kuwait. Since that time, UAR television managers have shown increasing interest in extending their assistance to non-Arab developing countries in Africa and Asia.[34]

The Nasser government's most spectacular international effort in television, however, has been its sponsorship since 1962 of a series of international television festivals, the first of their kind in the Asian-African area. The festivals are a highly conscious attempt to strengthen the UAR's standing in international circles. The political importance of the festivals is such that all of the major powers, including the United States, have sent representatives to them. Thirty countries were represented at the third festival, held in Alexandria in August, 1964.

We might now ask the question, which of our three video stars—Nasser, de Gaulle or Castro—is the most effective TV politician? Unfortunately, no Nielsen ratings for world leaders are available to give us a clue to the answer. There are, in fact, few reliable indicators of television's place, present or potential, in modern politics. "In the area of political television, we are all ignorant," newsman Edward R. Murrow once said, "We know a great deal about what will sell goods and services. We have spent vast sums on research . . . but we do not know enough. We have not been sufficiently interested to try to determine what sells ideas." Murrow added his own prescription for effective political television: "There is no substitute for the man who has at least mild fire in his belly and is able to pierce that screen with his own conviction."[35]

The three leaders examined here all share this trait. In individual ways, each has used television to project his own ideas and personality in an aura of charisma that spreads out to envelop vast unseen audiences. These men's success is a lesson in television's political power to influence. But it also carries a warning. Charisma is the most fragile of political emotions, difficult to generate and hard to sustain over a long period. When the leader finishes speaking, his televised image fades from the screen and with it goes some of the mystique that, only a few moments earlier, had held millions of people within his influence.

Television, happily, will never reach the mesmeric limits envisaged by George Orwell in his world of 1984. Nevertheless, its political powers should not be underestimated. No other mass medium has ever provided political leaders with such direct sight-and-sound contact with the mass of their followers. Because television is controlled by the political elite, the leadership can manipulate it in ways that permit them access to this mass audience on their own terms. Nasser, de Gaulle, and Castro all have shown themselves to be instinctive masters of the political arts in their TV appearances. Finally, television has a unique capacity to project a sense of personal identification between the leader and his audience. The gap that separates the average citizen from the inexplicable bureaucracy that controls his life is suddenly closed as his leader explains and simplifies it all on his own home screen. This is not, however, an automatic process; the inventory of politicians who have tried and failed to use television for their own purposes is already a long and growing one. The key element is the intangible one of personal dynamism, the fire-in-the-belly that is the precondition for political success in television.

7

U.S. Television's
Overseas Markets

Every evening millions of television viewers around the world sit before their sets to be entertained by such programs as "Espectaculo de Lucy," "Entgleiste Komische Stummfilmszenen mit dialog," "Arligt Byte," and "Dzsessz Szinhely U.S.A." These shows have one attribute in common: they were all produced in the United States.[1] As such, they are part of the largest and most visible American activity in the booming field of international television.

American commercial involvement in television abroad dates from 1939 when the Radio Corporation of America sold a transmitter to the Soviet government for experimental telecasting in Moscow. RCA and the other industry pioneers fully expected such equipment sales to be television's major activity abroad. And, in fact, through the early postwar period they were. After 1950, however, the pattern changed as the industry moved into other areas. Today, the range of overseas activities parallels domestic operations. It includes program production and syndication, equipment sales, management and technical services, advertising sales, and the outright control of television stations and related properties. A conservative estimate of current annual revenues from these overseas operations is 125 million dollars, with a yearly 10 percent rate of increase.[2]

The largest share of this business is the syndication of U.S. television programs ranging in style and content from "Sheena the Jungle Girl" to Walter Cronkite documentaries. American TV products—for better and worse—are setting the tone for television programming throughout the world in much the same way Hollywood did for motion pictures forty years ago. The United States now leads all other countries as a program exporter by a wide margin. From the sporadic export of a few features to Britain and Latin America ten years ago, telefilm sales have expanded to an estimated 1965 dollar volume of over seventy-five million dollars, spread through ninety countries. Foreign sales were, until a few years ago, a source of random profits peripheral to revenues from syndication at home. This casual attitude has since been reversed, largely as a result of soaring production costs and fierce competition within the trade. Today, overseas sales represent the difference between profit and loss for the telefilm industry.[3] Since the nature of the domestic telefilm production and distribution industry sets the pattern for its overseas activities, a brief review of its structure is useful.

Telefilm is the brash stepchild of American commercial television. In an economic system as complex as America's, new ventures usually start on an experimental note as they search for their niche in the scheme of things. The TV film industry was spared any such early doubts or hesitations. Its purpose was clear: to produce films, divided into thirty-minute segments, designed for maximum audience appeal. Above all, the trade had to meet the networks' need for a predictable product that could be marketed to advertisers. The obvious choice for producers of such films were the Hollywood feature-film studios. In the early fifties, however, the big studios were not interested. They were still riding the postwar feature-film boom. Moreover, they did not want to give aid and comfort to a competitor. Of the larger studios, only Columbia—through its Screen Gems affiliate—broke ranks and went into telefilm production.

As a result, TV film-making during the fifties was centered around a group of new independent producers. Many of the firms never got beyond producing an impressive letterhead for their stationery and a fantasy-filled brochure outlining their plans. The corporate mortality rate was high. By the end of 1956, 331 companies were listed as television program producers by *Tele-*

vision Factbook. Three years later the same publication reported that half these companies had gone out of business.[4] For the companies which survived, television production and syndication reached bonanza proportions.

The pattern of a relatively large number of independent producers selling films to the networks and to individual stations held through the 1950's. Sales to individual stations were at least as important as those to networks since the networks had not yet established strong control over the programing of their affiliates. As the networks tightened control, the focus of TV film syndication, particularly the all-important first-run sale, shifted to the networks. Marketing success or failure was tied to the fact that the entire industry had just three primary customers for new products.

Only the strongest independent telefilm producers have been able to survive and thrive. They have done so by accommodating themselves to two forces new to the field. One is the old-line Hollywood feature-film producers; the other is the national networks themselves.

By 1955, the leaders of the movie industry had concluded that television was here to stay and that they had better join it, rather than fight or ignore it. They were nudged into this conclusion by the hard facts of declining box office receipts, spiraling production costs, and the rise of foreign competition. They were also impressed by Screen Gems' successes in the field. By 1955, Screen Gems claimed to be the largest producer of serials for television.[5] During the late fifties, all of the major film companies began to produce television films. These included Twentieth Century-Fox, Universal, Metro-Goldwyn-Mayer, Warner Brothers, and Walt Disney Productions. Latecomer to the field was United Artists, which bought control of Ziv Productions, one of the largest and most successful of the early independent producers.

Television film production is now the major activity of the Hollywood studios. By 1965 they were grossing over four hundred million dollars from telefilm sales, or about one hundred million dollars more than their gross rentals for feature films in the domestic market. An earlier Screen Actors Guild report stated that two-thirds of the revenues of its members came from television work.[6] Almost 85 percent of the prime-time programs shown on the three major U.S. networks during the 1965/66 season were produced in Hollywood. West Coast producing firms were also moving into the production of filmed TV commercials, traditionally an East Coast function; in 1965 Hollywood had captured 30 percent of this lucrative market. After years of fighting the new upstart medium, Hollywood was now being molded into a new pattern by television's program needs. The marriage between the old-line producers and the telefilm industry was consummated symbolically in the spring of 1964 when the venerable Association of Motion Picture Producers merged with the Alliance of Television Film Producers.[7]

The other new entries into the television film production and distribution field were the three networks. Aside from gaining economic benefits, their intention was to provide themselves with "program protection"—a hedge against the failure of other producers to come up with what they regarded as suitable network programs. Directly or indirectly, each of the three networks has increased its interests in telefilm production and syndication in recent years.

As a result of the shaking-down process in the industry, Hollywood production companies and networks now dominate telefilm production and distribution both at home and abroad. Many of the independent companies have closed up shop, diversified their interests, or concentrated on the rerun syndication of their older products. The palm leaf in the last category goes certainly to Fremantle International, Inc., which continues to find a lively market abroad for the fifteen-year-old "Hopalong Cassidy" series.[8]

There will always be an active overseas market for old television serials. However, the biggest share of the market is preempted by new programs. Increasingly, program sales overseas are centered around the so-called "on-network" shows, those which are currently running on U.S. networks. By 1963, three-quarters of the prime-time shows on the three U.S. networks were being syndicated simultaneously abroad. The Motion Picture Export Association estimated in that year that such shows accounted for about 60 percent of all U.S. telefilm sales abroad.[9]

These developments have determined the present pattern of American telefilm syndication throughout the world. It was perhaps inevitable that such a wide-ranging and profitable business would be dominated by the twin giants of American entertainment—Hollywood and the New York networks. Unlike most independent producers, these organizations have the corporate stability and experience to set up the world-wide marketing organizations which telefilm syndication requires. Hollywood, in particular, has been able to draw upon its long experience in overseas selling. The networks have not been far behind in establishing strong sales organizations abroad. Supplementing these overseas sales offices, the major U.S. syndicators make extensive use of European trade fairs to display their products. The largest of these, the International Film, TV Film and Documentary Market, is held twice yearly in Milan.

The networks and the Hollywood producers each have a trade association to handle the political and economic barriers they encounter in marketing their telefilm products abroad. Hollywood's representative is the Motion Picture Export Association (MPEA), an affiliate of the Motion Picture Association of America. In 1960, the networks and the larger independent syndicators formed the Television Program Export Association (TPEA) to handle their overseas interests.[10]

Where do the television film distributors sell their wares abroad? The precise answer to this is obscured by the lack of definitive export statistics for these sales.[11] However, there is no doubt that the market is big and booming, and becoming more so every year. The best index, year by year, is the estimates prepared by the Television Program Export Association. The TPEA figures are a combination of various guesses combed from an industry inclined to infuse its estimates with a strong element of "show biz" optimism. However, the trend of TPEA and similar annual estimates provides a fairly accurate reflection of the telefilm export boom. In 1961, industry circles predicted a thirty-million-dollar market; a year later the estimate was increased to fifty million dollars; and in 1964, TPEA estimated a market of sixty-eight million dollars. Thus in four years, telefilm exports more than doubled.

The market for American TV films literally covers the world. Exceptions can be enumerated easily—Cuba, Bulgaria, India, the Soviet Union, Communist China, and the closed-circuit system in Macao which specializes in telecasting table-top cricket races. Viewers in most other television countries generally get a substantial ration of American products on their home screens. "Bonanza," for instance, has an estimated audience of 350 million viewers in fifty-nine countries.

In the absence of authoritative figures, it is difficult to identify the size of markets for telefilm exports. In roughly descending order of importance, the largest markets (in dollar volume) are Canada, Great Britain, Japan, Australia, West Germany, Italy, Mexico, France, Brazil, and Argentina. Many factors determine the size of these markets. Local audience preference for American television features is certainly a key element; by and large, U.S. products are popular with overseas viewers. There are, however, limitations in individual markets. Many countries impose a foreign-exchange restriction on imported television film—an extension of arrangements which have plagued U.S. motion picture distributors for decades. Other countries limit American telefilms by restricting the amount of time imported television products can pre-empt in local TV schedules.

This has been the case in Great Britain. The British market has been important to American telefilm distributors since the early 1950's. The BBC relied heavily on "I Love Lucy" and other popular U.S. features to strengthen the audience appeal of its early television operations. After 1955, the new commercial television stations took a quick lead over the BBC with a schedule that relied heavily on American cowboy serials and pratfall comedies. Both networks were limited, however, by a self-imposed regulation which restricts imported television products to 14 percent of their total schedule.

In recent years, both the BBC and the commercial stations have increased the British content of their schedules. American programs continue to hold their own during the more competitive nighttime and weekend hours. Typically, London's ATV commercial station developed a new late-night Sunday audience for itself by screening "The Beverly Hillbillies" during the 1963/64 season in the "quiet" 9:30–10:30 p.m. time segment. The show immediately attracted almost half the total London audience. However, American programs have generally been edged out of the "Top Ten" list in British television surveys in recent years, in favor of such run-of-the-bathos soap operas as "Coronation Street" and other home products.

Despite these setbacks, the British market continues to attract U.S. distributors because of its stability, as well as the general willingness of British stations to pay prime prices for American features. In August, 1963, the BBC paid CBS Films twenty-eight thousand dollars for the British rights to a documentary featuring Elizabeth Taylor in London. The commercial stations have similar resources, thanks to the fact that they now receive almost a third of the total revenues disbursed by all British advertisers.[12]

Canada is another lucrative market for U.S. telefilm distributors. However, the Canadian government restricts the amount of "foreign" programs to 45 percent of local program schedules. Some U.S. telecasts on Canadian stations are "live," transmitted at the same time they are shown on U.S. networks. However, U.S. telefilms are an important element in Canadian TV programing.

American entry into the Japanese market—second only to the United States market in size—was for years dominated by foreign-exchange restrictions imposed by the Japanese government. In 1959–60, for instance, the government set a fiscal ceiling of 1.1 million dollars on U.S. telefilm imports. In 1962–63, this ceiling was raised to 3.3 million dollars. As a result of heavy pressure by U.S. trade associations, the figure was doubled in the 1963–64 fiscal year. During the period of severe exchange restrictions, American film distributors had sold their products at relatively low prices in Japan, primarily to establish themselves in the market. With the virtual lifting of these restrictions, distributors raised their prices accordingly. An hour-long show sold to a Japanese station for several hundred dollars in the 1950's had an asking price of six to eight thousand dollars. This has led inevitably to Japanese complaints that U.S. distributors are pricing themselves out of the market. As a result there was a drop during 1964 in the number of American telefilms sold to Japanese stations—a trend which was reversed in 1965 as U.S. distributors adjusted their prices to more realistic levels.

As in Great Britain, Japanese television stations are using proportionately fewer American features as they develop a more stable pattern of local programs. American shows will continue to be an important part of the Japanese television scene. The trend will, however, be toward "quality" spectacle shows and toward those serial shows with very strong audience appeal.

The most widely open market for U.S. telefilm distributors is Australia. The daily schedule of a typical Australian television schedule is, particularly in peak listening hours, virtually indistinguishable from that of a station in Iowa or New Jersey. A 1963 survey of Australian TV schedules showed that only 10 percent of peak-time programing was local; the other 90 percent was largely American. [13] For the year ending in July, 1964, 76 percent of the films entering Australia were American, and most of these were intended for television use.[14] The primary reason for this heavy dose of U.S. programs is, of course, the affinity of the average Australian for things American. This is whetted by the intense competition for advertising revenues and audiences by the country's thirty-four commercial stations. (The government-controlled Australian Broadcasting Commission, with twelve stations, attracts a small minority of the viewing audience.)

The remainder of U.S. telefilm exports is segmented into dozens of small markets. Government-controlled television networks in Europe buy a substantial number of U.S. programs; this is particularly true in West Germany, Italy, and the Scandinavian countries. Commercial stations in Latin America are, collectively, an important U.S. telefilm customer. Individually, their operations—and their ability to pay—are generally too limited to provide a large market at the present time. The same is true of newly developing stations in Africa and Asia. However, the market for U.S. TV films can be expected to rise in dollar volume as these stations attract larger audiences and bigger advertising revenues in the coming years. Almost every major U.S. distributor is selling films at cut-rate prices in such countries against the day when these markets will become stronger.

Hollywood's interest in selling its products to overseas television stations is not limited to films made for television. An increasingly lucrative part of its overseas TV sales involves the redistribution of its vast stock of old feature films. The "late-late show" Hollywood film is an institutional fixture in U.S. television. It is an innovation to most overseas viewers. Perhaps the most significant difference is that, for most stations abroad, feature films are not considered "filler" programing, relegated to the middle of the afternoon or the late evening. They are reserved for peak-time viewing hours, in much the same manner as NBC has developed with its "Saturday Night at the Movies" network series in this country.

The overseas television market for what the industry calls its "vaulties" (*i.e.*, from the vault) is a booming one. A 1963 *Variety* survey of export prices for old feature films showed a wide variation. It ranged from a high of eighty-five hundred dollars per film in Canada to a low of three hundred dollars in Argentina.[15] The market is fluid enough to include many exceptions to these limits. The asking price for one twenty-year-old Hollywood film, *Rebecca,* on German TV was fifteen thousand dollars. At the same time, the Japanese TV market price for old U.S. films was about twenty-five hundred dollars.[16]

Hollywood's desire to exploit this market is tempered, however, by the attitude toward television of the overseas distributors of its new films. These distributors rightly regard the competition of television as a major menace both to their own prosperity and to that of the companies they represent. In the words of one Italian distributor, the appearance of old films on local TV is "premeditated homicide" by Hollywood. This feeling has resulted in a strong campaign by Hollywood's longtime overseas distributors to restrict the showing of any feature films on local TV.

The campaign has had some curious successes. In France, film exhibitors have tried to discourage TV showings of feature films by suing the French television organization for "unfair competition." Similar pressures in Italy forced the RAI-TV network to restrict feature-film shows to once-a-week appearances on each of its channels. In Spain, the exhibitors have demanded that the state-run network screen at least one Spanish feature film for every three foreign films. West German exhibitors have proposed that local stations pay a tax of five thousand dollars every time they run a feature film. Until the end of 1964, British film interests had a tightly run Film Industry Defense Organization to keep feature films off TV.

As a result of these controversies, U.S. feature-film distributors have moved slowly to exploit what is bound to be a good long-range market for their older products. The fiscal rewards, however, are too high to be affected for very long by the protests of their regular overseas distributors. When Universal Pictures negotiated with London's ATV station for the sale of 215 films made since 1948, the asking price was reportedly 20 million dollars.[17] A portent of things to come is the fact that the West German television network paid 200,000 dollars to a local film producer for one showing of a new film before it was put on the regular theater circuit.[18]

The Hollywood syndicators regard overseas markets primarily as an outlet for their films. The foreign interests of the Big Three networks are considerably broader. While film sales are their chief source of overseas revenues, the networks have extended their operations into such areas as equipment sales, advertising placement, technical and program consultant services, and direct investment in overseas television enterprises.

The international activities of NBC, CBS, and ABC are so diverse that it is difficult to establish their relative standings in the field. Each is strong in some areas, weaker in others. Their annual reports and other publicity do not always distinguish clearly between all of their domestic and overseas activities. ABC describes itself as "the world's largest buyer of programs for telecasting outside the U.S." The CBS 1964 year-end report claims that the network is operating abroad in 107 countries and that it is the world's largest exporter of telefilms. NBC, in a 1965 report, tells of sales in 300 markets in 80 countries. Whatever their relative standing in dollar volume or the sales-to-countries numbers game, there is no doubt that each of the networks is deeply involved in the telefilm export trade.

To handle this and other aspects of overseas business, each network set up separate divisions for its international operations. (However, CBS eliminated its overseas division in a 1965 consolidation move.) The bulk of their overseas activities, as already noted, is in telefilm sales. The networks, like the Hollywood syndicators, concentrate their sales efforts on light serial programs. CBS has a specialized interest in cartoon features, largely because of the products turned out by its Terrytoon affiliate. The networks have joined independent distributors in the practice of releasing new telefilm products abroad almost as soon as they have had their first-run showings on U.S. television.

In addition to marketing their own products, the networks are doing an increasingly thriving business as distribution agents for other U.S. and foreign telefilm producers throughout the world. These foreign arrangements generally result from the affiliations which each of the U.S. networks has developed with television firms abroad, involving either an ownership stake in the firm or a contract arrangement. ABC, in particular, has encouraged its overseas affiliates to produce films, offering market guarantees for world-wide exposure through its own sales channels.[19]

One area of telefilm exports where the networks have a virtual monopoly involves news and public affairs documentaries. Although these productions are a distinct minority of the networks' telefilm exports, U.S. public affairs shows are highly popular abroad. From a political viewpoint, they are a prime example to overseas television audiences of American democratic inquiry —and, in particular, Americans' ability to examine their own problems and those of the rest of the world objectively. Foreign stations welcome these documentaries as prestige additions to their schedules. The American networks are interested in this aspect of such shows, and in recovering, through foreign sales, part of their heavy investment in such programs.

One of the landmarks of early postwar British television was the CBS series of Edward R. Murrow shows presented by the British Broadcasting Corporation during the early fifties. Murrow's famous "See It Now" indictment of the McCarthy hearings created almost as much a stir in Britain as it did in this country. NBC's most successful early documentary was "Victory At Sea," the serial dealing with the naval war in the Pacific. NBC claims that the program has been shown in every free world country with television facilities during the past decade.[20] In recent years, all of the well-known U.S. television public affairs series such as "CBS Reports" and NBC's "Project 20" have been televised in the major television countries throughout the world.

A specialized "public affairs" area for the networks abroad is sports programs. The fact that many of the sports filmed by the U.S. networks are not well known to overseas audiences does not seem to matter. In 1963 NBC sold its "Celebrity Golf" series to a station in Thailand, a nation where golfers are possibly more rare than its best-known rarity, the white elephant. The same network extended its international sports coverage to the Olympic Games, through its appointment as Latin American distributor of the Japan Broadcasting Company's exclusive coverage of the Tokyo 1964 summer games.[21]

In the news field, the networks' export activities are limited largely to providing newsfilm coverage to foreign stations. An aggressive operator in this field is ABC which, until very recently, lagged far behind the other networks. In recent years ABC has invested heavily in strengthening its world-wide newsgathering facilities to service both its domestic and foreign affiliates.[22] However, CBS and NBC both have a strong lead in this field, particularly in the British, Canadian, and Japanese markets.

All of the networks face formidable competition in the newsfilm business from U.S. and foreign firms. United Press International has a world-wide clientele of over three thousand radio-TV subscribers to its news and newsfilm services. The networks also have newsfilm competition from two British firms— Visnews, a combine of Commonwealth news organizations, and ITN, a London firm that has recently moved into the American market as part of an overseas expansion program.[23] The greatest overseas competition in the public affairs field for the U.S. networks in the future may come from Japan. Each of the four major Japanese networks has documentary film units which are at least the match, in technical and newsgathering skill, of those maintained by any other networks in the world.

In addition to these telefilm activities, each of the U.S. networks is involved in a variety of affiliations with foreign television firms, ranging from technical and management contracts to outright ownership of at least part of the firms. A listing of these affiliations would take up many pages of small type. Some examples will, however, indicate the range. NBC has a management-advisory contract with Nigeria's federal television system. CBS has been involved in technical-advisory contracts with stations on all continents. ABC has affiliation arrangements with over twenty foreign stations, including the five members of the Central American Television Network (CATVN). Both ABC and NBC own shares in several Australian stations. Every month sees the networks diversifying further into the rapidly developing international market. Although these overseas operations are only a small part of their total network activities, their corporate eyes are on the foreign market's larger implications. The growth of regional, and eventually intercontinental, networks is no longer dismissed as a banquet-speech vision. The vision is being rapidly materialized as market potential in New York sales offices.[24]

One of the most lucrative overseas operations in the future may be the extension of domestic advertising sales by U.S. networks to their overseas outlets. American firms have begun to make substantial investments in television advertising abroad, particularly in the European and Japanese markets. General Foods and Lever Brothers have been, for example, heavy advertisers on West German television. The expansion of U.S. advertising agencies into the international market has served to spur this development. Within the past two years, the American networks have moved into this market. The leader in this case has been ABC. "You can," it promises American advertisers, "sell to a $136 million foreign market with ABC Worldvision."[25] ABC does not restrict itself to American products. It has placed advertising not only for American cigarettes in Tehran, but also for British soap and Japanese transistor radios in Latin America.

Certainly part of the reason why U.S. telefilm distributors have been so successful abroad is that they had the field largely to themselves for so long. Until 1960, there was almost no competition from foreign distributors in the international market. Not only did American distributors have a head start, but they also could draw upon a backlog of television features which had already been profitably circulated among domestic network stations. There was a ready market for these abroad, where new stations were hard pressed to find program material. Having recouped their profits on domestic sales, the distributors could afford to market these films abroad at low prices. The result was to give them a strong initial position in the world telefilm market.

This U.S. pre-eminence will continue for a long time. In both dollar volume and product placement, American television products are strongly entrenched in the international market. However, the days of little or no competition are ended. A dozen nations, ranging from Great Britain to Mexico, have gone into telefilm export markets throughout the world in recent years. Because of the continued world-wide TV boom, the volume of American telefilm exports will increase in the coming years. Its share of the world market can, however, be expected to decrease slowly but steadily as a result of rising foreign competition.

The countries that have entered the international telefilm markets are varied, but they have several characteristics in common. In all cases, they are countries with strong domestic television systems. They also have motion-picture production industries which have been affected adversely by box-office losses as a result of television. Finally, they are countries that have, in one way or another, a "natural" market for their telefilm exports.

The strongest competitors to U.S. distributors in this field are the British. Their "natural" telefilm export market is the Commonwealth and the United States. The British did not get into this market on a large scale until 1960, when the BBC-TV set up a "promotions department" to market its own films as well as those it had acquired from other countries. During the first year of these operations, the BBC sold more than twelve hundred program hours of film in over fifty overseas markets.[26] In the same year, the British commercial television companies also began selling program products abroad. Associated-Rediffusion, one of the largest of these firms, sold over nine hundred programs in thirty-three markets during its first year of operations.[27] These initial successes, coupled with the increasingly competitive nature of domestic British television, stepped up interest in the overseas market.

The result has been to put both the British television and the feature-film industries into the business of producing telefilms designed largely for distribution abroad. The largest commercial telefilm producer has been the Independent Television Corporation (ITC), a subsidiary of Associated Television. Other commercial stations, notably Granada and Rediffusion, have also stepped up film production with an eye on the export market. In most cases, they experienced uneven results, partly because they were novices in the business and partly because of the strong American competition in the overseas market. Nevertheless, they have been successful enough to confirm the importance of telefilm production and distribution in British television. In the fiscal year ending in March, 1962, Associated Television sold over four million dollars' worth of its products in the United States alone.[28]

These commercial firms are being pressed hard in the export market by the government-chartered BBC. In 1965, the BBC export division was marketing programs in eighty-three countries with sales totaling four and one-half million dollars a year.[29] For the corporation and its commercial rivals, the lucrative export markets have been and will continue to be in the Commonwealth and the United States. Most of their telefilm products are light-weight features, modeled in spirit, if not in form, on U.S. productions.

Despite this imitativeness, the British telefilm effort occasionally exhibits an interesting chauvinistic tone. In part, the British see their telefilm exports as a cultural counterweight to American domination of the world's television screens. The case was stated succinctly by the BBC's Director of Television, Kenneth Adams:

"The makers of TV programs in Britain," he declared, "who have a wish and a capacity to export will have to cooperate in the face of the dumpings of Hollywood and the increasing threat of Americanization of Commonwealth culture, at whatever level."[30]

This attitude was a factor in the plans of a group of British intellectuals, led by Malcolm Muggeridge and Lord Francis Williams, in 1963 when they formed a telefilm production company, Television Reporters International (TRI). A key objective was, in the words of one report, "to provide a balanced picture of the world today as a counterblast to American pulp entertainment" on the world's television screens.[31] The enterprise foundered financially in 1964 and was bought by a group of businessmen who shifted TRI's production pattern toward light entertainment.

British telefilm exports probably account for at least two-thirds of the foreign competition to American efforts in this field. However, other European countries are getting into the market. In France, the state network has encouraged French film producers to make serial films for domestic and overseas television. As in other countries, this effort is intended in part to offset the economic decline the local film industry has suffered, largely as a result of the competition of television. ORTF has made arrangements to produce films itself, to put up the money for private firms making telefilms, or, in other cases, to buy the French rights to such films before they are produced. The Italian state-run RAI-TV has also made similar production arrangements, with an eye on the export market. Its first film project, a serial called "Maestro Don Gesueldo," was completed in 1963. American telefilm distributors are also beginning to feel the competitive pinch in the Latin American market where aggressive Mexican and Argentinian distributors are beginning to exploit the possibility of regional distribution of their Spanish-language features. Canada is, however, probably the most active non-U.S. operator, next to Britain, in the international telefilm market. At the end of 1963, the Canadian Broadcasting Corporation reported that it had sold, over a three-year period, 416 programs in 14 countries. The CBC carries on a lively trade in French-language television products, since Montreal has been for years the largest "live" French-language television production center in the world. The CBC markets French programs to stations in France, Belgium, Luxembourg, Monaco, and Switzerland on a standardized exchange basis.[32]

Language can, however, be a barrier for foreign producers interested in strengthening their international telefilm sales. This problem has plagued Japanese efforts to break into the field. The Japanese are the equals of their Western television counterparts in program production and in marketing aggressiveness. Their problem is that they do not have a readily salable product. Language difficulties are only a part of this, however. The rest is that the average Japanese program, no matter how well produced, does not fall into the standardized format that draws mass audiences to television screens around the world. Japanese shows are Japanese. The international telefilm market is based, for better or for worse, on standards set by American producers which are imitated, with little variation, by other Western telefilm companies.

This American-oriented "internationalization" of the product is a formidable barrier for Japanese and other non-Western telefilm producers. They can either have a restricted market for programs of their own style or try to imitate Western telefilm efforts.[33] Although international television would be culturally richer if they chose the former course, Japanese producers have, by and large, taken the path of Western-style imitation in their export efforts. In searching out international telefilm markets, the Japanese have relied heavily on coproduction and codistribution arrangements with established American firms. The first such arrangement in 1963 involved NBC, which cosponsored the production and distribution of the "Astro Boy" cartoon serial.

During 1962, the idea of coproduction with other foreign firms blossomed in the American telefilm industry. The motivation was mixed. In part, producers and distributors saw it as a way to escape high domestic labor costs. It was also a useful way around the problem of quotas on purely American telefilms in Britain and other countries. A few also visualized a chance to utilize exotic foreign locales, not to mention foreign bankrolls, to enhance the acceptance of their products in the highly competitive U.S. market.

Most coproduction planning at the time turned out to be press-release talk: "*Herman Megaphone, the New York indie producer, said last night that he planned to write, direct and produce twenty hour-long TV spectaculars to be filmed in Paris, Baghdad, and Pago Pago. Mr. Megaphone said that arrangements were still fluid and that it was too early announce a firm production schedule.*" Once the relentlessly optimistic press releases were swept away, however, coproduction emerged as a new, and apparently permanent, part of the industry's international activities. However, the industry discovered, as the Hollywood feature-film producers did fifteen years earlier, that international coproduction deals are not an easy way out of either their artistic or fiscal problems.

The cornerstone of American coproduction efforts in the future will be the British television industry, and particularly the commercial television station operators. One of the largest of these, Associated Television, announced in November, 1963, that it planned to invest fifty million dollars with U.S. firms on coproduction ventures over a five-year period. However, it is already apparent that some of the bloom has fallen off the coproduction rose. The situation was summarized by Dennis Scuse, director of the BBC's export department, in a March, 1964, interview:

> Although we have not shut the door completely on coproduction, we will look at proposals very carefully indeed before we enter any more. Not that they were not carefully looked at before, but from now on they will be even more closely scrutinized.[34]

Mr. Scuse's sober comments were based on the fact that a number of cooperative arrangements made by the BBC with American and Canadian firms did not result in expected large-scale distribution of the films involved in the normally lucrative North American market.

The newest foreign venture for the U.S. television industry is "tollvision" or pay-as-you-see TV transmitted to home receivers. Here the industry's overseas and domestic interests are combined in fascinating and often conflicting ways. At home the prospect of pay-TV has set off a controversy whose outcome promises to affect the entire economic structure of the business. For years the industry had lightly regarded the pay-TV threat to what it calls "free television." The inconclusive results of the first U.S. pay-TV experiment in Hartford, Connecticut, seemed to confirm this judgment. However, the sanguine mood has changed in the past two years despite the industry's temporarily successful attempt to have a pay-TV system in California closed down by a referendum. More significant is the growing importance of the role of community-antenna systems (CATV). These systems were originally designed to boost the quality of fringe-area signals but they are readily adaptable to pay-TV circuits. An estimated one-quarter of the CATV systems in this country are already originating some form of closed-circuit telecasts, ranging from weather reports to local educational programs.[35]

Pay-TV faces formidable opposition both within the television industry and outside. The National Association of Broadcasters has taken a strong position, advocating federal restrictions against it. Perhaps the most active anti-pay-TV campaigners are the motion-picture theater owners. Their reaction to the California pay-TV system was to organize a "California Crusade for Free TV" as part of their "Anti-Pay-TV Committee of the Theater Owners of America." Although the film exhibitors and their allies in commercial television have different purposes in opposing pay-TV, each takes the public position that pay-TV will undermine the constitutional right of every American not to be denied a free look at Leonard Bernstein and Lawrence Welk, paid for by commercials, in his own living room.

These domestic threats to "free television" do not, however, inhibit the U.S. television industry abroad. Every segment of the industry is actively involved in pay-TV's foreign prospects. The world's first pay-TV experiment was carried out by a U.S. company in a foreign country when Paramount Pictures installed its telemeter system in three thousand homes in the Toronto suburb of Etobicoke in 1960. The Toronto test was limited in scope, as was the later Hartford, Connecticut, experiment conducted by RKO-General Phonevision Company. However, they have proved that pay-TV—like "free television"—needs a mass audience to be successful. The prospects for pay-TV are keyed to the question of whether such an audience exists, both here and abroad.

The most promising foreign pay-TV prospects seemed to be in Great Britain. Here five pay-TV companies were offered licenses by the government in 1963 to conduct tollvision experiments for three years. Unlike the American experience, British pay-TV is being encouraged by powerful elements in the commercial television and motion-picture industries in league with other financial and artistic interests. The roster of individuals and organizations involved in British pay-TV in recent years includes J. Arthur Rank, Sir Laurence Olivier, Dame Margot Fonteyn, the Manchester *Guardian*, the banking house of Roths-child, the Rediffusion Television Company, the London *Financial Times*, and the bookselling firm of W. H. Smith & Son.[36]

To these diverse British interests must be added a list of familiar American names, including CBS-TV, Paramount Pictures, David Susskind, and Time, Incorporated. In August, 1963, CBS purchased a two-thirds interest in a London pay-TV concern, British Home Entertainment, Inc. (BHE). At the same time, the ubiquitous Mr. Susskind was named BHE's American talent representative. Another British company with extensive U.S. interests is British Telemeter, an offshoot of Paramount Pictures' domestic Telemeter organization. In February, 1964, Time, Inc., the publishers of *Time* and *Life* magazines, bought a stake in British Telemeter. American participation in the firm was increased the next month when one of its original investors, British Lion Films, came under the control of an Anglo-American syndicate. The U.S. element in the syndicate is Walter Reade, Jr., a leading film exhibitor.

By the middle of 1965, however, the British experiment in pay-as-you-see television faced an uncertain future. Four of the five companies who had been invited to submit applications for licenses decided to bow out of the field. The only company left to continue the experiment was Pay TV, Ltd., a consortium which included Associated British Picture Corp., British Relay Wireless, and British Home Entertainment. The prospects were for a post-ponement of any large-scale pay-TV operations in Britain until some of the more hazy economic factors in the business could be clarified. However, most informed observers were reluctant to predict an end to British pay-TV efforts despite the apparent failure of the first attempt to encourage them.

The other major American interest in foreign pay-TV is in Canada. The four-year experiment with its Telemeter wired-television system in Toronto has encouraged Paramount Pictures to make plans for a similar service in Montreal. Other American interests have also moved into Canadian pay-TV and the related field of community-antenna TV. In November, 1963, the trade press reported that CBS-TV would exercise its option to acquire control of one of the largest Canadian community-antenna systems in Vancouver.[37] A month later, a combine of American, British, and Canadian interests announced the formation of Canadian Home and Theater Vision, Ltd. to promote Canadian pay-TV. The new firm plans to operate two hundred community-antenna systems throughout the country. The American and British financial stake in the new venture was reported to be twelve million dollars.[38] By 1965, however, there were indications that these and other investors were moving cautiously and that Canadian pay-TV would not be a reality for at least several years.

The development of pay-TV systems in other countries—and the prospects for American investments in them—would seem to be limited at the present time. The economics of pay-TV are such that it cannot expect to flourish until "regular" television has developed to the point where its mass audience is prepared to accept the idea of paying to view programs that, with some exceptions, it can now see free or by the payment of a small TV license charge. Outside of the U.S., Britain, and Canada, this potential exists only in Japan, West Germany, Australia, and possibly one or two Latin American countries.

Nevertheless, tollvision remains an important area for exploitation by U.S. television interests. Many countries have state-controlled television systems which they have no intention of turning over to private interests. However, they might look favorably on the tax-earning possibilities of commercial closed-circuit pay-TV, limited to entertainment purposes and directed at middle- and upper-income bracket set owners. An interesting experiment in state-controlled pay-TV has been carried out in the Netherlands. In 1963, Dutch postal authorities installed a pilot closed-circuit system in fifteen hundred houses in The Hague. The system carried not only Dutch television, but also programs from neighboring German and Belgian networks, together with transmissions from twelve FM stations. The test programs, like regular Dutch television, were noncommercial. However, it takes little imagination to see the entrepreneurial possibilities of such systems both to local financial interests and to American investors in the future.

Whether the field is pay-TV or straight film syndication, there seems little doubt that expansion will be the keynote for the U.S. television industry's international activities in the coming years. Although competition is increasing steadily American firms have had the advantage of being first on the scene. It will be many years before foreign television firms will be able to challenge the present marketing lead enjoyed by their U.S. competitors. This is particularly true of telefilm distribution, but it also applies to the rest of the spectrum of American television involvement abroad. The only area where foreign firms have overtaken the U.S. lead is in equipment sales. Although American electronic firms have a good share of the international market, they often cannot overcome the price and credit advantages provided, often with government support, by British, Japanese, German, and other foreign equipment manufacturers.

The counterpoint to the successful U.S. export drive in international television is, of course, the complaint that our telefilm exports are harmful to "the American image." This discussion results in more than the usual share of inane statements. On one side, we have the television industry's pious declarations that its export products are pure-gold Americanism. This is challenged by critics who take a valid fact—the blandness of many popular U.S. television products—and stretch it to an indictment of American culture. Their humorless carping is a poor answer to the industry's willingness to excuse the sale of Grade B products by claiming the prerogatives of free enterprise.

Short of a censorship system which no one wants, the solution lies in the market place, and in the willingness of industry leaders to recognize that the sale of second-rate goods in television, as in other services, does not help their business or its profit-and-loss statements in the long run. There will always be a strong export market for lightweight television features, primarily because television overseas, as in this country, is primarily an entertainment medium. However, there are interesting indications that the trend of American television exports in the coming years will be toward better quality programs. The most lucrative markets for U.S. telefilm exporters will continue to be the TV networks in industrialized countries. These stations have greatly improved their local program production facilities in recent years. They are also able to tap a considerably broader range of higher grade foreign programs, both American and non-American. Ten years ago, foreign networks relied heavily on any kind of American products to keep their schedules filled. They can afford to be much more selective now.

Recent surveys of market conditions, particularly in Europe and Japan, indicate that they are doing just that. In these markets, the trend in American telefilms is toward the special, high-budget productions such as "Bonanza" and "The Danny Kaye Show." It would be naive to suggest that, in the future, "My Little Margie" will no longer dimple her way through Brazil or that "The Beverly Hillbillies" will not continue to mine their lode of corn in Great Britain, and, eventually, Timbuctoo. The trend, however, is toward the merchandising of better programs to meet the new demands of overseas buyers. The future historians of television's development will find useful parallels here with the manner in which Hollywood shifted from its heavy production of Grade B pictures for export twenty years ago to its present reliance on high-budget, quality productions. Because of the pell-mell pace of television expansion throughout the world, this prospect faces U.S. telefilm distributors within the first decade of their overseas marketing activities.

In the *next* ten years, international television will have expanded to the point where regional and intercontinental networks connecting all areas of the world simultaneously will be a day-to-day reality. Never before in history will the peoples of the earth have been brought closer together, sharing the sights and sounds of events that affect us all. The American television industry, already deeply involved abroad, can play a key role in establishing and maintaining high goals for this development. The question to be decided is whether the industry sees international television simply as a profitable outlet for all those old "Loretta Young Shows" or whether it accepts a responsibility to use the medium to help strengthen American world leadership.

The BBC transmitted its first television play in June, 1930. Here actor Val Gielgud rehearses for the play, which consisted mainly of close-up shots of the actors. A BBC engineer holds a primitive "fading board" to improve the sound.

Although Laos is one of the few countries in the world without television, Laotians have been exposed to its impact. Here a large audience gathers before a demonstration of closed-circuit television at a United States government exhibit in a Vientiane fair.

October 11, 1960. A puppet show based on Indian folk tales is a feature on New Delhi's experimental television station.

Ingrid Bergman rehearsing for the title role in "Hedda Gabler," a joint BBC-CBS production presented in December, 1962.

Yugoslav television covers a concert at Zagreb's Handicraft Museum.

Sister Marta Lucía Godoy conducts a literacy class on a Guatemala City station as part of an Alliance for Progress educational project.

The most widely distributed American television program overseas is "Let's Learn English," produced by the United States Information Agency. The filmed series is combined with "live" lessons adapted to local audiences. Here Ann Wood, an English teaching specialist, conducts a televised lesson for viewers in Lisbon.

September 22, 1961. Children in an East Anglian primary school watch a BBC "enrichment" educational television program as part of their classroom activity. Illustrations relating to the program are mounted on a nearby blackboard for use after the telecast.

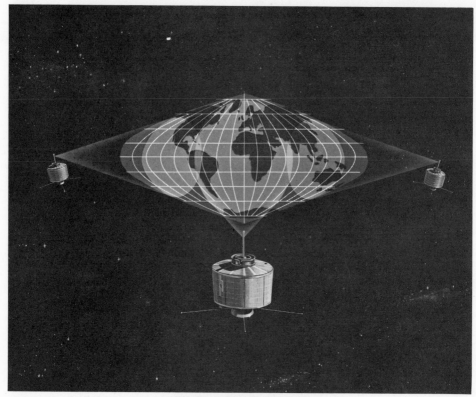

This schematic drawing shows how three stationary type satellites can provide a global communications network with uninterrupted, twenty-four-hour-a-day television and telephone service. Each satellite, at an altitude of 22,300 miles, can "see" a third of the globe. Microwave signals can be relayed via the satellites from any ground station to any other within the network. Traveling at a speed that is synchronized with the earth's rotation, the satellites appear to hang motionless in the sky.

A mobile camera unit of the Nigerian Television Service pro-vides "live" coverage of the 1964 opening of the country's Federal Parliament for Channel 10 viewers in Lagos.

Every afternoon the affiliated stations of Western Europe's international television network, Eurovision, exchange news-film of the day's major stories. The exchange is coordinated in the Geneva office of the European Broadcasting Union shown below.

NATIONAL BROADCASTING COMPANY

In 1963 Soviet authorities set a precedent in television exchanges by permitting an NBC camera crew to film an hour-long documentary, "The Story of the Kremlin," emphasizing the historical treasures to be found in the centuries-old complex of buildings.

With a sterilized camera, a CBS news team films a tumor operation by Dr. Gordon Seagrave, the famed "Burma Surgeon" of World War II. Taken at an American missionary hospital run by Seagrave in northern Burma, one mile from the Red Chinese border, the film was used as part of a CBS documentary series in 1961.

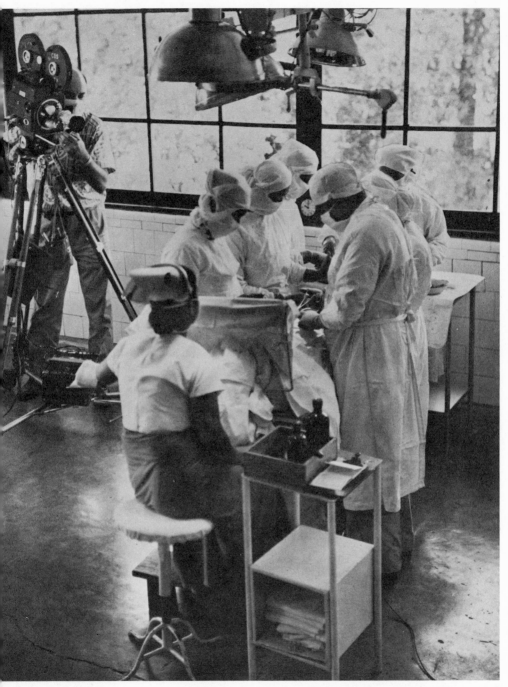

A television production unit in Cologne prepares a historical drama for ARD, West Germany's major network.

The British song-and-dance man, Roy Castle, who has often appeared on American television shows, performs in Scottish Television's Glasgow studios.

A Swedish family gathered for an evening of television viewing.

A postwar European phenomenon is the "tele-café," where viewers gather for communal television viewing, as in this Brussels neighborhood café.

Kyu Sagamoto, one of Japan's most popular singers, is host of a westernized musical variety show every Saturday night on the Mainichi Broadcasting System's commercial station in Osaka.

Although only a few Latin American countries are now linked by television relays, there are increasing exchanges of performing artists between countries. Here a Mexican variety troupe performs for Caracas television viewers.

In a 1965 communications-satellite television experiment, British and American police authorities exchanged photographs of "most-wanted" criminals. The initial exchange resulted in the capture of one suspect. Above, Scotland Yard officials in London carry out their part of the exchange.

Female announcers are a long-standing tradition in European radio and television. This young woman is a "speakerine" for the French station network. Speakerines generally introduce programs or describe what is going to be presented at various times during the day.

An Australian television newscaster broadcasts the results of a parliamentary election.

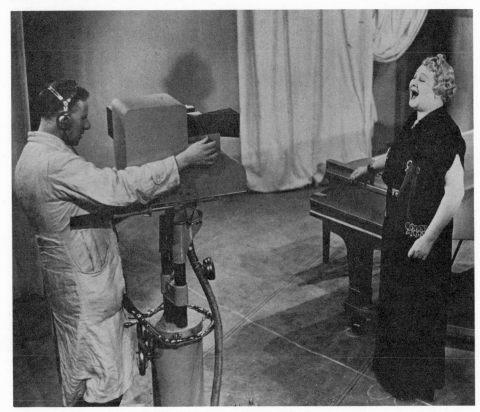

Sophie Tucker in a December, 1936, BBC show, "Starlight."

8

Communist
Television

It is evening in Moscow. After the supper dishes have been cleared away, families gather before their television sets, which occupy an honored place in their apartments. Across the city, larger groups gather to watch television in Komsomol (Communist Youth Union) and workers' clubs. Outside the metropolis, in ramshackle wooden halls crowded with farm workers, faces turn upwards to the televison set perched on a platform above them. The screen lights up, holding forth the promise of an evening's entertainment and relaxation.

The first program of the evening is a special tribute to Zoia Kosmodemianskaia, a partisan fighter of the Great Patriotic War (World War II), on the anniversary of her death. A photograph of the heroic *Komsomolka* appears on the screen, followed by a narrator standing against a backdrop of a studio curtain. He is the first of several speakers who will extol Kosmodemianskaia's deeds. She volunteered for the front in the darkest days of the German advance, he explains, and later was hanged as a spy by the Fascist invaders. Her last words were: "We will defeat you!" She is an immortal example to the children of the Moscow school named after her and to the workers of the machine-building factory where she worked before going to the front. In commemoration of her death, the Komsomol members at the factory have taken a pledge to overfulfill their production quota. More speakers follow, saying much the same thing, and the program ends.

179

Next comes a light entertainment program called "Blue Light," the most popular variety show on Soviet TV. This week's program features the "Atta Boys," a conservative version of the Beatles, together with a juggling act, a puppet band doing a pantomime of the old Glenn Miller song hit, "In the Mood," and finally a line of lightly clad chorus girls.

Moscow viewers are next invited to watch a documentary film about a new steel mill at Rustavi in Georgia. The film opens with views of the mill's impressive exterior and then moves indoors where brawny, mustachioed Caucasian mountaineers are pouring steel. "They are struggling to fulfill and overfulfill the plan," the film's commentator says. "They are proud to bear the title of 'Communist Brigade of Labor.'" The film now shifts from the mill to the adjoining workers' housing area, to children in school and at play, and then back to the mill again as the commentator gives a concluding assurance that the workers will press on in the never-ending battle to give the party and the people more and more high-quality steel.

The popular "News Relay" program follows. Tonight it offers a special treat—a visit to the apartment of the distinguished composer, Aram Ilich Khachaturian. The audience is first introduced to Olga Lepeshinskaia, a slim, pretty announcer who will interview Khachaturian from a studio at the Moscow television center. The scene shifts to the composer's apartment where the camera finds him seated casually in a large chair, wearing a smoking jacket. He responds easily to Miss Lepeshinskaia's questions about his work, then walks over to the piano to play excerpts from his recent compositions. After some further conversation about his collection of musical clocks, the interview ends.

The television evening comes to a close with a summary of current news events. It is a verbatim presentation of the day's reports from Tass, the official news agency, read by *diktors*—staff announcers who are the closest thing to TV personalities on Soviet television. Their reports are interspersed with film clips. The news is heavy with details of a new plot by West German Fascists to undermine world peace. After the news, television sets are switched off in the farmers' halls, the workers' clubs and in private homes. It is not difficult to imagine a home viewer turning to his wife and saying: "Imagine that! There was Lepesh-inskaia, talking directly over the wire to Khachaturian in his apartment, and we saw them both. How wonderful television is, that we can see such things while sitting in our own apart-ment!"

This enthusiasm and wonder are doubtless shared by millions of viewers in scores of cities across the Soviet Union. Television is the newest and most popular mass medium in the country, already reaching an audience of over 40 million people daily. The Soviet television network consists of over 100 key stations, linked to over 40 large relay transmitters and about 250 smaller relay installations. These facilities served 12.9 million receivers in April, 1965.[1] The figures, like most Soviet statistics, have to be accepted with some caution but there is little doubt that the Soviet government has decided that nationwide television is important enough to justify the heavy capital investment in-volved.

The Soviet Union has had television facilities since 1939, when experimental transmissions began in Moscow, using equip-ment purchased from the Radio Corporation of America.[2] Tele-vision operations were suspended during the war but were re-sumed on a limited scale in 1946. For a number of years thereafter, little was done to expand TV broadcasting facilities, partly because of more pressing economic needs and partly because Stalin and his associates did not appreciate the potenti-alities of the new medium. That leaders who are presumed to be past masters in propaganda should have had such a blind spot may seem strange, but it is understandable in terms of the party's historic bias in favor of the written word, particularly the press. It has been said that even if television had been an important medium of communications in Stalin's day, he would have con-fined its activities to reproducing daily editorials and articles from *Pravda*.

It was only after Stalin's death in 1953 and the liberalization of Soviet policies restricting consumer goods production that television really began to develop in the USSR as a mass medium. Even when the increased emphasis on consumer goods was cut back again later, the output of television sets continued to expand and their increasing availability became one of the few tangible evidences for Soviet citizens of the new liberality of the regime. In 1959, when prices of many luxury items were raised, the cost of television sets was actually lowered. The market is still by no means saturated, and even in the cities those who have sets of their own are in the minority. There are, however, enough sets in workers' clubs, hostels, and other public places to make television viewing a fairly common experience for the inhabitants of the larger cities.

Notwithstanding some audience criticism of programs, television is clearly a popular form of entertainment in the Soviet Union—a welcome diversion and means of relaxation in a society where such amenities have been in chronic short supply. The very fact that Soviet citizens can now enjoy television is, by itself, of propaganda value to the regime since it symbolizes for the public the gains of the post-Stalin period.

The policy of making television more widely available has gone hand in hand with a change in Soviet propaganda methods since Stalin's death. By and large, this change reflected Nikita Khrushchev's insistence that while the party line must remain inviolate, it should be presented to the people in as palatable a form as possible. The result has been a noticeable effort to produce livelier propaganda products. Newspapers and magazines are appearing in new formats that can almost be called sprightly in comparison with the leaden-footed efforts of the Stalin era. The film industry has been partially revivified after almost total collapse in the last years of Stalin's rule, and radio broadcasting has generally been made more interesting.

Television, too, has benefited from this change since the late 1950's. Far from being restricted to the transmission of *Pravda* editorials, Soviet television programing began to emphasize sports and other entertainment subjects during the Khrushchev period. Although normal precautionary steps were taken to see that the medium did not violate any ideological norms, there was little apparent effort to exercise close control of programing or to exploit television more assiduously as a propaganda weapon. There were no news programs on Soviet television until 1957, and then only once daily.[3]

Any assumption that television would somehow escape being made a cog in the Soviet propaganda system would have been naive, however. During the late 1950's, the regime took a fresh look at the new medium and decided to upgrade its propaganda role. Accordingly the Seven Year Plan (1959–65) called for an expansion of facilities which, if they had been fulfilled, would have given Soviet television a larger daily audience—somewhere in the neighborhood of 125 million—than that of all the other propaganda media combined, excepting radio. The Plan came within striking distance of fulfillment as far as TV was concerned: the 13 million sets in operation by the end of 1965 were just 2 million short of the goal.

Clearly this "entertainment medium" is meant to do more than entertain in the Soviet Union. The first detailed definition of television's role in Soviet society was spelled out in two resolutions adopted by the party Central Committee during 1960. The earlier of these directives, issued in January, ordered changes in the form and content of all party propaganda so as to emphasize the need for greater efforts to build up Soviet world power, and it outlined the parts that the various media would play in this new drive.[4] The newspapers were given pride of place among the media, but for the first time television received special mention. Its role was more fully detailed a month later when the Central Committee issued a special resolution defining the functions of television and radio. The resolution opened with a sharp attack on "soft" trends in television programing:

> Television presents new opportunities for the daily political, cultural and esthetic education of the population, including those parts of the population seldom reached by mass political work. The Party Central Committee believes, however, that it is being far from adequately used to propagandize the achievements of the Soviet people in political, economic and cultural life and to exhibit Soviet man, the builder of communism.[5]

The Central Committee's litany of complaints about the utilization of television covered a wide field. Programs were "dull" and "unconvincing"; reporting of Socialist achievements in the provinces was "rare and generally handled unskillfully"; television production was badly organized; and, above all, not enough was being done to propagate the party line. The resolution decreed a series of reforms, ranging from a proviso for more "propaganda on healthy living" to the requirement that special children's programs be broadcast by every television station at least one hour every day. But the most important effect of the directive was to apprise Soviet television managers that their primary assignment was an ideological one.

The Central Committee's comments were addressed principally to the organization responsible for the over-all direction of Soviet radio and television—the State Committee for Radio and Television Broadcasting, attached to the USSR Council of Ministers. Responsibility for the bulk of actual television operations is dispersed among the local stations, which have considerable autonomy in adapting their programs to regional needs. This practice is explained in Soviet political literature as a reflection of the "Leninist policy of equality among the many peoples inhabiting the Soviet Union."[6] However, aside from the desirability of tailoring programs to specific audiences, such as workers in virgin lands and various national groups, another practical reason for allowing local stations substantial operating autonomy is the lack of country-wide relay facilities for transmitting Moscow-originated programs. Although such facilities are expanding in European Russia, progress will be much slower in the central and eastern areas. The target date mentioned by Soviet commentators for a full linking of the system has been 1980, but this schedule may be speeded up as a result of the first successful Soviet communications satellite in 1965, linking TV relay centers in western Russia with Vladivostok. Exchanges of films, kinescopes, and magnetic-tape programs between stations have been minimal, although this deficiency is undoubtedly being remedied since it was a major object of criticism in the Central Committee's February, 1960, resolution.

Local autonomy in television programing, however, does not mean any relaxation of centralized ideological control, which is a function of the State Committee and the party apparatus. Since the issuance of the 1960 resolutions, party organizations have had a more clearly defined responsibility for overseeing the ideological content of local television programs. In spite of this, a relatively small percentage of shows have thus far been directly political in content. At least two-thirds of any Soviet newspaper is generally devoted to political news and commentary, and about a third of radio output falls in this category.[7] The proportion of directly political programs on television is somewhat smaller than on radio, although a strong ideological thread runs through most of the broacast material, particularly the news.

In the earlier days of Soviet television, news programs consisted solely of the unadorned reading of bulletins from Tass. In recent years, however, they have become more varied, with greater use made of news film prepared especially for television. The Moscow main channel telecasts three news shows—two fifteen-minute segments and a half-hour show in the late evening. The three programs are made available to stations on the growing relay network, all of which are required to rebroadcast the half-hour program.[8] Local stations supplement the Moscow-originated news programs with special political features of their own. The titles of these features are frequently indicative of their propagandistic flavor, e.g., "We Shall Fulfill the Seven Year Plan Ahead of Schedule," "Lenin's Ideas Are Becoming a Reality," "Listen to Advice from Scientists, Comrades," and "Through Heroic Labor, We Shall Carry Out the Grandiose Communist Assignment." Many are straight "talks" with guest appearances by workers who are successfully fulfilling their production quotas. Although available evidence on the preferences of Soviet viewers is meager, it indicates that such programs generally are not popular. Even an official Soviet listing of most popular television shows in 1965 is realistic enough to indicate that these programs do not rate high:

> The most popular Moscow TV programs are the news reports; The World Today, on international affairs; the Quiz and Fun Club show; the Blue Light revue; the Travel Club film showings of professional and amateur travelogues; Forgotten Films, which deals with cinema history and shows the best of the old films; and the News Relay, a kaleidoscope of news at home and abroad.[9]

Filmed and on-the-spot reports of Soviet economic, scientific, and social achievements seem also to be well received, probably because they present visible proof of national progress. Television has, for example, been particularly effective in reporting Soviet space feats, one of its triumphs having been the first transmission of a live sequence from an earth-circling manned satellite in August, 1962.

But while Soviet viewers may get dramatic pictures from space they see little of the terrestrial world outside their own national borders. There are occasional program exchanges with television stations in the Communist bloc countries of Eastern Europe, carried out through the Soviet-sponsored Intervision regional network, the Communist counterpart of Western Europe's Eurovision system. In February, 1963, the Russians completed the last link in their television hookup with the East European bloc countries, Albania, however, being excluded. There are increasing indications that the Soviet government is considering the propaganda advantages of more TV exchanges with non-Communist countries. Since April, 1961, programs have been exchanged with West European countries via Finland and East Berlin. The Soviets have also relayed programs to the United States through the Early Bird satellite; in 1965 the annual May Day parade in Red Square was seen "live" by U.S. viewers shortly after the first Early Bird experimental transmissions were made across the Atlantic. Although the first communications satellite put into orbit by the Russians has been used only to transmit messages within the Soviet Union, the day may soon come when Soviet "comsats" will be able to relay international TV exchanges in much the same way as the American Telstar, Relay, and Early Bird satellites have been doing. The prospect of demonstrating Communist achievements and power to the rest of the world by live television broadcasts certainly must be a tempting one to Soviet propagandists. They also have to face the less pleasing prospect that such international programing would undoubtedly be reciprocal, requiring the presentation to the Soviet public of foreign transmissions giving an uncensored view of life beyond Communist borders.

What impels most Soviet viewers to switch on their sets is

not so much the desire to be informed of events as it is the desire to be entertained. In the absence of Muscovite versions of a Nielsen Poll or other program-rating system, one must rely on scattered evidence in assessing Soviet viewer preferences. If they were given a chance to be polled, they would probably vote for light entertainment variety shows and for costume plays as their top choices. Both types of programs are presented in sufficient quantities to evoke official complaints that TV programs do not measure up artistically to party standards. In a critique of eighty-six drama productions televised by the Moscow station, a commentator in the leading party magazine, *Kommunist*, once complained that only twenty-nine dealt with present-day topics and that even less attention was being devoted to plays about "our wonderful contemporary—the builder of Communist society."[10] Most stations also have special programs that are popular with particular groups. These include programs for women (*e.g.*, "For You, Women"), for children ("Tales by Grandmother Television"), and for farmers ("Seminars for Corn Growers"). Sports programs are universally popular and are given a prominent place in the schedules of all Soviet stations.[11]

For foreign observers the most impressive aspect of Soviet television programing is the large number of current plays, dance productions, and motion pictures offered to viewers. Soviet commentators often cite this as evidence of the superior cultural tone of TV broadcasting in the USSR compared with that in the United States and other "capitalistic" countries. In one year Moscow television has presented over eighty plays produced especially for television, in addition to over sixty others from the repertoires of Moscow theatrical companies. During one fifteen-month period, the Riga station televised the entire repertoire of that city's theatrical companies.[12]

Despite these efforts to provide good programing, Soviet television often finds itself under attack in the party press. The emphasis in these critiques is usually on the poor quality of the programs. In a typical review of local TV, *Pravda* has charged that productions are "artistically weak" and "trite," adding that "the wealth of possibilities of our television is poorly utilized."[13] Foreign observers have made similar criticisms:

When they are not transmitting a film, the Russians are photographing a stage play or a radio lecture or a concert or a dance performance as if the function of the medium was merely to make visible what was previously only heard or read. . . . Everything is taken straightforward and head-on, with no manipulation of angles, or lights, to create fluidity and surprise, no feeling at all of the special idiom of television.[14]

This general mediocrity can be explained in part by the deficiencies in equipment of most Soviet television studios. These weaknesses are more a reflection of Soviet production faults than of the competence of the engineers who design the equipment. Soviet engineers have, in fact, made important technological contributions to television's development. The most dramatic of these was their design of the first system to transmit live pictures from an orbiting manned spacecraft. Their first communications satellite, "Molniya I" ("Lightning"), launched in April, 1965, transmitted color TV pictures from Moscow to Vladivostok shortly after it was sent into space.[15] In 1964, Soviet engineers unveiled a color TV set that also provided three-dimensional pictures. The set, displayed at the National Economic Exposition in Moscow, showed films of a railroad train that seemed to be coming out of the screen. Other engineers have experimented successfully with multiplex sound systems that permit television sets to receive audio signals in several languages—a potentially important development for multilingual nations like the Soviet Union and also for international transmissions from one language culture to another.

The root cause of Soviet television's artistic weakness is not, therefore, primarily technological in nature. It is better explained by the hobbling of creative artistic imagination imposed by the need for ideological conformity in everything that is seen or heard by the public. Soviet TV producers and directors shy away generally from any attempt at innovation that might invite attack by the authorities or by the party press. This constricted atmosphere may well explain why Soviet television has not attracted the small group of talented film directors who have been involved in efforts to achieve at least a partial restoration of the best traditions of Russian cinematography.

In recent years the non-Communist world has witnessed the great impact of television on political and social affairs. To what extent will the medium have a comparable effect on Soviet society? The answer lies shrouded in the mists that envelop any attempt to assess the mass media in a totalitarian society. However, the subject deserves attention along with others relating to the current rapid pace of change in the Soviet Union.

There is, first of all, television's already impressive role as a major mass medium in Soviet life, in terms of both its geographical spread and the size of its audience. Although there are as yet fewer than fifteen million sets available to a population of over two hundred million, there is little reason to question the official claim that within a few years the medium will be available to almost every Soviet citizen. A great many sets are in public places where the viewing audience can run to a hundred or more persons, and the audience ratio for home receivers is also high. Thus, the "blue screen," as television is known colloquially, is becoming an increasingly important source of news and entertainment for Soviet citizens, particularly in the larger cities where it has already begun to surpass radio.

One of television's foremost effects will be to give Soviet citizens a greater awareness of their own vast country. Although the unity of the peoples of the USSR has been a perennial propaganda theme since Lenin's day, it has never had as effective a propagator as the television screen, with its ability through film and live transmissions to bring a panorama of the whole nation into workers' clubs and home parlors. Television should prove an influential force in this regard, particularly when the transcontinental relay link is completed in a few years.

In the coming years, it is also possible that Soviet television viewers may be permitted more frequent glimpses of the world beyond Communist borders. Although the government can be expected to exercise careful control over the pace of television exchanges with non-Communist countries, the fact that it has already set in motion a number of such projects may be a hopeful sign. The most significant of these projects is the slowly developing pattern of cooperation with Western Europe's Eurovision network. Soviet officials have also negotiated bilateral agreements with Western countries for television program exchanges; an agreement providing for such exchanges was concluded with the British Broadcasting Corporation in July, 1963.[16] A similar plan for such exchanges was included in the original Soviet-American cultural agreement in 1958 but it has never been implemented. Soviet officials are still wary of the prospect of foreign programs on local television although enough minor precedents have been set in recent years to indicate that there will probably be a measured increase in such glimpses of the outside world in the next few years.

The most intriguing aspect of Soviet television is perhaps its increasingly important role as a link between the Soviet rulers and the ruled. The rapid expansion of TV facilities during the early post-Stalin era has been continued by Nikita Khrushchev's successors. They have continued the practice he began of making television reports to the people. When his successor, Premier Aleksei Kosygin, returned from an Asian tour early in 1965, his TV report to Soviet citizens was handled like that of Western leaders, with an advance text of his speech made available to the foreign press, background maps to which he referred during his talk, and even a teleprompter.[17]

Such high-level interest in the medium is not always reflected by lower Party officials. In large part this is due to the persistence of the Communist belief in the primacy of the press as an ideological and agitational weapon. Lenin laid down this dictum in his classical treatise on propaganda, *What Needs to Be Done*, in the early years of this century and there are many Soviet officials who see no reason to challenge a thesis they have grown up with. The view that television's role is not to originate but merely to repeat what has already been said by the press and the local party agitator has been deplored in a revealing statement by a Soviet television official:

> Television has not always found support with everyone nor has it been properly appreciated by everyone. . . . It is sometimes considered more important to issue a small pamphlet in 10,000 or 15,000 copies than to televise a program on the same topic. There are those who feel that delivering a lecture on television is not particularly important, that it is a far more responsible task to speak in a hall that accommodates 300 to 500 persons. After

all, you can count the number in attendance and the number of questions asked. It seems somehow not the thing to do, after a television lecture, to write that it was heard by six or eight million people and that hundreds of questions were asked in various places, sometimes in letters sent across hundreds of kilometers.[18]

There is much here to explain the wariness with which many party officials still regard television. Reliance on personal contact, on being able to answer the question directly, is an important part of the traditional pattern of Soviet propaganda and agitation activities. Television eliminates this element. It can be controlled at its source but not in the millions of homes where it is received. The guiding hand of the Agitprop organizer is not present to lead the discussion and to resolve hesitations. This is a psychological weakness in the view of old-line party bureaucrats who have had it drilled into them that the goal of propaganda and agitation is to eliminate any possible doubts about current socialist reality.

Official fears that television may get out of control ideologically have yet to be justified. Even during the most turbulent intellectual controversies that have rocked Soviet cultural life since the death of Stalin television has played a passive and obedient role in serving the current party line. In December, 1964, however, television had a moment of artistic notoriety. This occurred on Poetry Day when Moscow television covered a poetry reading. The highlight of the program was the reading by Yevgeny Yevtushenko of one of his new poems. It turned out to be a veiled attack on the instability of the Soviet political situation at the time. Two Moscow television officials were fired as a result of their public exposure of this breach of cultural decorum.[19]

In the long run Soviet television does pose an ideological threat to the regime. Its propaganda value to the party is considerable—but so, too, is its capability as a mirror of everyday reality. It is this quality, potentially threatening the very foundations of Soviet ideology, that will no doubt impel the party to persevere in its efforts to confine TV's functions, as long as it can, to that of just another transmission belt of cut-and-dried ideas and emotions.

Television in Eastern European countries, as in the Soviet Union, is a direct reflection of current political realities. The so-called "liberalization" that has taken place in the political, economic, and ideological affairs of the region's Communist governments shows up on the living room screen. Thus TV in Poland, Rumania, and Czechoslovakia is, by Communist standards, somewhat more relaxed in its approach than is the medium in East Germany and Bulgaria where Stalinist norms of conduct still persist. Yugoslavia, claiming a nonaligned position between East and West, is a special case, as is Albania, the only Chinese Communist satellite in the West, where a ramshackle television station in Tirana offers an unenviable schedule of Sino-Albanian propaganda shows.

East European television compares directly with the Soviet model in at least one important respect. In every country, the medium is operated as a direct instrument of the state propaganda machine. Whatever form political "liberalization" may take in each of these countries, it has not affected television's standing as a state-controlled—or, more specifically, party-controlled—medium. When liberalization has, in the party leadership's opinion, gotten out of hand, there is a crackdown and the offenders are properly punished. In 1964 East German TV's top political commentator, Karl von Schnitzler, was dropped after making a series of blunders on his anti-western "Der Schwarze Kanal" (Black Channel) show.[20] At about the same time, three popular singers on Prague television were ruled off the air by the Ministry of Education and Culture for allegedly "violating norms of common decency." Their crime had been making satirical remarks about food and clothing shortages in Czechoslovakia, according to reports at the time.[21]

While this form of political and cultural censorship is a continuing fact of life in East European television, the more important fact is that the medium is also developing as a powerful force for ending the party-imposed isolation that has separated Eastern Europe from the West for the past two decades. In the first place, East European TV has a higher degree of Western content than any other medium in the region. The level of this programing from Western sources is still relatively low, but the

mere fact that it is permitted in such a popular medium is significant. At times the amount of Western programs is considerable.
Twenty-two percent of the weekly program schedule of Warsaw
television in 1962 was American in origin, ranging from "Disneyland" to "Danger Is My Business."[22]

The percentage of shows from Western sources varies in
Poland and other East European countries but such programing
has tended to increase each year in most cases. This development
is partly due to the aggressive salesmanship of American and
West European TV program distributors, but the most important
reason for it is that local station managers, with the tacit approval
of the local Communist party leadership, are being forced to
give their viewing audience what it wants.

Two other factors also contribute to the "Westernization"
of East European television. One is the continuing exchange of
programs between the Communist Intervision regional network
and Eurovision, its West European counterpart. The two systems
link more than two dozen countries throughout Europe in simultaneous relays of important events ranging from a May Day
parade in Moscow to the Changing-of-the-Guard ceremony in
London. Most of the program exchanges between the two networks involve sports events but there is also a useful trading of
programs dealing with political and cultural happenings. The
other contact with the West takes place primarily in East Germany, Czechoslovakia, and Hungary where millions of TV viewers can eavesdrop on programs transmitted from nearby stations
in West Germany, West Berlin, and Austria.[23]

Thus television plays a role in the changes now taking place
in the relations between Eastern European countries and the
Atlantic community. More than any other medium it offers large
numbers of East Europeans a true "window on the West." This
development is a challenge to local Communist leaderships who
are fully aware of the pitfalls of permitting even limited contact
with non-Communist countries. They are even more painfully
aware of the dangers of trying to stop or slow down the present
trend toward greater contact with "the outside." In order to get
a better measure of the role that television can play in this push-
pull of political and ideological factors, it will be useful to review

briefly the TV situation in each of the East European countries.

Czechoslovakia was the first Communist country outside the Soviet Union to inaugurate television. Experimental telecasts were begun in Prague in May, 1953; within a year a regular broadcasting schedule was started.[24] By 1962 over a million receivers were in operation and by 1965 a second million had been added, providing one set for every two families. Czechoslovakia was also the first Communist state to develop a nationwide network, although there is a rather marked disparity in the distribution of sets throughout the country. The Slovak region, with almost a third of the population, reportedly had only 15 percent of the country's receivers in 1964.

There were fairly reliable indications by 1965 that TV had become the most influential mass medium in Czechoslovakia. One survey stated that 60 percent of the population regularly looked at television for two to three hours nightly. Only 20 percent of the populace regarded radio as their primary source of information. More significant was the survey's implicit criticism of government TV propaganda programs. The most popular programs, according to the viewers polled, were motion-picture films, drama, sports, variety shows, and audience-participation shows. While there may be some propaganda content in each of these types of programs, they are relatively innocuous; the survey did indicate, at least indirectly, that news programs and commentaries, where party indoctrination touches are more evident, did not rate high among viewers.[25]

Czechoslovakia's general pre-eminence in East European television is underscored by the fact that Intervision, the regional network, has its headquarters in Prague. Czech technicians have primary responsibility for the complicated technical operations coordinating live relays between Intervision's member networks. The Czechs have indicated that they intend to maintain their TV lead by building a second national network, consisting of fifty-nine high-powered transmitters, in the next five years.

The Poles started their first television operations two years later than the Czechs, but they have developed their network almost as rapidly. After Warsaw TV went on the air in the middle 1950's, enthusiastic television buffs in several provincial areas built their own relay transmitters from spare parts in order to receive the Warsaw video signal. By 1965 Polish transmitters covered over two-thirds of the country, including all the major cities. Although there were fewer than 2 million sets for a population of 30 million people, television was a common feature of Polish urban life. TV is a major investment for the average Polish family since receivers normally cost the equivalent of two to three months' salary. In rural areas community receivers with audiences up to 150 persons per set are a common sight. In 1965 the Warsaw economic weekly *Zycie Gospodarcze* claimed that 77 percent of the populace had access to television.[26] The precise statistic may be suspect but there is no doubt that the medium is widespread and very popular.

The evidence of its influence is found in the new and still controversial Polish practice of conducting public-opinion polls and other sociological investigations throughout the country. (A decade ago such practices would have been forbidden as un-Marxist.) One opinion survey, announced in 1965, gives some indication of television's role in Polish life. Among children and adults over thirty, TV was listed first in their media choices; it was given third place by young people, following films and books. However, television was ranked second by all groups as a source of information on current events and first as a means of acquiring knowledge.[27]

Other polls indicate, however, that radio is also a major media source for information. A 1964 poll by the Polish radio's Public Opinion Research Center found that only a quarter of Polish listeners and viewers rely on television for *international* news events while almost 90 percent rely on radio. This would, of course, include the popular BBC, Voice of America, and other Western radio systems which broadcast to Poland.

As in Czechoslovakia, films of various sorts make up the major portion of the Polish viewer's program diet. The most popular of these films are undoubtedly serial programs imported from the United States. "Bonanza," presented once a month, is a leading favorite; "Disneyland," offered every Saturday, is another. In 1964 the Polish television magazine *Radio i Telewizja* carried a résumé of six of the "most interesting" film serials then being shown. The six programs listed were "Robin Hood," "Wagon Train," "The Saint," "The Globetrotter," "Alfred Hitchcock Presents," and "Huckleberry Hound," all American or British productions although the article did not mention this fact. A month later the magazine published an article decrying the great number of programs from the West on local stations. It suggested that they be cut back since they imposed on Polish children the ideal of the American hero.[28] There has, in fact, been a general reduction in the number of American programs on Warsaw TV since 1962 when they made up almost a quarter of the station's schedule.

The rest of the Polish TV schedule consists of dramatic productions, how-to-do-it shows, children's programs, and a quiz show patterned on the American models of a half-dozen years ago, complete with an "isolation booth," a smooth-tongued master of ceremonies, and a grand prize of twenty-five thousand zlotys, the equivalent of about a thousand dollars at the official exchange rate.[29] The government keeps a close eye on the content of news shows but is otherwise restrained in utilizing the medium as a propaganda mouthpiece. In April, 1963, for the first time the proceedings of a government party meeting in Warsaw were taped and presented on the local station.[30]

Television developed more slowly in Hungary, largely because of the aftereffects of the 1956 antiregime uprising. By the end of 1965 the country had three-quarters of a million receivers tuned into a nightly program schedule featuring quiz shows, American and British adventure serials, and vintage Tarzan movies. The same pattern is found in Rumania where the Bucharest station and its relay transmitters service about four hundred thousand receivers. Among the Soviet-oriented East European regimes Bulgaria has been slowest in developing a television capability and the most persistent in using the medium as a propaganda outlet. In December, 1963, the Sofia station featured a spy drama when it broadcast films of an alleged rendezvous between a Bulgarian official and an American Legation officer in which the former was said to have passed on secret information. A more welcome form of fiction on Bulgarian TV, however, is American programs such as "My Friend Flicka," one of the popular shows of the 1965 season.

Yugoslav TV is faithful to the Titoist philosophy of international nonalignment in its melding of features of both Communist and Western television. Alone among Communist countries, Yugoslavia is a member of both the Eurovision and Intervision networks. On the programing side, however, the taste of the country's million viewers does not accurately reflect political nonalignment. Next to local programs, the popular favorites are shows from the United States and other Western countries. Productions from the Soviet Union and from other East European countries usually have a low rating.

The most extensive TV operations in Eastern Europe are carried on by the East German regime. Over half of East Germany's seven million households have television receivers, the highest set-per-family ratio in any Communist country and one of the highest anywhere. The regime's TV organization, Deutscher Fernsehfunk, is the professional equal of any similar organization in the world; its productions of operas, plays, and similar programs are often superior to those mounted by West German stations. The flaw in East German television is the Pankow regime's heavy-handed attempts to use it as a propaganda outlet. The program schedule is spotted with indoctrination shows, many of them using the traditional German "political cabaret" technique of witty satire on interesting current events. In most cases the East German versions are neither witty nor interesting; their emphasis is on such themes as West German fascism, NATO warmongering, and American imperialism. The intended audience for these programs is only partly East German. The regime has a lively awareness of the medium's influence on millions of viewers in West Germany and West Berlin. West German authorities have a similar interest in East German audiences although they do not attempt to tailor their program to East zone viewers. However each side has sought to discourage its citizens from looking at the other's TV programs. For years West German publishers honored an informal agreement not to publish East German TV schedules in their newspapers. The agree-

ment broke down in 1964 when several leading publishing firms
—including the powerful Springer group—began publishing the
schedules. The Springer firm's radio and television guide, with
a 12.5 million weekly circulation, was instrumental in breaking
the ban.[31]

East German leaders have taken more stringent measures to
limit the impact of West German TV in their territory. For
several years it was a crime, punishable by a jail sentence or a
fine, to listen to television from the West; this regulation reportedly was eased in 1964 because of difficulty in enforcing it.[32]
However, reports from East Germany indicate that a TV set
owner still runs the risk of being identified as politically unreliable if he keeps his set tuned to West German programs. In spite
of this pressure such programs continue to be popular in East
Germany, although nonpropagandistic programs on East German
television also attract large audiences on both sides of the border.[33]

Despite the misgivings of local Communist leaderships, East
European television contact with the West is increasing every
year. A small part of this involves the exchange of live programs
through the Intervision network. The great bulk, however, consists of Western films bought by stations to meet the ill-con-
cealed audience preferences for such programs. Although
American productions are generally popular, they have strong
competition from British, French, and German programs in Iron
Curtain markets. Britain's BBC and its commercial rivals have
each made important gains in the Eastern European market for
TV material in recent years. The French have relied heavily on
formal cultural agreements at the government level providing
for exchanges of television programs. One such agreement between France and Czechoslovakia, signed in June, 1965, called
for the exchange of short and full-length films, documentary
productions, and cartoon features; moreover it assured general
assistance to TV editors, newsmen, producers, and cameramen
sent to one another's country.[34]

American distributors have been hampered at two levels in
their attempt to expand their market for TV programs in the
region. The first block is the general unwillingness of local sta-

tions to pay what the distributors regard as a reasonable price for U.S. products. In 1965 the going prices for half-hour American films in Eastern Europe ranged from a high of three hundred dollars in East Germany to one hundred dollars in Rumania.[35] By New York standards, these are giveaway rates. The second block is the difficulty in getting foreign-exchange remittances for their sales in these dollar-short countries. The American government provides some relief in this area through its Informational Media Guaranty program, which has made exchange arrangements between soft currencies and dollars for TV film distributors operating in Poland and Yugoslavia. Despite these difficulties—and the ever-present threat that the local Communist party will order a cutback in foreign TV programing—American and other Western distributors can probably expect to expand their markets throughout Eastern Europe in the coming years.

The world's largest Communist nation, on mainland China, has only begun to take television seriously. In 1959 Red Chinese authorities sanctioned the first experimental station in Peking; a year later another small facility was opened in Shanghai. At the end of 1960 mainland Chinese sources reported that stations had been opened in five other cities—Harbin, Tientsin, Shenyang, Changchun, and Canton—and that sixteen other stations were beginning experimental operations.[36] The number of stations does not seem to have increased significantly since that time; Peking authorities have been reluctant to publicize statistics on television transmitters or receivers in recent years. This would normally indicate that their plans for the medium's expansion, after the initial spurt in the early sixties, have been held up for some reason. The most likely cause of this leveling-off is the regime's desire to concentrate the resources of its hard-pressed broadcasting equipment industry on radio rather than television. Radio will probably be the most widespread mass propaganda medium in China for another generation. Most Chinese citizens get their share of ideological indoctrination each day through the more than six million public loud-speakers connected to a closed-circuit government radio system.[37]

The Peking regime is not, however, ignoring television. Several factories turn out a ten-inch-screen receiver, named the "Peking" and modeled on an earlier Russian set. There are probably several hundred thousand sets in operation throughout the country, most of them placed in schools, workers' clubs, and other locations which permit public viewing. Although receivers are displayed in stores, a potential set owner goes to the local broadcasting station to arrange his purchase. The set is installed by government technicians once he gets his allotment.[38]

Communist China's TV program schedules are divided between educational self-improvement, sports, cultural shows, and outright propaganda news and commentaries. Chinese overseas propaganda emphasizes the work of a "television university," sponsored by Peking University, which offers correspondence courses. A 1962 article in Peking's *People's Daily* stated that over twenty-seven thousand students had enrolled in the courses at that time and that plans were being made for a "television education network" with a thousand locations in the Peking area where students could gather for their lessons. "After about four years of spare-time study," the article declared, "students can complete courses equivalent to those offered in basic subjects by a general university."[39]

Although educational TV undoubtedly figures in the regime's plans for the medium, the government is obviously more interested in TV's propaganda capacities. Some of the flavor of this interest can be found in the following description of the Peking station's daily news program from an English-language Peking magazine, *China Reconstructs*:

> On six days a week the station broadcasts a 20-minute newsreel program. It covers local, national and international events, filmed by the station's corps of cameramen throughout the country, by Chinese cameramen in Asia, Africa and Latin America, and by services in more than 20 countries with which China has exchange relations. A typical local newscast may show a vineyard with a good crop of grapes, the opening of a new synthetic fibre plant, visiting Algerian students. Recent international coverage included

shots of the Tenth World Conference Against Atomic and Hydrogen Bombs held in Japan, and the American Negro people's protests against discrimination in Philadelphia. Thus TV sets bring the people of Peking closer to the world-wide fight for peace and against imperialism and colonialism.[40]

Party leaders in all Communist countries continually express high hopes for TV as an instrument of Marxist-Leninist propaganda. Whether the medium will serve this end or whether it will actually loosen party control over local public opinion in Communist states is one of the fascinating uncertainties in television's global development in the near future.

9

ETV: The European and Japanese Experience

Television is well on its way to becoming the greatest mass educational instrument of all time. This is one of the great truths about the medium; it is also one of its greatest clichés.

No other facet of television's potential has been so bedeviled by a combination of rickety assumptions, banquet hall rhetoric, hazy facts, and other loose thinking. For the New York advertising agencies, television education means cajoling millions of people into buying hair spray, detergents, and soup strainers. Nowhere in television are the words "creative" and "educational" more generously used than along the Madison Avenue axis when TV commercials are being planned. School administrators throughout the world emphasize the use of television to teach Italian, mechanical drawing, physics, and scores of other academic subjects. Sociologists in Sweden extol the medium for teaching sex hygiene. Self-appointed cultural uplifters stress its role in bringing Bach cantatas, Inca dancers, and Macedonian ikons to Everyman. Politicians gleefully embrace the opportunity television offers to educate their constituents about the rightness of their causes.

When all have had their conflicting say about television's educational value, the fact remains that television does educate. Every day hundreds of millions of people move beyond the narrow compass of their lives through the sights and sounds of television. African tribesmen stare at Walter Cronkite documentaries; Mexican housewives follow the scandals of "Peyton Place"; Moscow clerks watch live relays of Soviet cosmonauts orbiting in space; Indiana teen-agers review French idioms with their television screen teacher.

Television is shaping lives and thoughts in ways that have not yet been measured. How much and how well the medium influences its audiences is, in fact, largely a moot question. Answering it is the prerequisite to understanding TV's role both as a social force and, more specifically, as an educational instrument. After two decades of experience, the research evidence in this field is still scanty. In large part television's impact is masked by its bland façade of light entertainment. Here we will examine the medium's more structured attempts at enlightenment—the vast amorphous field known as educational television (ETV) which has expanded in size and in influence both here and abroad during the past decade.

The United States has a major stake in television's global development as an educational tool. In advanced countries, the medium can play a role not only in childhood education but also in the sophisticated retraining of adults to meet the challenge of rapid technological and social changes. In underdeveloped areas of Asia, Africa, and Latin America, ETV has an even more fundamental role to play. The endemic instability in these areas reflects the fact that over two-thirds of their populations are illiterate. Of the remaining third, over half of the people lack the skills for sustaining a minimum living standard. The viable world order we seek awaits a massive change in these conditions, and this in turn involves applying radical educational methods. Television will be one of these methods. Like all the other tools brought to the job, it will not be a panacea; like them, it may simply permit us to keep our collective heads above the water while we form islands of order from which to proceed against the disorder that will dominate most of the less-developed areas for the next generation. We will examine this situation in the next chapter; here we will review television's role as a new educational force in the industrialized nations.

Before surveying the situation in Europe and Japan, however, it is relevant to look at American ETV. The reason for this is that, more than any single nation, the United States has set the pace both in experimenting with and in applying a wide range of educational television techniques. The American experience is a bench mark against which we can measure ETV's development abroad and, in particular, the opportunities open to us both in applying our own experience to foreign situations and in learning from them.

The American lead in this field is based on more than a half-century of experience in applying audio-visual techniques for educational purposes. This experience was readily transferred to television; as early as 1945 the Federal Communications Commission began planning for full-scale allocation of television channels for educational uses. Television's rise coincided with the postwar baby boom and the greatest expansion of educational facilities in U.S. history. Inevitably, the question was raised as to the medium's role as a tool for reaching more students being taught more complex subjects.

American ETV's development has been shaped by the decentralized character of U.S. education. Of all the major television countries, the U.S. has no master plan for the medium's educational use. With some exceptions, American ETV has followed the national educational pattern of localized operation and control. The only country-wide ETV effort is the loose federation of more than one hundred local community stations which make up the National Educational Television (NET) network. U.S. educational TV is a collection of hundreds of individual ETV systems, operating at all levels from the six-state Midwest Airborne Television System to the scores of small closed-circuit systems run by individual schools. Each state and local community has sought its own answers to the proper use of television. The result has been to make the United States the center for the liveliest and most far-ranging experiments in educational uses of television.

The range of experimentation is impressive. Much of this is due to the American technological lead and diversity of educational resources; most other large countries, with more centralized school systems, have settled on a relatively uniform national ETV system. American educators have had no such inhibitions, and the resultant proliferation of different systems has explored some of the best (and, it might be added, worst) possibilities for television as a teaching tool. The most familiar of these are the NET community stations, which form the largest television educational network in the world, offering programs to schools during the daytime and to adult audiences at night. Closed-circuit television systems serve individual schools and entire states. The South Carolina Educational TV Center transmits lessons to over 250 schools in that state; its ultimate aim is to link all of the state's 1,200 public schools in a 6-channel network providing a complete kindergarten-to-college curriculum. The most intensive experiment in closed-circuit teaching has taken place since 1956 in the Hagerstown, Maryland, area where 37 schools make use of a complete TV curriculum. A more specialized experiment in New York City's Chelsea section has linked the local school, health center, and neighboring homes in a test of television's ability to serve specialized needs of a low-income, high-density community. Dozens of colleges and universities have turned to closed-circuit television as a means for effectively stretching limited resources to meet the problem of burgeoning enrolments. Los Angeles Station KCET has used a unique scrambler system to transmit medical demonstrations for in-service training courses at local hospitals.

There are a number of gaps in this otherwise impressive development. One has been the general confusion of purpose about educational television's role in U.S. life. Almost no one questions the principle that local communities should control ETV content, particularly that portion of it going into classrooms. However, this does not solve the financial problem: educational TV, like its commercial counterpart, is an expensive proposition. Indecision and doubts about who is going to pay the bills have adversely affected both the quality and quantity of ETV operations during the past decade.

These questions of financing and control over program content relate to another problem that will have to be resolved before educational television takes its rightful place in American life.

This is the question of ETV's relationship to commercial television's power structure. Most of the inhibitions that have plagued ETV's development are tied, directly or indirectly, to the ambivalence which commercial television interests have felt toward it.

Theoretically, there should be no problem. The public interest and U.S. broadcasting tradition call for television's development as a private system which provides a healthy balance between commercial and public needs. In part, the confusion is caused by the parochial viewpoints of the factions involved. One is the commercial broadcasters' claim to be on the side of the angels (and, more specifically, on the side of the FCC regulations) on the issue of their public service responsibilities. At another extreme are the critics who castigate the private broadcasters because they refuse to televise lectures on Spinoza or Cambodian dance festivals during prime evening network time. Meanwhile, the imbalance that exists in this area continues. It will never be solved neatly, and there is no particular reason why it should be, since a neat solution would probably involve government-imposed restrictions that could be harmful to both commercial and noncommercial television. Nevertheless, a better pragmatic balance between the two is needed.

U.S. television pioneers had a clear idea of the medium's public service role: they were intrigued by its programing possibilities as a cultural and social force. This high-mindedness was trampled in the gold-rush commercialism that seized the U.S. television industry beginning in 1948. Plans for the orderly pace of the cultural development of television were discarded in the high-stakes battle to get commercial channels. The least glorious chapter in U.S. broadcasting history involves the attempts by the industry to throttle modest government plans to set aside a small number of channels for educational broadcasting after the war. In 1952, after a bitter struggle, the FCC assigned eighty-two VHF channels for educational stations. Even this small victory was threatened by the inability or unwillingness of universities and other institutions to claim these channels. For a while it appeared as if commercial broadcasters were justified in arguing that TV's educational chores and channels should be left to them. However, American educational broadcasters found their patrons, led by the Ford Foundation which has contributed over eighty million dollars in grants to ETV enterprises. More than any single factor, Ford funds gave stability to American ETV in its first decade. The passage of federal legislation in 1962 authorizing grants for the construction and equipment of educational stations added a significant new element of support. By 1965, U.S. educational television was rapidly expanding with over one hundred local community stations and hundreds of small closed-circuit systems.

The growth of U.S. educational television has forced some changes in attitudes by the commercial broadcasters. By and large, they have welcomed ETV's expansion for reasons that are partly altruistic and partly hard-headed business. The altruism has expressed itself often in substantial assistance for ETV stations; a 1964 survey showed that commercial broadcasters had contributed over eight million dollars in grants, equipment, and services to educational stations.[1] This is somewhat less than a tenth of 1 percent of the net profits of the commercial broadcasters during the period involved, but it spelled the difference between success and failure for many stations during ETV's early years. The dark side of this altruism should also be noted. Supporting ETV stations with an occasional gift seemed a useful way of relieving commercial broadcasting's obligation in public service programing. Moreover, the mere existence of an ETV channel in larger cities has a market value all its own: it blocks the use of that channel to a potential commercial competitor.

Thus American ETV is big business, no longer a poverty-stricken egghead ghetto surrounded by the shiny towers of commercial television. ETV still ranks far down the list in terms of audiences and facilities, but its growth has aroused the commercial broadcasters to a new appreciation of its possible competitive role. The two or three million people who listen to ETV programs on any given day are a small percentage of the total U.S. television audience, but their loss cannot be dismissed lightly by the commercial broadcasters. Educational stations tend to attract better-educated middle- and upper-income adults whose attention is sought by most television advertisers. A 1965 survey by the Louis Harris Poll indicated that television viewing by this group has declined in recent years because "the taste preferences of the better educated and more affluent adults bear little resemblance to the trend of program changes which the networks are planning."[2]

ETV's early efforts to attract this group—its "natural audience" —were plagued by the generally amateurish quality of its programs. This situation is changing, to the concern of some commercial broadcasters. An amusing example of this occurred in 1963 when a community ETV station operated by the University of Georgia showed a Gina Lollobrigida film. The Georgia Broadcasters Association protested strongly against what it considered unwarranted competition. "You are not educating, you are entertaining and amusing," the head of the broadcasters' group warned the station solemnly.[3] The University regents later sustained the station's claim that the use of the Lollobrigida film was educational.

Perhaps the most sensitive area of commercial broadcasting attitudes toward ETV involves the so-called "commercialization" of educational stations. In their search for operating funds, the ETV stations have tapped a broad range of sources. Grants provided by the private foundations and by government agencies have been supplemented by the stations' specialized money-raising efforts. One California station has raised funds by auctioning off items owned by famous movie queens and other celebrities. A Los Angeles station thrives on the profits from a local rock 'n roll radio station. Other stations solicit yearly memberships from their listeners. In recent years, however, a particularly lucrative new source of funds has developed which represents a distinct threat to commercial broadcasting revenues. This is the practice of having corporations underwrite part or all of an evening's ETV programing on community stations in exchange for a discreet mention of the sponsorship. Although no outright advertising of the firm's products is permitted, the sponsorship is a useful way for a company to shore up its public service image. Since this arrangement usually involves companies that are normally commercial television advertisers, it is reasonable to assume that every dollar they spend on ETV programing is a dollar lost by commercial television. Increasingly ETV stations are seeking this type of financing, and increasingly the commercial networks are resisting them. In 1965 New York's Station WNDT announced a plan for raising three million dollars per year through contributions from large corporations that would be identified as the station's sponsors for an entire season. The National Association of Broadcasters, trade group for the commercial broadcasters, protested the plan as a violation of the Federal Communications Act.[4] More than any single development in American ETV's early history, this trend may force a more realistic relationship between commercial and ETV broadcasters.

The fact that American ETV has had a difficult time finding its niche in the over-all television scene should not, however, obscure its many accomplishments. It is the most intensive educational television system in the world, with the significant exception of Japanese ETV. More important, its managers have taken the lead in experimenting with and applying new concepts for television as an instructional and cultural tool. This alone makes American ETV a significant factor in international television.

Any survey of educational television abroad must begin with Europe. School systems in Britain and on the continent have a long tradition of utilizing radio for classroom "enrichment" teaching. The BBC began school broadcasts in 1924; by the end of World War II three-quarters of British schools used broadcast lessons regularly.[5] The Scandinavian countries in particular had developed an extensive pattern of radio broadcasting for schools. It was inevitable that this pattern would be extended to television.

The American ETV pattern was formed largely around the concept of a "fourth network" of locally operated community stations which would serve both school children and adults. This reflected both the American concern for local control over educational facilities and also the general reductance of commercial stations to become involved in educational broadcasting. In Europe, educational telecasting from the start was regarded as a responsibility of all stations, whether or not they were controlled by a government department. Thus in Britain, the commercial Independent Television Authority stations supplement BBC efforts in offering ETV programs to local school authorities.

The European approach to school television during the 1950's was, however, a cautious one. School administrators gave very little thought and attention to the use of television for direct instructional purposes, the area in which American educators were doing their liveliest experimentation. In part this reflected the generally more conservative European educational practices. It also mirrored a general reaction toward television's growing reputation as a baleful influence on children. A number of surveys made in Britain and on the continent provided lurid grist for the mills of those who feared the effect of the medium on young viewers.[6] These somewhat overwrought reports led to counter-excesses: in Sweden a booklet was issued with every new television set, emphasizing the responsibility of parents to control their children's viewing.[7]

The BBC and Radiodiffusion Télévision Française began experimenting with "enrichment" programs for classroom use in the early 1950's. By 1955, RTF was supplying several hours of programing to schools weekly. The BBC's efforts were augmented after 1955 by the ETV activities of a second, commercial network. Most other European countries, beset by more pressing problems of organizing their television systems, shied away from inaugurating school broadcasting during the fifties.

The exception was Italy. Unlike their counterparts in other European countries, Italian educational authorities looked upon television not simply as a useful "enrichment" tool. They also saw it as a possible instrument for ameliorating the lack of school facilities, particularly in the rural areas of southern Italy. These shortages were acute at the secondary school level, affecting the government's efforts to give teenagers the technical and vocational skills they needed to break the region's poverty cycle. A unique attempt to cope with this problem was the inauguration in 1958 of "Telescuola," the "television school." Operated by RAI, the national network, in cooperation with the Ministry of Education, "Telescuola" set a new pace and defined new horizons for educational television efforts abroad. It was the first significant effort to apply direct instruction by television to a mass audience. While American educators had been experimenting in this field for several years before "Telescuola" went on the air, their efforts were limited to relatively small pilot projects. "Telescuola" applied these direct-teaching lessons to an entire country. More significantly, it was directed at a problem largely alien to the earlier U.S. experiments, namely the use of television as a mass medium for teaching in an economically underdeveloped area.

The first "Telescuola" programs, begun in November, 1958, concentrated on direct instruction of courses given in *scuola di avviamento professionale*—vocational training schools. The project was directed at two groups—teenagers who lived in areas where such schools were not available, and high school "dropouts." In both cases, most of the prospective students lived in southern Italy. During its first year "Telescuola" enrolled fifty thousand students who viewed two half-hour vocational courses daily, taught by Ministry of Education specialists. In order to create a classroom atmosphere, students were divided, whenever possible, into "viewing groups" under a group leader. Over sixteen hundred such groups were formed during the first experimental year. At the end of the year, the students who finished the course took a regular final test at a state school. Seventy percent of them passed these tests—a record designed to give "Telescuola" the fillip it needed to answer its early critics.

In 1959, the "Telescuola" course was expanded to two and a half hours daily, with successful students granted a regular "certificate of vocational preparation (industry)" at the end of the course. The televised technical lectures were broken up by short breaks used variously for choral singing, religious instruction, or a pep-talk series entitled "A Word Among Ourselves" in which student problems were discussed. This segment was later expanded into a series of vocational guidance lectures, "Your Future." By 1961, "Telescuola" was broadcasting 34 hours weekly, with a range of courses that included not only vocational subjects but history, mathematics, geography, French, domestic science, drawing, art, and civics. Special textbooks for the televised courses were developed by the Ministry of Education and published by RAI.[8]

By 1961, "Telescuola" had almost two thousand "listening posts," almost half of which were located in southern Italy and on the islands of Sardinia and Sicily. About one-third of the students were high-school "dropouts"; a surprising 50 percent were girls. As "Telescuola" expanded, its administrators discovered that their biggest problem was in keeping their pupils' motivations high, and, specifically, to encourage them to finish the course and take the state examinations. This theme was stressed in the vocational guidance lectures, in monthly bulletins from "Telescuola" headquarters, and in student contests (first prize: a trip to Rome). The importance of motivation was underlined by the fact that, among those who finished the courses and took the examinations in 1961, only 15 percent failed to pass.

"Telescuola" branched out into another area of TV teaching in 1960 when it inaugurated a reading-and-writing course for illiterates. During the 1950's, an intensive campaign reduced the number of illiterates in Italy from twelve to two million. The remaining illiterates were "hard core" cases, mostly older people who could not be reached by regular training because of their sense of psychological isolation. The possibility of using television to lower this barrier was tested first with a program called "It's Never Too Late." Developed in cooperation with the Ministry of Education's Central Service for Adult Education, the initial "Telescuola" literacy project consisted of three half-hour shows a week emphasizing reading, writing, simple counting, and arithmetic. The first "semester" attracted a regular audience of about forty thousand viewers, enough to convince "Telescuola" officials that the project was a useful one but also one whose major problem was "a question of attracting into the school and into a habit of study adults who had no interest whatever in any form of learning."[9]

With this in mind, the programs were designed more directly to catch and retain the interest of their illiterate audiences. Each viewer was provided a packet of materials from Rome, containing a specially edited textbook, notebook, ruler, and pencils. Viewing groups were formed to lessen the sense of isolation and also to get over a major hurdle, the general lack of television sets among poorer families who supplied the bulk of the audience. Puppets and short dramatic sketches were introduced into the program format; a "Victory Panel" of letters lit up when the lesson was learned. Follow-up lectures were devised to check backsliding. Slowly but steadily, "Telescuola's" pupils began to show up to take the state literacy examination; most of them came away with the certificate that testified to their admittance into the wider world of those who could read and write.

"Telescuola" was a relatively obscure project until the end of 1961. At that time, the European Broadcasting Union held its first international conference on school broadcasting in Rome. Representatives from eighty-two television organizations in sixty-five countries came to Rome for the first organized exchange of views on the educational role of television. The purpose of the meeting was, in the words of one delegate, "to see what 400 million radio sets and 100 million television sets around the world could do to help 600 million illiterates and 700 million school-age children."[10] "Telescuola," by then a thriving three-year-old project, stole the show. The Italians were able to provide a live demonstration of how ETV was being used every day to meet some of their own pressing educational requirements. Their demonstrations had the most dramatic impact on delegates from Asia, Africa, and Latin America; a number of them returned home and attempted to apply "Telescuola's" lessons, not always successfully, to their fledgling television stations.

"Telescuola's" international debut at the Rome meeting also had its effect on teachers and TV experts from other European countries. They recognized that the project was, in many respects, a limited response to the particular educational problems of one of the less affluent European countries. However, they were also impressed by its general capabilities as a direct teaching tool. They had tended to dismiss earlier American experiments in this field as too specialized for European adaptation; "Telescuola" made them pay greater attention to the possibilities of direct instructional television methods.

The new ideas discussed at the Rome conference turned the European educational broadcasters toward thoughts of expanding their television activities beyond the limited diet of enrichment programs they were offering at the time. Their interest coincided with the dramatic expansion of television facilities and audiences throughout the continent during the early 1960's. Thus they had both the means and the motivation to demonstrate the role that educational telecasting could play.

West European ETV is a mosaic pattern, formed by the variations in both educational systems and television operations from country to country. There are, roughly, three types of combinations which determine the specific form of educational television in Europe. The first involves those countries whose educational systems and television networks are under central government control. These include France, the Netherlands, Belgium, the Scandinavian nations, and a number of smaller countries. The second category includes decentralized publicly operated television stations and decentralized school systems as in West Germany. The third category involves decentralized school systems and a television system divided between commercial and noncommercial stations as in Great Britain.

France provides the best European example of a state television network serving a centralized school system. ORTF, the national network, works directly with the national Ministry of Education and the Institut National Pédagogique in developing school broadcasts that are related directly to the ministry's curriculum planning. The French inaugurated the first formal educational television in Europe in October, 1951, with two weekly programs for primary schools in the Paris area. By 1961 this had expanded to eleven programs serving five thousand schools throughout the nation, in addition to a growing adult education audience.[11] These early French efforts were concentrated almost exclusively on "enrichment" programs designed to supplement classroom activities rather than provide direct instruction. Beginning in 1960, however, French educational authorities began experimenting more intensively with direct ETV instruction.

During the 1960/61 school year, a pilot project for teaching mathematics in this fashion was begun in the Lille district. The results were so successful that the mathematics course has become a permanent feature in French educational television. The program series was shared with nearby Belgian schools, thereby qualifying as the first international ETV experiment. Since that time, French ETV officials have developed a wide variety of direct-instruction programs both for the state network and for individual closed-circuit systems. A special series of in-service training courses for teachers has been given since 1961. Other instructional programs are designed for students at technical institutes. An unusual refinement was added to this series in 1964 at the École Nationale de Radiotechnique et d'Électricité near Paris with TV receivers installed in the classroom ceilings. Mirrors on the student's desk permit him to watch the program directly without having to look from his text to a receiver across the room.[12]

The French have also taken a broader view in recent years of television's possibilities in adult education. French television conducted the first mass experiment in cultural programing aimed directly at organized viewing groups, the so-called "tele-clubs" organized under UNESCO sponsorship in the early 1950's.[13] With the spread of television receivers, programing for groups has been dropped in favor of more individually tailored series. The French have experimented in particular with televised correspondence courses for adults in recent years.

These approaches to educational television have had a strong effect on the ETV plans of other European nations with state networks. Belgian ETV efforts closely parallel the French system, except that school programs have to be prepared for each of the country's two educational systems, one taught in French and the other in Flemish. By the early 1960's all of the Scandinavian countries had instituted school broadcasting on their national TV networks. The Dutch television system had to solve a knotty problem of curriculum planning before it could begin ETV programing in 1962. Since Dutch TV programs are prepared by a group of five religious and secular organizations, each with its individual ideas on education, the problem was to get a consensus on the content of school broadcasting programs. After several years of discussion, an elaborate system of controls was agreed upon whereby any of the individual "confessional" organizations may accept or reject programs prepared by the others.[14]

The most complex problem faced by a state television network in serving local schools occurs in Switzerland. The national network is expected to serve twenty-five separate cantonal education systems, plus assorted religious and secular schools. These schools use four languages—French, German, Italian, and Romansch. "The fact remains," one Swiss educator has noted, "that it seems easier to exchange (programs) between Switzerland and Dahomey than between the different regions of the country."[15]

West German television offers another special type of educational broadcasting. The Germans are the only Europeans who have opted for the American system of a separate network of locally controlled ETV stations. In large part this reflects the fact that both German education and television are, like their American counterparts, highly decentralized. The German ETV "third network," unlike the NET "fourth network" in the United States, is operated by the same management which runs regular German television stations. The first ETV station, operated by Hessischer Rundfunk, began operations in September, 1964, in Munich. A second station was inaugurated three months later in Frankfurt; during 1965, several others began operations. Initially, each station emphasized regional interests of its viewers although eventually they will all be linked more closely in a national ETV network. Unlike the other European networks, German ETV programing in its early stages concentrated almost exclusively on adult "enrichment" programing rather than school programs. However, each of the new "third network" stations has plans for more intensive school broadcasting.[16]

Tradition, politics, and network rivalries have made British educational television a pacesetting model of its kind. In 1952, the first experimental broadcasts were transmitted by closed circuit to six secondary schools in the London area with results that were sufficiently promising to encourage the BBC to undertake a fuller schedule of ETV programs for schools. A 1957–58 series of four broadcasts a week extended the experiment to 350 schools. In 1959, the BBC, in cooperation with the Ministry of Education, announced plans for "the first nationwide and permanent service of school television anywhere in the world."[17]

These words were somewhat hyperbolic; the French, not to mention a dozen or more American educational television systems, could challenge the BBC's claims as an ETV pioneer. Nevertheless, the BBC deserves considerable credit for the manner in which it has phased school telecasts into all levels of the decentralized British educational system. The 1964–65 schedule of BBC educational broadcasts, both on radio and on TV, took sixty pages to list the corporation's offerings for that school year. Over seven thousand schools throughout Britain and Scotland were equipped to take these programs. BBC has taken a long lead in the production of supplementary reading materials for students and teachers viewing its programs.

Most of the BBC's fifteen hours of weekly daytime school broadcasting is enrichment programing. During the 1962/63 school year, however, BBC experimented with a direct teaching course in pure mathematics for fifth and sixth form grammar school students. The course was successful enough to warrant a permanent place in the BBC schedule. However, British educational authorities have, in general, shown little enthusiasm for other proposals to expand dramatically the amount of direct instruction television being offered to their schools. The BBC, following their lead, has indicated that it intends to move slowly in this field.

The tone and content of what is taught on BBC school programs is set by the Schools Broadcasting Council, an independent advisory body composed of national and local education officials. Although program ideas can originate either with the council or with the BBC, all program plans must be approved by professional committees sponsored by the council. Liaison between local education authorities and the BBC is maintained by fifteen field education officers appointed by the BBC from the teaching profession. The system has been criticized by some educators as being poorly designed to give classroom teachers the television materials they need, adequately prepared and at the proper time. "The advisory council method of coordinating teacher and camera seems to be incapable of bringing about the proper relations," Dr. Peter Laslett of Cambridge University has noted. If the system is to work, he says, "the teacher would have to be given access to the camera himself, instead of being informed, as he is now, by a distant institution devoted to television as a general entertainment service, what he is being offered for his class." Laslett believes that only with closed-circuit systems, capable of providing programs at the direct request of classroom teachers, can television be utilized as a classroom teaching tool.[18]

In 1963, the corporation took its first steps into the field of adult education television with a five-hour-a-week schedule running for thirty weeks. The programs ranged from a series of demonstrations of molecular biology to a short course in maintaining the family car. This program was expanded in 1964 with the inauguration of the BBC second channel (BBC-2) which scheduled, from its beginning, several hours of adult educational programing during prime night-time hours. Designed for "discreet audiences of serious viewers," the BBC-2 series are generally free of the condescending popularization that characterizes many American efforts in the field. A special monthly publication, "Tuesday Term," gives BBC-2 viewers program notes on each of the courses, with suggestions for further reading. In 1965, the BBC was planning to extend its adult education series to include correspondence courses.

The BBC's efforts in educational television have been motivated, in part, by the fact that it has competition in this field as well as in regular TV broadcasting. The competition is provided by the Independent Television Authority (ITA), the central regulatory body for over a dozen commercial television stations throughout the country. ITA stations have attracted the bulk of the British "telly" audience since they began operations in 1955; in almost all instances, they have been an impressive financial success. It is for this reason as much as any other that the British commercial stations have shown a special interest in educational broadcasts. With the ITA charter subject to regular Parliamentary scrutiny, the commercial stations try hard to maintain their "public service" image in the face of continuing charges that commercial telecasting has lowered British broadcasting standards. Educational broadcasting has been a useful way for the ITA stations to demonstrate their cultural *bona fides*.[19]

Associated-Rediffusion, operator of one of the largest ITA stations, began an experimental school broadcasting series in

1957. By the end of 1961, three other large commercial companies —Associated Television, Granada, and Scottish TV—were directly involved in ETV production for their own outlets and for transmission by other commercial stations. By the following year, the ITA network was offering its stations ten series of school programs weekly. Like the BBC, ITA stations rely on advisory committees of national and local educators to set the pattern and subject matter of the network's school programs. As a result ITA school broadcasting has proved to be an important supplement to the somewhat more extensive BBC efforts in this field.

The commercial stations have not taken second place to the BBC in the field of ETV programing for adults. Not only did ITA pioneer in this field but its stations have shown a lively awareness of the role adult ETV can play in their schedules. In 1963, several ITA stations began experimenting with early-morning scholarly programs at the university level. Scottish TV offered a professional medical series for doctors. By 1964, commercial stations were experimenting with adult ETV shows during prime nighttime hours. An ITA audience research survey of the first series indicated that it was seen at one time or another by 7 percent of Britain's adult viewers. An average of 730,000 persons watched the once-a-week series, the survey showed.[20]

Although both ITA and BBC have made important advances in school broadcasting, the final form of ETV's role in British education has still to be decided. The commercial broadcasters have generally taken the position that school broadcasting should be the responsibility of a "fourth network" designed specifically for ETV activities. In 1961, interests associated with ITA sponsored an "Institute for Educational Television" in London which actively promulgated this viewpoint. Some observers saw the institute as an organization less concerned with the future of educational television than with a plan for blocking further expansion of the BBC's share of the regular television audience.[21]

The BBC has defended the position that educational broadcasting should be part and parcel of regular television transmissions, not segregated into a separate channel. Underlying this viewpoint has been the BBC's concern that it would be relegated to the status of the educational and cultural-uplift network while the commercial stations pursued their goal of attracting the vast bulk of British viewers in search of light entertainment. The BBC's views were pungently outlined by its director in a 1963 speech:

> As the national instrument of broadcasting, we cannot be what the Americans would call an egghead channel. To keep our place in the nation's life we must concern ourselves with the whole of that life, with mass interests and with minority interests. . . . We are firmly opposed to the segregation of education into a sort of broadcasting ghetto on the American model, so much praised by those who do not understand, as Americans do, that it was devised to meet the needs of a country where broadcasting is completely dominated by commercial interests. That is not the case with us in this country and there is now no danger that it ever will be.[22]

Whether or not his prediction holds good for time immemorial, Sir Hugh's position was supported by the government at the time. Following the general recommendations of the 1962 Pilkington Report, the Conservative government rejected the idea of a separate ETV network, authorized a second BBC channel, and postponed any action on a second commercial channel for a number of years. These decisions reaffirmed the BBC and ITA responsibilities for expanding their educational television activities within their existing channels.

In the election campaign leading up to its October, 1964, victory, the Labor party proposed that television should be treated more intensively as a national educational resource. Although the party's plans for doing this were vague at the time, they drew upon the increasing interest of British educators in television. In 1960, a group of Leeds University scholars had urged that a "universities' teaching corporation" should be set up to operate a new network which would broadcast without the obligation "to entertain or to pander to some theoretical lowest common multiple of viewers."[23] Other British universities became acquainted with television's possibilities while preparing adult education programs for ITA stations. In October, 1962, Cambridge University facilities were used to telecast a series of college-level lectures to the general public over a commercial station and, by closed circuit, to classes at the University of East Anglia.[24]

The most dramatic proposal in this field was made in 1961 by the editors of *The Economist*. Surveying the prospects for educational television, they proposed "some sort of British Television University (or universities) which could revolutionize spare-time adult education" with televised instruction leading to extramural university degrees. They saw the proposed "televarsity" as a useful step toward filling the gaps in Britain's overcrowded, inadequate university system:

> There would never be a really mass audience for any one of these lectures, because only an absurd swot would try to take all the courses at the same time. But each course, involving say four or five lectures or demonstrations a week, coming into people's own firesides, would be very likely to attract several times the number of people who can at present take similar courses in all the existing colleges and other places of advanced education in this country. . . . If it caught on, this could be a device for trebling or quadrupling the number of reasonably well-educated people in Britain within a relatively short span of years.[25]

These and similar proposals provided fuel for the Labor party's plans for a nation-wide "university of the air" and other expanded uses of television for education. Once in office, Prime Minister Harold Wilson and his advisers had to decide whether their plans should be carried out within the current framework of British television or by setting up a separate ETV network. In a policy statement issued in April, 1965, by Miss Jennie Lee, undersecretary for education and science, the party rejected the idea of a fourth network which would leave the other channels "impoverished."

"Whether there is to be a fourth channel or something else," Miss Lee told the House of Commons, "we have got to the point where we must deploy the hours of listening on educational grounds and not simply take what is left from every other purpose." The more the government examined the problem of setting up a "university of the air," she said, the more it realized that "ultimately, if there were to be degree courses on TV, they would have to have some control over peak time."[26] Whatever form the government's final recommendations on educational television take, it was evident that British television would have a more scholarly look in the coming years.

Several Commonwealth countries have looked to British ETV practices as a guide for their own activities in this field. Australia has had a long tradition of school broadcasting by radio as part of its effort to reach isolated schools and children in its vast outback regions. This experience was transferred to television beginning in 1958 when the Australian Broadcasting Corporation (ABC), in cooperation with local authorities, inaugurated an ETV schedule. By 1961, ABC stations in each of the Australian state capitals had educational television programs. In the same year ABC introduced its "university of the air," offering college-level lectures and demonstrations. Similar adult education programs have dominated most early Canadian efforts to develop ETV programs for that country's two networks. In 1963, Dr. Claude Bissell, president of the University of Toronto, proposed massive use of university-level ETV to provide home schooling for students who could not otherwise be accommodated by Canada's crowded schools of higher education. He suggested that these students could tune in on lectures at home and then spend a week receiving direct instruction at a local university during Christmas, Easter, and summer holidays.[27]

Although Communist television systems in Eastern Europe have lagged behind their Western counterparts in school broadcasting, the gap is now being closed. The first ETV experiments by a Communist regime took place in Yugoslavia in 1960 when a series of enrichment programs were broadcast by the Zagreb station.[28] Polish television began school broadcasting at about the same time. During the 1962/63 school year, about forty-five hundred schools were being served by these programs, according to Polish sources. By 1965, most of the other East European countries had initiated school broadcasts on a regular basis.

The rapidly expanding Soviet television system has given increasing attention to both adult and school ETV programing since 1962. The Russians are experimenting with both direct instructional and enrichment programs. In one 1962 experiment, fifty-two thousand farmers in the Moscow region were formed into listening groups to view a televised series of lectures and demonstrations on scientific agronomy.[29] Soviet television authorities have indicated they plan to set up separate educational channels in major cities throughout the country; the first of these was inaugurated in Moscow in October, 1964. They have also tried a new approach toward ETV programs for children. Instead of broadcasting into classrooms, enrichment lessons are transmitted to home receivers in the afternoon after school hours. The lessons are coordinated with the school curriculum in ways that assist students to prepare their homework and review the day's school lessons.

The Chinese Communists have also explored the possibilities of ETV programing for their small but growing television network. A 1962 Chinese report claimed that the Shanghai station offered university-level courses in physics and chemistry and that stations in Peking, Tientsin, Canton, and Harbin were also sponsoring "television universities" as part of the regime's national worker education drive.

A new dimension in ETV was opened to broadcasters and educators who gathered for the second international conference on school broadcasting in Tokyo in April, 1964. Most of them were acquainted with reports about Japanese ETV efforts. What they saw in Tokyo confirmed the fact that Japan is the first country in the world that has fully integrated television into its educational structure from kindergarten to university-level studies and into the broad field of adult instruction.

After several years of experimenting, the government-chartered Nippon Hosai Kyokai (NHK) network inaugurated the first station of a separate national ETV network in 1958. By 1965, there were 46 ETV stations originating programs throughout Japan. NHK operates 25 of these outlets; the rest are run by commercial companies whose stations are permitted to transmit general programs when the ETV schedule is completed each day. The NHK stations retransmit their educational programs over 238 smaller relay satellite stations designed to reach schools and home receivers in isolated areas. The commercial ETV stations have about 40 such satellite relay transmitters for their own stations. These facilities permit the most extensive school broadcasting schedule in the world. In 1965 almost all Japanese schools were equipped with television receivers; NHK surveys showed that over 90 percent of the schools actively used ETV broadcasts as a regular classroom teaching tool. The range of Japanese ETV programing is as broad as the school curriculum itself; almost every subject taught in the classroom has its television counterpart. Outside the classroom, Japanese TV also provides adult education programs beamed to 18 million home television sets reaching an audience of almost 90 million people.

Teachers and school administrators have formed a National Federation of the Study Group of Radio and TV Education to advise NHK and its affiliated stations on ETV programing. NHK also has its own advisory committee of Ministry of Education officials and other experts to assure that its programing is coordinated with school curricula.[30] Because Japanese school curricula are centrally controlled, NHK and its affiliated ETV stations can schedule their broadcasts with the assurance that they will fit directly into classroom activities throughout the week.

Almost all of the early Japanese school broadcasting efforts were devoted to enrichment programing. Television film crews produced an extensive series of programs designed to supplement classroom instruction; in one 1958 series, cameras were attached to a submarine to provide visual material for a program about life on the ocean floor. In the early 1960's, however, NHK shifted its programing emphasis toward more direct instructional efforts. This trend has affected all levels of instruction. It is most evident, however, at the secondary school level where NHK operates the first school in the world which grants a fully accredited diploma based on radio and television instruction.

The school, known as the NHK Upper Secondary School, was inaugurated in 1962. It has its own campus in Tokyo where students come to take tests, to receive guidance, and, when they finish their course, to attend their graduation ceremonies. Their classroom, however, is their home and their teachers are the NHK instructors who appear on their television screen. The NHK school is one of seventy correspondence schools offering senior high school credit courses under a 1947 law designed to encourage part-time education of teen-agers who leave school after the required nine-year primary and junior high school courses. In 1963 about 15 percent of all senior high school students in the country were enrolled in these correspondence schools.

NHK began experimenting with televised instructional courses for these correspondence school students in 1959. Since most of the students had full-time jobs, the courses were telecast on Saturdays and Sundays. Before these broadcasts were introduced, correspondence students were required by the Ministry of Education to spend twenty days a year at a full-time high school getting direct classroom instruction. The television and radio courses proved so effective that the ministry lowered this requirement to ten days a year for those students following the television courses and to eight days for those following the courses on both radio and TV. As a result, working youths could finish their courses without losing too much time from their job. By 1963 NHK was offering twelve hours of high school instruction weekly to students at its own school and the seventy other correspondence institutions throughout the country.

NHK research studies of this project indicate that televised correspondence school instruction may have its most important effect in continually motivating students to complete their course of study. Loss of interest is a perennial problem in such courses: in 1963, fewer than 4 percent of correspondence school students in Japan successfully finished their course. Since that time, this percentage has edged up as television instructors have emphasized vocational and personal guidance along with the orthodox instructional courses.[31]

The NHK research department—the largest operated by any television system in the world—also keeps a careful eye on the effectiveness of the network's other educational ventures. One of these is the extensive adult education courses sponsored by NHK and its affiliated ETV stations during evening hours and on weekends. However, research on the influence of educational programs of any kind is at best an elusive thing. Once the charts and statistics are put aside, it is perhaps easier to get some idea of the impact of television from the following poem, written by a Japanese child in a rural school, shortly after the teacher announced that the school would have to give up its rented television set:

> We have to return the television soon,
> We have studied cheerfully with TV.
> But if there were no more TV in school,
> It is like a day without sunshine.
> I am sad as if our house is going to be sold.
> Even if there were no television,
> I will imitate the act of switching it on.
> I will recall the time when we had television
> Because it was like love itself.[32]

Educational television in Japan, the United States, and the countries of Western Europe is developing as a sophisticated new ingredient in an already highly developed educational pattern. American leadership in experimenting with a wide range of ETV possibilities will continue to be an important influence on the medium's future in industrialized countries. Most European and Japanese educators recognize pacesetting U.S. developments in this field; they are also aware that at least part of our activities reflect (as one British commentator put it) "the fatal American preoccupation with novelty and change for the sake of change." The other side of this coin is, of course, that American educators and broadcasters can draw useful lessons from abroad in making our ETV operations more responsive to U.S. educational needs.

In educational matters, however, the West and Japan are an affluent minority. Television and other audio-visual teaching systems are important steps in the harnessing of technology for the improvement of educational methods. The situation is completely different in the underdeveloped areas of Asia, Africa, and Latin America. Here television and its electronic allies are potentially revolutionary weapons in the battle against a staggering educational deficit. No review of television abroad would be complete without taking a closer look at its educational impact in these areas.

10

ETV: New Tool for Developing Nations

Among all of television's prospects in the coming years, none is more intriguing than the potential educational role of the medium in Asia, Africa, and Latin America. How can TV's unique capacity for informing and persuading be applied to the massive modernization problems of the underdeveloped world? Finding constructive answers to this question could have important implications for the political and social evolution of sixty new nations in the next decade.

As the leading free world power, the United States has a stake in those answers. In part, they involve television's potential as a classroom teaching tool that can strengthen meager educational resources in the new nations. American ETV offers these countries the most extensive inventory of the medium's teaching uses. Another consideration is television's wider potential for informing entire populations about twentieth century political, social, and economic realities. Here TV can be a conscious instrument of social change, utilizing its sight-and-sound powers to project a persuasive model of what needs to be done to bring the new nations into the full stream of modern life.

Television is already performing part of this function in most of the forty-five underdeveloped countries that have TV facilities. Day and night, TV provides a tempting image of a materially better life, largely in programs imported from the West. Dr. Kildare, Lucille Ball, and the men from U.N.C.L.E. are the bearers of a promise of affluence to vast audiences throughout Asia, Africa, and Latin America. TV screens in the new countries are a powerful addition to the "revolution of rising expectations." The opulent images these screens show are, however, less than half the story television must tell if it is to serve its full potential. The revolution of rising expectations quickly leads to the revolution of rising frustrations when people are not made aware of the obligations as well as the rewards of modern life. Most of the dilemmas facing the new nations relate to failures in the social reorientation of two billion people as they begin to move beyond old patterns of village, tribe, and caste into the quick pace of political and technological change.

The United States has relatively little influence over this vast movement. We can, however, play a useful role by assisting these countries with ideas and technological help in the field of social modernization. Some helpful initiatives are already under way in this area; obviously, more needs to be done.

This approach calls for radical methods designed to help strengthen modernization programs in the new nations. Our problem is, in large part, one of a garbled dialogue, a stubborn inability to understand fully each other's interests. Despite our extensive record of assistance to the new nations, the gap in mutual confidence often remains. This is by no means all our fault; much of the blame lies with the other side.

But the gap also is caused by our own cultural obtuseness and, in particular, our tendency to believe that political and economic modernization in these countries will take place only on the conditions we set. We insist that development is a slow, hard pull, requiring years of sacrifice. The core of hard truth in all this is obscured by the stubborn refusal of the peoples of Asia and Africa to postpone the day they reach some measure of economic and political equality with the West. Not only do they question our motives in talking about the long, hard pull; they are also skeptical whether their developmental problems do in fact involve transposing the West's historical experience to their current reality.

Our experience has indeed been different. It is rooted in the circumstances of European evolution from a feudal society during the past five centuries. A central fact in this evolution was the growth of literacy, based on the printed word. The movable type printing press was the module on which we built the most advanced political and technological systems the world has yet seen.

For all these accomplishments, the West did not complete its revolution. It stopped short of becoming a world movement while the more powerful European nations colonized Asia and Africa. Political oppression and economic imperialism were only part of this pattern of exploitation. The European colonialists controlled their empires by withholding literacy and more advanced education, a policy far more effective in stifling opposition than putting "the natives" in chains. Education was limited largely to the training of clerks to serve the colonial administrators. (The exception to this was the missionary school system which trained a small elite out of which came many of the independence leaders of Asia and Africa.) This heritage of limited education opportunity still hampers Western efforts to provide realistic assistance in former colonial areas. Its most obvious effect is a massive inventory of illiterate and undereducated people, the legacy of centuries of neglect. More damaging, however, is the rigidity with which we are attempting to close this educational gap. With some notable exceptions, our approach to this problem emphasizes the transfer of traditional forms of Western school systems to the developing areas.

However, if Asian and African countries are to meet the schooling needs of their expanding populations, this pattern of Western-modeled education will have to be heavily modified. There is, of course, much in our educational tradition that has been and will continue to be valuable to Asians and Africans. These include our contributions to the development of academic freedom and rigorous scholarship, and our concern for education as a weapon of individual and collective liberties. Within this tradition there are many techniques which may be adaptable to other cultures, from IQ tests to school-building planning.

It does not follow, however, that the general forms of Western education can or should be adapted by the new nations of Asia and Africa. There may be some self-satisfaction for us in the imitation of our methods, but this is poor compensation for the fact that such imitation often perpetuates rather than resolves development problems. There are several reasons why this is so. The first is that the curriculum needs for school systems in newly developing societies call for a different set of subject matter emphases than those of more developed countries. The second reason is that developing nations need an educational pattern that can train more people more quickly than is possible in the Western pattern, keyed as it is to a sophisticated progression of education levels stretching out over fifteen or twenty years. Finally, Western-modeled schooling is based upon elaborate educational plants and auxiliary resources—from books to Bunsen burners— that will be beyond the economic resources of the new nations for a generation or more. The realistic need in these countries is for new forms of educational short cuts that provide as much quality as possible, given the gap that exists between the number of people to be trained and the resources available to do it.

One of the anomalies of this situation is the preference of leadership elites in the new countries for an educational system based on Western models. Most of them were educated, at home or abroad, in American or European schools. Not only is this the only type of educational system they know, but they have a vested interest in preserving its prestigious forms to maintain their own status. Thus we need not only to revise our own ideas about the efficiency of Western-oriented schools in underdeveloped countries but also to change the attitudes of a large part of the leadership which controls these schools.

As long as the pattern of education is tied rigidly to traditional Western techniques, the chances for a decisive breakthrough to political and economic viability are reduced. These chances will be enhanced only through a new framework of training techniques that matches the historical circumstances in which the developing nations find themselves.

This is the framework in which we should place television's potential role in the new nations of Asia, Africa, and Latin America. Educational TV is only one of many techniques that must be structured into the school systems of these countries to meet their modernization needs. Radio, films, and other audio-visual ms also have their part to play in this effort. None of them, ver, can match TV's effectiveness in informing and persuading mass audiences. /Television can bring one good teacher and all his teaching tools to the attention of millions of people, erasing at least part of the burden of a chronically short supply of trained educators/ He can appear in formal schooling situations, and he can also bring his lessons to the hundreds of millions of illiterates who have never in their lives stepped inside a classroom./

At least one American specialist believes that ETV's greatest potential in underdeveloped countries lies specifically in this area of fundamental education for the billion or more people who live beyond the pale of formal education. Writing of ETV planning in Chile, Jesuit sociologist Father Neil Hurley declares:

> Television's finest educational possibilities at present seem to be at those levels where as yet there is no pedagogical tradition: the training of the illiterate and the unskilled. Here we are on virgin soil with no problems of reorienting educational philosophies, of displacing personnel, or rearranging curricula, and of coping with students caught in a transitional phase. Chile's "revolution in liberty" will meet its acid test in the area of the underprivileged, those who eagerly want to read and write, to learn a craft and vocational skills, who want to be incorporated into Twentieth Century life. It is precisely at this level where TV can leap the literacy barrier and barriers of space and time to carry light into the darkness of the lower classes and those in remote areas. This is where TV can prove revolutionary by feeding the ravenous hunger for life, for vicarious experience, for moral example, for inspiration, for emotional release, and for schooling.[1]

Whether it is used for the training of illiterates in Chile or of university students in Pakistan, television can bring a significant new dimension to the modernization of the world's newly independent nations. In the rest of this chapter we shall examine what these countries are currently doing in this field and how the United States and other more developed countries are beginning to assist them.

Despite its great potential, ETV has developed slowly in Asia, Africa, and Latin America. When television was being introduced into most countries in these areas, the public pronouncements of its promoters stressed the medium's educational capabilities. Once the stations began operating, however, these high-minded promises about educational broadcasting were largely forgotten. The reasons for this were, in part, economic. Most TV stations in underdeveloped countries are operated, directly or indirectly, by commercial interests which were initially concerned with keeping their enterprise solvent. Educational programing was a luxury that tied up their facilities without producing revenue. They received little help from local educational ministries which had neither the funds nor the trained personnel to cope with the expensive and complex requirements of educational broadcasting. As a result, most stations passed off their early ETV obligations with a few documentary films broadcast in off hours.

/ This state of affairs is, however, slowly changing. Since 1963, educators in a score of developing countries have taken active steps toward utilizing television as a teaching tool./ Many of these educators "discovered" ETV at two international conferences on school broadcasting sponsored by the European Broadcasting Union in Rome in 1961 and in Tokyo in 1964. These meetings gave Asian and African delegates a chance to see "live models" of European and Japanese school broadcasting. A number of them also saw a wide variety of experimentation in this field during visits to the United States. Their initial reaction, in many instances, was to apply the attractive Western and Japanese models they saw to their own educational systems. These early efforts to transpose advanced techniques to less developed educational systems have generally failed. Almost all these attempts, for instance, underestimated the technical and fiscal difficulties involved in installing and maintaining television receivers in schools. Nevertheless, a number of significant starts have been made in applying ETV in developing countries.

The earliest experimentation in ETV for developing countries took place in Latin America. A number of ETV projects were begun throughout the region in the late 1950's; by 1961, interest in the subject was sufficient to encourage educators and broadcasters to set up a regional commission on ETV problems.[2] A UNESCO regional seminar on educational television, held in Mexico City in 1964, attracted delegates from seventeen countries. At the meeting, most of these countries reported that their ETV plans were beginning to move beyond wishful thinking to active operations.

The most extensive application of ETV in Latin America by 1965 had taken place in Colombia. Relying heavily on their observation of the Italian "Telescuola" project, Colombia educators inaugurated an experimental ETV project in 1961. The experiment was later expanded to include a full range of primary school subjects relayed over the full national network during school hours. In 1962, the project was made eligible for Alliance for Progress economic assistance. The U.S. government has since supplied equipment for the project, including receiving sets to be placed in rural schools. In addition, the Peace Corps assigned ninety American television technicians and program directors to work with the Ministry of Education and the national network in planning and carrying out ETV programs. In 1965, an estimated four hundred thousand children were viewing classroom television throughout the country.

The Colombian ETV project has had its full share of growing-pain difficulties and setbacks. However, by the end of 1965, ETV was well on its way toward establishing itself as a permanent feature in a country whose educational resources can accommodate only 40 percent of school-age children and which needs thirty thousand more teachers to meet its full primary school requirements. ETV's role in helping reduce these awesome deficits is enhanced by several factors. One is that the Colombians have a television network that covers 85 percent of the country. The second is that the project is receiving some useful foreign assistance. The third, and most important, is that local educators and broadcasters appear to have a realistic idea of ETV's opportunities and limitations and are proceeding accordingly.[3]

Argentina is another Latin American nation which drew its original ETV inspiration and techniques from Italy's "Telescuola." In April, 1963, the Ministry of Education inaugurated a television series of high school courses on the state channel in Buenos Aires. "Telescuela Tecnica Argentina" was intended, like its Italian counterpart, to provide direct instruction for students who were "dropouts" or who lived in remote areas where there were no high schools. Unlike "Telescuola," the Argentine courses did not set an age limit on enrollment. This led to some surprising results: among the students in the first series of courses, half were over the age of thirty. Fourteen of those enrolled were seventy years old or older. The original series, telecast three hours every weekday, offered a "major" in electrical mechanics for men and in fashion design for women. These technical courses were supplemented by regular high school lessons in literature, English, mathematics, and Spanish. By the end of 1963, "Telescuela Tecnica" had an estimated "look in" audience of six hundred thousand viewers. Although only a small portion of this group were actively enrolled in the courses offered, the fact that an ETV series could attract hundreds of thousands of people encouraged Ministry of Education officials to plan to make "Telescuela" a permanent part of Argentine television.[4]

Educational television ranging in scope from illiteracy training to university-level lectures is offered in Guatemala under a project sponsored by the Ministry of Education, the U.S. Information Service, and Radio-Television Guatemala, a commercial station. A literacy course of eighty-five lessons has been presented weekdays on the station three times a year. Another series, entitled "TeleAula" has provided daily lectures on educational theory and methods to students in Guatemalan teacher-training institutes. The courses are also utilized for in-service training of practicing teachers throughout the country. The Ministry of Education has made the "TeleAula" course a compulsory subject for second-year students in normal schools. The third ETV series presented on Guatemalan television is "TeleU" a series of college-level lectures prepared by the University of San Carlos.

During 1964 and 1965, a half-dozen other Latin American nations inaugurated ETV programing on local television stations. In Brazil, the Joao Baptista do Amaral Foundation sponsored a literacy program modeled on the Italian network's "It's Never Too Late" series. Cuban television offered primary and secondary level school programs, with the added feature of publishing the texts of the lessons in local newspapers. Peruvian educators and broadcasters experimented with direct-instruction telecasting in the provincial city of Arequipa and have set up a separate ETV channel in Lima under Ministry of Education auspices. In February, 1964, the Mexican government announced that it planned to construct five ETV stations in the central part of the country over a period of several years. Although these and other plans were still experimental and vague, they indicated a growing interest in the educational role of television throughout Latin America.

The educational problems facing newly independent African countries have added a sense of urgency to the search for effective short cuts in this field. A 1960 UNESCO survey indicated that about 85 percent of Africa's population was illiterate, compared to the world-wide average of 50 percent. At that time, seventeen million African children were receiving no schooling at all. The survey noted that, despite the need for vocational and technical training, there was not a single institute for training teachers in these subjects throughout tropical Africa. Although there has been some improvement in these conditions in recent years, Africa is still laboring under the burdens of a major educational deficit. Increasingly, television's role in easing this burden is being examined.

Over a dozen African nations had begun experimenting with television as a teaching tool by 1965. The leading nation in this field is Nigeria, where ETV's capabilities were first tested in 1959, a year before the country became independent. The first experiments were conducted by WN-TV, the country's first television station, under a grant from the regional Ministry of Education in Western Nigeria.[5] The programs were serviced to 120 schools in the Lagos and Ibadan areas. After independence in 1960, the central government organized a National School Broadcasting Service for radio and television with the aid of a Ford Foundation grant. This permitted Nigerian stations to develop a modest inventory of classroom telecasts, most of which involved enrichment programs rather than direct teaching. In 1963 these efforts were strengthened when the United States government agreed to underwrite a large part of the costs of a five-year program significantly expanding Nigerian ETV efforts. Since that time, a team of U.S. educators, working with their Nigerian counterparts, have developed a curriculum of ETV lessons at the primary and secondary school levels for transmittal during school hours by four Nigerian stations. The result has been to give Nigeria a long lead in educational television in Africa.

Experiments in educational broadcasting are also being conducted in several former French colonies in West Africa. A first step toward measuring ETV capabilities in the field of adult education is being made by the Center for Mass Information and Education in Dakar under a 1963 agreement between UNESCO and the government of Senegal. Other African educators, working with French audio-visual experts, are experimenting with "radiovision"—a hybrid that combines educational radio programs transmitted to rural receivers with picture slides illustrating the radio lecture.[6]

The only other significant practical work in educational television in Africa has taken place in Southern Rhodesia. Rhodesian educational officials have experimented with ETV's capabilities since 1962 in the capital city of Salisbury. Most of the experiments have been limited to schools attended by children of the white minority which controls the government; only a token number of sets have been placed in African schools. Despite this anachronistic effort to apply racial standards to television, Rhodesian ETV efforts could have a useful influence on ETV's general development in East Africa. In 1965, Kenya, Zambia, and Uganda were experimenting with classroom broadcasting.

Educational television was inaugurated in the Middle East during the summer of 1960 when the Iranian Ministry of Education sponsored a series of direct-teaching science programs on the Tehran commercial station. The programs were designed as a "summer school" session for students who had failed their regular classroom science course during the previous year. Of the students who followed the televised course, 72 percent successfully passed their "make-up" examination at the end of the summer. Since that time, Ministry of Education officials, working with American technical assistance officials, have expanded their range of ETV programs on stations throughout the country.[7]

Among the Arab states, Egypt has taken the strongest lead in encouraging educational TV. Cairo television has emphasized both child and adult education in a heavy schedule of enrichment and how-to-do-it series which was being expanded in 1965 to include a separate third channel solely for ETV programing. Saudi Arabia education officials experimented with the medium's teaching possibilities before their government opened its first station. Using the facilities of the Arabian-American Oil Company station in Dhahran, they presented a series of televised courses for schools in the eastern part of the country in 1964.

ETV in Israel is unique in that it will be, officially at least, the only type of television offered to local viewers when the country's first television channel begins brodcasting sometime in 1966. The event will be a turning point in a ten-year-old debate about the need for television in Israel. The early years of the debate were dominated by David Ben Gurion, the nation's first Prime Minister, who dismissed television as an "unnecessary evil" which would drain too many resources from Israel's already hard-pressed economy. In 1962, the Rothschild Foundation, philanthropic arm of the famed international banking family, offered to install an educational television channel and maintain it for three years. The offer revived the TV-or-not-TV controversy. Opposition to television centered around the medium's supposed harmful effects on Israeli culture. During the parliamentary debate on the Rothschild offer in the Knesset, television was variously denounced as an "illegal immigrant," a "golem," and a "sponsor of vulgarity." Both sides in the debate called upon sacred Scripture in support of their claims; the most ingenious of these Biblical references was made by one pro-TV debater who referred to a verse in the twentieth chapter of Exodus: "And all the people saw the thunderings. . . ." Surely, the speaker noted rhetorically, this verse implies simultaneously viewing and hearing a phenomenon—in other words, the principle of television.

In March, 1963, the Knesset voted to accept the Rothschild television station, with the proviso that its program offering be limited to educational and cultural shows. It became apparent, even before the ETV channel began its transmissions, that the station would eventually be used for general television programing. In the meantime, however, Israel will be the only country in the world which officially limits its TV to educational subjects.[8]

A somewhat similar situation exists in India where the government has emphasized the educational uses of television in its cautious approaches to the development of the medium there. All of the early Indian experiments with television broadcasting centered around pilot projects designed to measure TV's educational potential. The first project carried out in 1960 was a UNESCO-sponsored test of the medium's role in adult education. A more extensive experiment, sponsored jointly by the Ford Foundation and the Indian government, attempted to measure the medium's capabilities as a direct classroom teaching tool.[9] However, it was apparent by 1965 that India did not have the fiscal or technical resources to support a television system solely for educational purposes. It remains to be seen what role, if any, will be assigned to educational television in the various proposals the government is considering for some form of commercial TV in India. Meanwhile the government is expanding its school broadcast experiments; a grant of four hundred thousand dollars from the West German government in May, 1965, will permit the Delhi station to increase its ETV schedule from four to six hours a day.

The only other developing Asian country where ETV has seriously been considered is the Philippines. In 1961, the National Science Development Board sponsored the first Asian experiment in college-level direct instruction by television. Ten colleges in Manila participated in the experiment, which involved a physics course presented three times weekly over Manila's Channel 9. The test was successful enough to encourage planning for wider use of instructional television.[10]

This planning process was strengthened in 1962 when a local university, the Ateneo de Manila, opened a graduate-level institute, the first of its kind in Asia, to train educators in the use of television and other audio-visual devices as teaching tools. This led in 1964 to the formation of the Metropolitan Educational Television Association (META), a consortium of Philippine and American organizations in Manila whose purpose is to utilize available daytime facilities of local TV stations for direct classroom broadcasting. META'S pioneering efforts, limited for the present to offering instruction at the high school level, give the Philippines an important lead in educational television among developing Asian countries.

Despite these hopeful signs, ETV's record in Asia, Africa and Latin America is still a spotty one. There are a number of reasons for this. One is the virtual domination of local television in developing nations by commercial interests. The prospects for educational television are dimmed considerably when it has to be measured primarily by its ability to pay its own way. Local educators, already harassed by inadequate budgets, are unwilling to invest in an expensive new teaching system when its advantages still have not been proved.

ETV's greatest hurdle, however, is a psychological one referred to earlier. This is the reluctance of many Asian, African, and Latin American elite groups to accept new technologies for mass education. Educated in traditional Western ways, they see their status as *the* educated class threatened by the introduction of effective universal education. These mandarin attitudes are not, of course, shared by all members of these groups; it would, however, be a mistake to underestimate the tenacity with which the leadership of these areas cling to old educational forms. Many Indian universities are fortresses of Victorian educational attitudes; schools in French-speaking Africa often reflect the attitudes of the Second Empire, and the last strongholds of medieval university education are in Latin America. It is one of the wry paradoxes of the end of the age of colonialism that many of the newly independent nations have sought refuge in outmoded forms of education while the former colonial powers have radically revised their own educational systems to meet the demands of a new era.

The intensive application of ETV and other new teaching tools in underdeveloped areas will depend largely on the willingness and ability of these leadership groups to revise their rigid attitudes on local educational needs. These revisions will involve not only attitudes on classroom instruction but also those on general problems of nation building in an increasingly interdependent world. The responsibility for meeting these challenges rests primarily with the elite leadership; the myth that such attitudes could, or should, be imported wholesale from the West has been a long time dying but it has finally been interred. Nevertheless, the United States and other industrialized countries do have a role to play across the whole spectrum of realigning old attitudes in Asia, Africa, and Latin America to meet the demands of a new age.

This involves some direct technological assistance together with the adaptation of ideas that have worked in the West to the needs of the East. In order to understand better educational television's prospects in the underdeveloped world, it is useful to examine the effort being made to provide such help.

At the international level, the United Nations, through the auspices of UNESCO, has made a useful contribution both in helping the new nations define their ETV needs and in sponsoring pilot model demonstrations of teaching possibilities using television. In recent years UNESCO has sponsored a series of seminars and conferences on educational radio and television in Asia, Africa, and Latin America. The meetings have covered the possibilities, and the limitations, for the growth of ETV in these areas and have also provided a forum for the exchange of information about ETV in other countries. UNESCO monographs on educational television and other mass media are often clogged with the obscurantism of international civil-servant prose, but they are the best general compilations available on this subject. At the end of 1965, UNESCO expanded its ETV horizons literally into outer space by sponsoring a seminar in Paris on the world-wide educational and cultural implications of communications satellites.[11]

The European Broadcasting Union (EBU) is another international organization which has played a role as a bridge between the developed and developing countries in ETV matters. Although it is primarily an organization of Western European broadcasters, EBU has organizational links with broadcasting organizations in over twenty Asian, African, and Latin American countries. EBU has sponsored the two most significant international conferences on school broadcasting—one in Rome in 1961 and another in Tokyo in 1964—at which educators from less developed countries had a unique opportunity to meet with their Western and Japanese colleagues. (A third conference is scheduled to be held in Paris in 1966.) These contacts encouraged the EBU in June, 1964, to set up a study group to examine ways in which the organization could assist broadcasters in developing nations.[12]

The most important practical assistance for ETV in developing countries, however, has come from Great Britain, France, Japan, and the United States. In varying ways, and for varying motives, each of these countries has taken an increasingly active interest in making its ETV expertise available to Asian, African, and Latin American nations. Some of these projects have been mentioned earlier; it is useful to examine these, and others, more closely here.

The British government has the longest tradition of assistance to Asian and African broadcasting largely as a result of its prewar policy of developing radio stations in its colonies. These assistance projects were continued after most of these colonies attained independence; in recent years it has been extended to include aid to television operations in these new nations. As a result, British advice and material assistance have been important factors in television's development in East Africa, South Asia, and parts of the Far East. British government scholarships and grants for study tours at the BBC and other television organizations have provided useful training opportunities for broadcasters in these areas. In 1964 a training institute for overseas broadcasters was opened near Glasgow by the Thomson Foundation, the philanthropic branch of Roy Thomson Enterprises, the largest British investor in commercial television projects throughout the world. In addition to providing full training scholarships for foreign broadcasters, the Thomson Foundation also makes British experts available to foreign TV stations.

Specific training in ETV theory and practice is provided by another British organization, the Center for Educational Television Overseas (CETO), located in London. CETO began operations in 1963, supported by a 544,000-dollar grant from British foundations and a 400,000-dollar grant from the Ford Foundation. It was, and remains, the only organization which trains Asian and African broadcasters in specific ETV techniques during study tours in Britain. It serves as a clearinghouse for these visitors, assigning them to specific training courses in British schools or in on-the-job assignments with British stations. In 1964, CETO provided training for 26 broadcasters from 21 Asian, African, and West Indian nations. Supplementing this direct training is a project for providing overseas television stations with

ETV "program kits" designed to assist local directors to prepare programs covering a wide range of academic subjects.

French government assistance to overseas television is limited largely to the new nations of French-speaking West Africa and to the Malagasy Republic, the former French colony of Madagascar. Unlike their British counterparts, prewar French colonial administrators were generally uninterested in developing local broadcasting. The main radio channel to their overseas territories was Radio-Colonial, a short-wave station located in France. After the war, the French government recognized the role radio and the newly developing medium of television could play in maintaining traditional French political and cultural influence in Africa. A ministerial commission in 1950 recommended an extensive technical assistance program for radio broadcasting in overseas French territories. After a series of false starts and reorganizations, the government set up a state organization called SORAFOM, la Société Radiodiffusion de la France d'Outre-Mer. By 1962, when all of the former French colonies in Africa had achieved independence, this title was changed to OCORA, l'Office de Coopération Radiophonique. With the change went a new emphasis on the role television would play as both a political and a cultural force in France's relations with its former African territories.

OCORA is uniquely designed for this purpose. At one level, it provides French-speaking African nations with transmitters, studios, and other technical equipment. At another level, it is a supplier of programs, making French productions available to African radio and TV stations and arranging the placement of African programs on French stations. Finally, it trains African broadcasters in its Studio-École in Paris, founded in 1963. Over three hundred Africans were trained at the school during its first year of operations.

Although the French government has made ETV programs available to stations throughout the world, its primary interests in this field are in French-speaking Africa. A considerable amount of OCORA programing efforts involves educational series prepared by the Ministry of Education and ORTF, the French national network. The emphasis is often heavily Francophile, but these programs are a useful first step toward the development of local ETV capabilities in the former French colonies.[13]

In Japan the state-chartered NHK network has taken the lead in training Asian broadcasters in ETV theory and practice. The network's Central Training Institute held its first ETV course for foreign broadcasters in August, 1962. The Japanese have also shown ingenuity in melding their considerable experience in educational television with their export drive for television equipment sales in Asia and Latin America. Offering to help a country set up its educational television facilities is sometimes part of the "package deal" made by the Japanese to meet stiff competition in international markets. In one such arrangement, reported from El Salvador in 1963, a Japanese delegation coupled its offer of ETV assistance with long-term credit if the local Ministry of Education agreed to use Japanese equipment for the project.

The leading nation in providing both ideas and material assistance for ETV efforts in developing countries is, however, the United States. There are no coordinating organizations for American international ETV projects comparable to the United Kingdom's Committee for Educational Television Abroad or the French Office de Coopération Radiophonique. The American approach to overseas ETV is considerably more pragmatic, with the disadvantages that result from uncoordinated programs but also with the advantages that flow from spontaneity and experimentation.

In its first decade (1953–1963), American ETV's contacts with foreign television systems was limited largely to visits by foreign broadcasters to U.S. television centers. The visitors' interest stemmed only in part from the fact that the United States had taken an early lead in educational telecasting. More significant for them was the American emphasis on experimenting with different ETV methods to determine the most effective use of the medium with both adult and younger audiences.

American ETV's international involvement could not, however, be restricted to a showcase for visiting educators and broadcasters. Since 1960, the pace of more active involvement has increased steadily. There were two reasons. The first was the recognition by American ETV broadcasters of the need to enrich their own programing efforts with material from other countries, and to make their own programs available to stations abroad. The second reason has been the growing interest of U.S. educators in ETV's potentialities in developing countries. American ETV efforts abroad have largely emphasized the role of the medium as a tool of constructive social change in less developed regions.

The dominant influence in these early overseas activities has been the Ford Foundation, the largest U.S. philanthropic trust. The Foundation's interest in overseas educational television stems in part from its commitment to the development of ETV at home. In the past ten years, it has invested over eighty million dollars in a wide range of domestic ETV projects. About half of the community educational stations in the United States were given their financial start with Ford funds. In addition to this "seed money" for community stations, the Foundation has also supported special instruction TV projects, including the Hagerstown experiment. This support for ETV at home complemented its equally strong commitment to exploring new ways to strengthen the modernization process in developing countries. The combination of interests was undoubtedly a major factor in the foundation's decision to examine ETV's potential in Asian and Latin American countries.

The first, and largest, of the Ford Foundation's overseas projects was in India. In January, 1960, a foundation team surveyed ETV prospects at the invitation of All India Radio (AIR). The team recommended that a foundation grant be made to support direct ETV instruction in science and language studies at the ninth class level in the Delhi State school system.

Subsequently the foundation approved a grant of 470,000 dollars to AIR and the Indian government for a four-year experimental project. The Indian government also supported the project with its financial share increasing each year and the foundation's share decreasing. The funds were used to purchase six hundred TV receivers and studio and test equipment including a five-kilowatt amplifier to strengthen AIR-TV's signal, and to underwrite in-service training for Indian broadcasting and educational personnel.

In October, 1960, AIR assigned seven program and technical officers for ETV training in the United States. The following June the Delhi Directorate of Education and AIR organized an in-service workshop for all ninth-class teachers of physics, chemistry, Hindi, and English who were to take part in the experiment. More than 650 teachers participated in the three-week course. They began their teaching-by-television duties in September, 1961. By the following spring, ETV programs were being received in 152 schools in the Delhi area. Twelve thousand boys and girls were given Hindi and English language training; over 30,000 took part in televised chemistry and physics lessons as part of their studies curriculum.

At the end of its four-year commitment the Ford Foundation phased out its participation in the Delhi State project. The result of this largest ETV experiment yet to be completed in a developing country was evaluated by an Indian-American research team in a report issued in 1965.

The Ford Foundation has also assisted an ETV project in the Philippines which is similar in spirit, if not in details, to the Delhi experiment. The foundation is one of several U.S. organizations helping the Ateneo de Manila University, a Jesuit school, in two projects designed to give the Philippine Republic a strong ETV lead among the developing countries of Asia. The projects involve the training of Philippine educators in the use of television and other audio-visual devices and the development of a phased program for school telecasting throughout the country.

In its training program, the Ateneo has set up an educational media section in its graduate school of education. Educational television features prominently in the course of studies which leads to the granting of a Master of Arts degree in education. Classroom theories in this new field are tested by the students through practical experience at the Ateneo's Center for Educational Television. The center is the most extensive ETV training facility yet to be established in a developing country; inaugurated in May, 1964, it has complete TV studio facilities to train the Ateneo's own students as well as educational administrators, studio instructors, and classroom teachers from outside the university. Initial financial costs were met by the Ford Foundation and two Manila businessmen, Eugenio and Fernando Lopez; a group of Manila business firms have agreed to underwrite the center's operating expenses for its first three years.

The Ateneo center has two other ETV projects currently under way. The first is its own closed-circuit teaching system for the Ateneo and the adjoining Maryknoll College. Programs for this internal ETV system can be produced at the center and "piped" into the nearby classrooms. During it early experimental phase, the center is evaluating the range and types of instruction best suited for university conditions. The center is also actively associated with Manila's Metropolitan Educational Television Association, Incorporated (META). Supported by a 160,000-dollar (Philippine) organizing grant from the Asia Foundation, META uses the transmitting facilities of Manila commercial stations for daytime ETV programing to local secondary schools.[14] The Asia Foundation grant covers the costs of an ETV training seminar for school administrators and teachers involved in the project, as well as for the production of a physics course consisting of a series of 100 half-hour lessons. Although META is currently limited both by facilities and funds to operations in the Greater Manila area, its organizers hope to extend its program activities to secondary schools in Bacalod, Baguio, Cebu, Davao, and Iloilo —and eventually to elementary and collegiate levels of instruction.[15]

Besides providing partial support for ETV projects in India and in the Philippines, the Ford Foundation has made funds available for two smaller projects in Latin America. These are a closed-circuit science teaching program at the University of Buenos Aires and another project at the Monterrey Institute of Technology in Mexico.

The Ford Foundation pioneered the extension of American educational television techniques and facilities abroad. Within the past several years, however, other organizations have begun to operate in this field. One of these is National Educational Television (NET), the coordinating association for most U.S. community educational stations. Largely as a result of a six-million-dollar Ford Foundation grant it received in 1963, NET has made a series of cooperative arrangements for the production and exchange of program materials with a dozen or more overseas television systems. In some cases, this has involved the direct purchase of programs from foreign stations for use by NET affiliates. In other instances, it has been extended to coproduction of programs with foreign stations. In one such coproduction arrangement, NET teamed up with Swedish television to produce "Portrait of a Small Country," a documentary series about Sweden. Collaboration with French producers has resulted in a highly successful series of art programs. NHK, the Japanese national network, produced for NET a series of thirteen programs whose purpose was to answer questions Americans most frequently ask about Japanese life and culture. In exchange, a similar series, answering typical Japanese queries about the United States, has been prepared for NHK viewers.

Japanese-American collaboration in ETV program exchange has reached the point where clearinghouses for such exchanges have been set up in New York and Tokyo. "The clearinghouse is intended to facilitate the showing of the more significant productions of this country, whether made by educational stations or groups of commercial stations or by independent producers on foreign screens," NET President John F. White stated at a 1964 conference held at Fordham University. "If successful, this experiment may be a model for exchange centers involving other countries."

In cooperation with the commercially operated Westinghouse Broadcasting Company, NET is the American representative of the "Intertel" program exchange plan. Intertel members in Canada, Australia, the United Kingdom, and the United States produce documentary programs for showing on member country stations. Another NET activity which has had some influence abroad is the National Instructional Television Library, a central repository for many of the thousands of ETV shows prepared by NET and its affiliated stations in recent years.

While these privately sponsored efforts will continue to be important, the most significant trend in American ETV's international activities is the U.S. government's new role. Until 1961,

Washington limited its overseas ETV involvement to facilitating visits of foreign broadcasters and educators to the United States, and sending American experts abroad, under the State Department's cultural exchange program. In the year ending June, 1963, seventy-seven TV and radio specialists came under this program to observe U.S. broadcasting methods, including ETV.

In 1961, the Kennedy administration proposed a small ETV technical assistance program for developing countries under the foreign aid program. The proposal quickly foundered on congressional opposition which centered around charges of alleged irregularities in contracts made by the government in preparing to implement the project. The Agency for International Development (AID) revived its proposals a year later, this time involving technical assistance for educational TV ventures in Nigeria and Colombia.

The Nigerian project is designed to study ways of utilizing the rapidly expanding Nigerian radio and television systems for instructional programs. An agreement signed between the American and Nigerian governments in June, 1962, provided for a study mission of American specialists to make recommendations on this subject. The U.S. government selected school officials from Washington County, Maryland—location of the Hagerstown ETV experiment—for the survey. Following the 1963 survey, AID and the Nigerian Ministry of Economic Delevopment agreed to extend the project on an experimental basis until June, 1967. Specialists from the Washington County school system and their Nigerian radio-television counterparts inaugurated the country's first instructional broadcasting system in the fall of 1964. The total U.S. contribution to the project is 897,200 dollars.

U.S. participation in the Colombian ETV experiment, described earlier in this chapter, includes technical personnel and equipment. The latter consists primarily of fifteen hundred television receivers for schools in the project. The Americans assisting Colombian educators and broadcasters are all Peace Corps volunteers. In 1965 there were about ninety Corps volunteers assigned to the project.

The results of the Nigerian and Colombian ETV projects will influence the American government's plans for future technical assistance to similar projects in other developing countries. U.S. private and public experience in this field is already extensive enough to demonstrate clearly that ETV is no panacea for the problems the new nations face in the educational field. The technical difficulties are in themselves formidable. One of these is the lack of adequate power supplies in rural areas where ETV is often most effective. This problem may be solved by such devices as transistorized receivers developed by American, Japanese, and other engineers. One such system designed by an American firm can be operated in a village with the power supplied by a generator hooked to a small children's carrousel in the village school playground. By turning the carrousel during their play, the children can provide the generator with enough power to operate a group of television sets in the village for a full day.

A more difficult problem is that of training local school administrators and teachers in the proper use of television as a teaching tool, and of getting television broadcasters to prepare programs suitable for schools. These problems are still far from solution in countries which have had ETV for a number of years. They are only beginning to be faced in most developing countries which have expressed an interest in ETV.

American educators and broadcasters are still making up their minds about ETV's long-range potential in developing countries. This is a time of experimentation, of determining the opportunities—and the limitations—of educational TV as an instrument of social change. Once these factors are better understood, American private and public organizations can define more clearly their possible contributions in this area of international cooperation.

Educational television abroad has developed to the point where it is no longer simply an interesting novelty. The next decade will witness a dramatic expansion in ETV activities at all levels of education both here and overseas. However, the most important task facing educators and broadcasters in the coming years will be to set a clear course for TV's future as a teaching tool. The creation and transmission of ETV broadcasts are, in the words of French educator Henri Dieuzeide, "nothing but two constituent aspects of an infinitely more complex educational process" which will have to accept being measured against other teaching techniques.[16]

This review calls for a more precise definition of the benefits and limitations of television-as-teacher in a complex variety of learning situations ranging from a university lecture hall in California to a dirt-floor schoolroom in the middle of Africa. Educational television in the United States and abroad is still limited largely to one technique—the so-called "enrichment" programs broadcast to primary and secondary schools in an unstructured pattern that often has no relation to the day-to-day classroom problems faced by individual teachers and their pupils. Under these circumstances, ETV is, at best, frosting on the educational cake, a diversion that may disrupt rather than enhance the learning process.

Educators and broadcasters will have to move far beyond the simplicities of enrichment programing if ETV is to fulfill its potential. This will, in turn, involve the use of more sophisticated technologies such as closed-circuit multichannel systems and other devices which permit teachers to use television materials flexibly rather than confining them to the rigidities of a station schedule. These systems will include such innovations as taped programs which teachers can order from an audio-visual library for individual classroom viewing. Another promising innovation is phonograph records, developed by American electronics firms, which project television pictures from a portable turntable. These technologies in turn will require that teachers be better trained in ETV methods than is the case with the simpler levels of educational television now in use here and abroad. A closer professional relationship between educators and broadcasters involved in ETV programing will be necessary. For the present, collaboration between the two groups is largely a committee affair with each side attempting to mesh its individual expertise into a new pattern that neither fully understands. To reach its potential, ETV must be managed by a new type of professional—broadcasters who are educators and educators who are broadcasters.

These sophisticated approaches represent a quantum leap above the present level of ETV development in the United States and other technically advanced countries. Under normal circumstances, it will take a generation or more for these new technologies to be applied to educational systems in newly developing countries. The United States, however, has a stake in seeing that this time span is shortened in ways that bring TV's full advantages quickly to bear on Asian, African, and Latin American development. This speeding-up process should not be carried out on a crash-program basis, however. Educational TV is no cure-all for the underdeveloped world's problems. Imposed without proper preparation, ETV can have the undesirable effect of enshrining mediocre teaching under the shiny symbol of technological progress. However, this danger should not be used as a perennial excuse for postponing a hard look at the advantages educational television offers in meeting the modernization needs of Asian and African countries. The pilot projects which the American government is currently supporting in Colombia and Nigeria have already demonstrated ETV's usefulness in this field. Both projects have suffered setbacks; this is inevitable in any attempt to apply a new technology to impoverished economies. The lesson learned from these experimental projects is the need for greater attention in adapting ETV techniques to local conditions. This process is never easy, but once it is understood it could provide a significant breakthrough in American and other free world efforts to stabilize the development process in Asia and Africa.

Beyond this possibility lies ETV's almost totally unexplored potential as an instrument for strengthening the forces of international law and order. By the end of this century the nations of the world will have to begin to surrender their current options of unrestricted international violence and nuclear escalation in favor of some form of enforceable international law. Whatever form this new world order will take, it will involve a massive educational effort to convince billions of people that their personal and collective interests lie in surrendering some of the prerogatives of tribal nationalism and adopting new methods of security and order. Even in its present, relatively primitive state of world-wide development, television can begin to play a part in bringing about this turning point in human history.

With the technology presently available, it is not too fanciful to imagine an ETV communications satellite system with multiplex channels providing live global coverage of daily peace-keeping activities of the United Nations and its specialized agencies. As more definitive arms control agreements are reached, world-wide television could transmit regular reports on their implementation including international inspectors' on-the-spot reports of how each nation is complying with the agreements. This kind of television would serve not only to reassure the world population that "the other side" is keeping its agreements but also to deter possible violators of the agreement. It would be a dramatic form of "open diplomacy" to fit the public opinion needs of a massive shift in world security arrangements.

Such programs would be transmitted by regular communications satellites to television stations throughout the world. Later comsat networks will also provide closed-circuit TV transmissions for specialized purposes. International meetings might be convened by linking regional groups through television. World-renowned scholars can make their lectures available to universities across the globe. News film and tapes of current events can be transmitted to individual TV stations for presentation on local news shows. These and other forms of satellite television could provide a powerful stimulant to the adoption of English or another language as a universally accepted tongue.

Under any circumstances, satellite television will be a new tool of international education, leading us to a new understanding of the world outside the narrow boundaries of our daily lives and thoughts. This will be as true for Americans looking at a program relayed from Central Africa as it will be of Soviet citizens watching us or of Pakistanis watching Brazilians. Television could be the new school where we learn about the world as it really is and where, for the first time, the risks and the opportunities of a more peaceful international order are made understandable to every man. There is no guarantee that television will be used for this high teaching purpose. In our own national interest, the United States has every good reason to see that it will be.

11
Television Signals
from Space

On a hot summer's night in 1962, millions of Americans were watching a run-of-the-channel television drama about a Scotland Yard detective when a CBS network announcer broke in. "We interrupt this program . . . ," he said. "The British are ready to bounce a program off Telstar."

On their screens, viewers saw an unpretentious communications control room with three men seated at a table. Without introduction, one of them spoke up: "On my right is that dour Scot, Robert White," and, as he waved a hand toward the other man, "John Bray, who is in charge of our planning in the space field. . . . It is half-past three in the morning. Good luck."

On this understated note, the first experiment in intercontinental television by space satellites ended. The image and voice of Capt. Charles Booth, deputy chief engineer of the British Post Office, and his colleagues were being transmitted from a telecommunications station in the south of England through a microwave relay sent via the Telstar satellite to a ground station in Maine which then relayed them to American television viewers. The date was July 11, and the occasion was a historic move toward the development of an adequate world dialogue of men and nations.

Telstar was the first of many similar satellites that promise a revolution in world communications. Orbiting the earth at heights of from two hundred to twenty-two thousand miles, they will serve as microwave relay stations, receiving and sending telephone, television, telex, and other types of messages to scattered points all over the globe. The present international pattern is based on heavy traffic between a small number of traditional communications hubs—New York, London, Beirut, Tokyo, etc. —with only minimal service to other points. The high-flying satellites are no respecters of tradition, however. They will double and triple the capacity of the heavily used traffic lanes. More significantly, they will open a new communications era in other regions, tracing an invisible cable with a thousand or more channels between Anchorage, Mogadiscio, Tierra del Fuego, and any places in between.

The ultimate effect of this quantum leap in world communications is difficult to see. It will, however, be deep and abiding. The new satellites will give us the channels to match our space-age requirements, and they will do it thirty years ahead of the time we would otherwise have had remotely comparable ground facilities. Some of the opportunities they offer have been only dimly imagined. They could operate orbital post offices, handling transoceanic correspondence by instantaneous facsimile, or relay an orbital newspaper dialed to a high-definition home screen. Or they might serve as electronic libraries which could flash any piece of reading matter in existence from a central "memory bank" to a home screen. The satellites can transmit messages in any language but they could be a powerful impulse to develop a world language. Their politics will be neutral; they can be used to relay the solitary commands of the head of a world-wide dictatorship or the noisy give-and-take of free men talking. More than any other space-age development, they will affect our earthbound search for a consensus upon which to build a world order.

The most intriguing immediate capability of the new satellite system is, of course, world television. The great bulk of communications satellite business in the foreseeable future will be taken up with telephone, telex, and other more specialized electronic exchanges. None of these, however, has stirred men's imaginations as much as the satellites' capability of beaming world events by television to every part of the earth. The idea of so many people sharing so directly in events ranging from a world soccer championship to the coronation of a pope has its own drama. A foretaste of this was provided by the first Telstar and Early Bird satellites, which tested a wide range of experimental demonstrations, from two-way telephony to the relaying of business-machine data at a rate of nearly 1.5 million words a minute.[1] It was, however, the Telstar television transmissions that had the greatest impact on both sides of the Atlantic, whether the transmission was the *"Folies Bergères,"* a baseball game, or a presidential press conference. For the first time, something had come from space that was recognizably familiar to millions of people; more important, they were touched by the human spark of confrontation with other people and events which, heretofore, they could have seen only in their mind's eye. "It was," stated one Stockholm newspaper, "America we were introduced to in all its greatness, beauty and simplicity." The use of satellites for world communications "is the first product of space research which will have a direct and tangible link with the people," a Karachi journal noted.[2]

Beyond these intriguing first probings into world television, there are a number of practical difficulties in its realization. Not the least of these is the fact that the state of the communications satellite art is still in its infancy. Once the system is operational, satellite television will present particular problems. One of these is its wide-band technical requirements, involving the use of many telephone channels during each of its transmissions. The economics of the new satellite system in its early years may inhibit any large-scale pre-emption of profitable telephone channels for television transmissions. Some early estimates indicated the problem: in 1961, one Federal Communications Commission official put transmission costs alone for a transoceanic program at twelve thousand dollars a minute.[3] Another estimate, submitted to Congress in 1962 by the U.S. Information Agency, put the cost somewhat lower—a quarter of a million dollars an hour for a transoceanic transmission, projected from current rates for submarine-cable relay to Europe.[4] Fortunately these and similar projections proved to be unduly pessimistic. However, there is no doubt that television-by-satellite will be an expensive proposition.

There are other inhibiting factors. One of these is simple

chronology. It is one thing to transmit a world-wide program by satellite relay and another to imagine people sitting up in the middle of the night in a different part of the globe to watch it. Even the five-hour time differential between the eastern United States and western Europe will be a limiting factor in exchanging programs. A program sent at prime evening time from New York will be seen in Britain or France at two in the morning. It would be less costly and more convenient to tape the program and send it to Europe by scheduled jet flights for transmission a few hours later.

There are good arguments for the proposition that satellite television will never be more than a propaganda stunt, trotted out to add a prestige touch to special occasions. How often, these critics say, can you show foreign audiences scenes of Niagara Falls, the Radio City Rockettes, or the inauguration of an American President? The inauguration and the Olympic Games are most often cited as events which will be covered by world television, yet they both happen only once every four years. What, the critics ask, comes in between? And who will pay for it? These and other bearish views on the future of satellite television will have to be met with concrete answers in the next few years.

There is a case to be made for satellite television, and particularly for American support of its development. It can be divided roughly into three segments. The simplest part of the case is that communications satellites with television capabilities exist. As a sort of Parkinson's Law corollary decreeing that the use of facilities is directly related to their availability, the satellites will be used for television transmissions. The second part of the case is that if we do not take advantage of the satellites' television capability, someone else will. It is usually good form to point to the Russians and to our need to stay ahead of them for prestige reasons, particularly in the so-called space race. The Russians have the technological capability to produce a space communications system, having orbited their first comsat in 1965.[5] The usual reason given for their apparent lag in this field is that they have given priority to other space tasks, notably the man-on-the-moon project. It is also possible that they are inhibited by the implications to their closed society of a communications system that opens thousands of new channels to the outside. In fact, our most formidable competition in the space communications field may eventually be the Europeans who have already organized a regional space organization to consider, among other projects, a communications satellite put into orbit by European rockets.[6]

The more convincing argument for our involvement in satellite television, however, is the role that it can play in the larger area of American world responsibilities. The key to this responsibility has been our commitment to the need for greater dialogue in the search for political and cultural patterns of a new world order. Television, global or otherwise, offers no panaceas for this task. It has, however, already shown its effectiveness as a medium with special capabilities for cutting across national boundaries and attitudes. The most striking example has occurred in Europe where the fifteen-nation Eurovision network has been one of the factors in setting the pace toward West European integration in the past decade. More than any other medium, Eurovision has brought to Europeans a sense of their common involvements in recent years. The development of transatlantic television by communications satellites will bring this connective link to the entire North Atlantic cultural community.

The most challenging potential for international television, however, may well be in strengthening the dialogue with nations outside our own immediate cultural heritage. Here is where television's unique usefulness for explaining and persuading may do us the greatest good. If we show sufficient imagination, it can bring the full force of our sights, sounds, and convictions to the home of a Tokyo clerk, a coffee house in Tehran, or a sports club in Lagos. The traditional impact of Hollywood as a purveyor of America's image abroad pales before the sense of immediacy and involvement that transoceanic live television will bring to hundreds of millions of people in Asia, Africa, and Latin America. Above all, it can bring about a new recognition of our common human involvement, lowering the barriers of geographical, cultural, and spiritual isolation that are our greatest stumbling blocks in the search for a pattern for a democratic world order.

Looked at in this light it would be unfortunate if we, in our present role as free world leader, were to turn our back on the advantages of live global television. The real question is not whether we should be involved. Inevitably, we will be—either directly as the nation which takes the initiative or, as a poor second, participating in a world network established by another country or group of countries. The problem lies in determining a realistic level of global television and in setting an operational pattern for it. How will the new network be operated? Who will pay for it? What types of programs will be best suited for it?

The answers to these questions are tied directly to the development of communications satellites. Their capabilities will determine, to a large extent, the shape of international television. It will be useful, therefore, to review the history of world television, with particular emphasis on the satellites, to get some perspective on the problem.

The idea of international television has captured men's fancies since the early 1920's when television first began to emerge from the laboratories. The first crude transatlantic television signals were transmitted on February 4, 1928, between a radio laboratory in London and a basement short-wave station in Hartsdale, New York. The New Yorkers watched a postage-stamp-sized tube as Mrs. Mia Howe moved her head back and forth while seated in front of a scanning device three thousand miles away.[7] This experiment in transmitting television by short-wave signal, and others which took place later on, attracted the attention of scientists working on television developments in the United States. The Radio Corporation of America (RCA), one of the pioneer companies in the field, petitioned the Federal Radio Commission in 1928 for an allocation of experimental broadcast channels "to span oceans and continents and to carry the television image from one country or continent to one or more countries or continents."[8] However, further experiments demonstrated that short wave was an unreliable carrier of television signals. The subject was dropped for almost twenty years, not to be revived until an imaginative British writer decided that there was a connection between spaceships and television.

Fanciful stories about space ships have made good journalistic copy since the days of Jules Verne—a fact which must have been uppermost in the mind of the editor of the British publication *Wireless World* when he accepted an article by science writer Arthur C. Clarke in 1945.[9] The article was squarely in the space-fantasy tradition. Clarke outlined a proposal—the first of its kind—for a series of spaceships which would serve as relay stations for a world-wide communications system broadcasting telephone, telegraph, and television signals. Two men would be stationed in each ship to guide it and to repair the communications equipment. The ships would orbit the earth at a height of 22,300 miles on an equatorial orbit, completing a circuit of the earth in one sidereal day. To a ground observer, they would appear to be stationary in the sky, providing a fixed point for transmissions to and from the earth. Signals from the ships could provide line-of-sight coverage of all parts of the earth's surface except for small parts of the two polar regions. To strain the credulity of his readers even further, Clarke added that there was no reason why such a communications system would not be completely feasible once the then-infant science of rocketry was better developed.

In less than twenty years, most of Clarke's predictions have moved from journalistic speculation to space reality. By the end of 1965, the United States had carried out experiments on five space-communications systems. Although they are varied in their techniques, each fulfilled the conditions of Arthur Clarke's basic predictions—an orbiting space terminal which relayed line-of-sight electronic signals. These satellites ranged from the hundred-foot-diameter Echo balloon, whose aluminized surface merely bounced the signals, to the smaller, more sophisticated Telstar, Relay, and Early Bird "active repeater" satellites filled with electronic gear that could both receive and send messages on command.

Anyone with a slide rule and a fair knowledge of Newtonian physics and electrical engineering in 1945 could have projected these high-flying descendants of Clarke's original speculations. But no one—not even the imaginative Mr. Clarke—could have predicted the events that brought them to reality in so short a time. On the one hand, there was a tremendous impetus given to space developments by the pressure of cold-war rivalry. On the other hand, there was the confluence of two streams of scientific development. One of these streams involved a stunning series of advances in the field of communications equipment, utilizing such newly hatched components as transistors, masers, and solar batteries. The other was the progress made in the expensive and uncertain art of rocketry. By 1955, American scientists were making their first probe toward a workable combination of the two, pointing toward the technological possibilities of orbiting communications satellites.[10]

The simplest of these possibilities was the passive satellite— a large balloon placed in random orbit around the earth, with a metallized surface from which line-of-sight signals were reflected from one ground transmitter to another at a distant location. In a second group were the so-called active-repeater satellites which would contain their own electronic equipment and power supplies for receiving and transmitting signals on command between two ground stations.[11] By 1959, American rocketry had proved its ability to put satellites into orbit. For scientists working on communications satellites, the problem now was to fit their complex electronic gear into the small payload limitations imposed by the new rockets.

These efforts were given an additional fillip by the fact that communications satellites were beginning to look like big business, particularly to the burgeoning new aerospace industry. These expectations were well founded. By the middle of 1962, almost half a billion dollars had been appropriated by Congress for research and development projects in the field under Defense Department and National Aeronautics and Space Administration (NASA) sponsorship.[12] Beyond this lies the potentially more profitable prospect of the role that the new satellites will play in the international communications industry once a fully operational system comes into being sometime in 1967.

The new satellites are showing up just in time to play a major part in the greatest expansion ever to take place in international communications. The general rate of expansion is between 15 and 20 percent yearly at the present time. The American Telephone and Telegraph Company (AT&T) expects an increase in its international telephone volume from 1960's four million calls to twenty million in 1970, and to nearly one hundred million in 1980.[13] Even more spectacular is the increase in nontelephone traffic, particularly in the transmission of telex and nonvoice leased circuits. A Lockheed Aircraft Corporation study has projected a 23–28 percent annual rate of increase in international telex communications during the 1960's.[14]

Not only do the new satellites have the potential of providing cheaper and more efficient service, but they also ease the pressure that the new expansion in communications has brought upon the limited frequencies available in the high-frequency spectrum used for radiotelephone communications to most areas abroad. The present alternative to radiotelephony—submarine coaxial cables—is technologically efficient and does not, of course, require radio frequencies. However, cables are expensive, and they do not have the most unique characteristic of the satellites, which is their ability to provide service between any two points on the globe. The high cost of laying submarine cables has largely limited their use to the North Atlantic area and a few other high-volume traffic routes.

Reviewing the current growth in international communications, one industry spokesman told a congressional committee in 1961: "There seems to be little doubt that satellite communications are the solution for the additional channel requirements which are developing now and during the next two decades."[15]

By 1961, a half-dozen American companies in the communications and electronics industries had entered the sweepstakes for a reliable satellite system that could meet these new demands. The leader in the field was, predictably, the American Telephone and Telegraph Company, whose dominance in international communications gave it a major stake in any plans for closing the gap between inadequate facilities and rising demands. AT&T Bell Laboratories had begun studying the practical possibilities of communications satellites in 1954. The company decided to concentrate its research energies on a system of active repeater satellites (later dubbed "Telstar") which would be placed in random orbit around the earth at a relatively low level of from six hundred to three thousand miles. At these heights, somewhere between forty and fifty satellites would be needed to provide full line-of-sight coverage to all parts of the earth.

Variations on this low-flying-orbit system were also being proposed by the Radio Corporation of America, Lockheed Aircraft, and International Telephone and Telegraph. Two other firms, General Electric and Hughes Aircraft, put their research resources into a high-orbiting system requiring only three satellites. Westinghouse Electric was experimenting with a completely different system called "ultracom," described as an "ultra-violet space communications system."[16]

None of these companies, however, had the technological head start that AT&T enjoyed in the field. By 1960, when the problem of matching satellites to the payload capacities of existing rockets began to emerge into practical solutions, the Bell Laboratory Telstar satellite was the only one ready to move off the drawing board into experimental production. The telephone company confirmed this in December, 1960, when it announced that it proposed to launch, within a year and at its own expense, an experimental relay satellite using NASA launch and rocket facilities. (NASA had earlier offered such facilities at cost to U.S. industry for space experiments.[17]) It appeared that the communications satellite prize had gone to "Mother Bell," as the company is known with mixed awe and respect in American industry. However, the technological, economic, and political stakes in the new satellites were too high to permit such a simple solution. The decisions on the satellites—what system was to be used, who was to build it, and who was to operate it—was lifted from the laboratory and corporation board room into the political arena.

By early 1961, the need for a workable public policy on the satellites was evident. In its search the new Kennedy administration set a number of priorities. The most important of these was the need to get a reliable system operating as quickly as possible. The prestige benefits for the U.S. in being first in space with a world-ranging communications system gave this view added weight.

Tied to it, however, was the hard fact that, at the time, the U.S. had not yet put up a single communications satellite even experimentally.[18] Orbiting a satellite was one problem; a more difficult one was assuring that its electronic equipment would operate in the cold reaches of outer space. There was little beyond laboratory calculations to confirm this. At the time, no American rocket had yet lofted equipment as elaborate or as sensitive as that required by the communications satellites. Also undetermined was the question of which pattern of relay satellites was the most suitable among those proposed. Active or passive satellites? High orbit or low orbit?

The administration took steps to assure a fair test of these possibilities by authorizing contracts for experimental work in each. During the spring and summer of 1961, NASA contracted with RCA for the low-orbit Relay system and with the Hughes Aircraft Company for its proposed high-orbit synchronous Syncom system. It also authorized study of an improved balloon satellite system proposed by the Douglas Aircraft Company. At about the same time, it signed an agreement with AT&T (which had bid unsuccessfully on the low-orbit contract won by RCA) to provide launching and rocket facilities for the Telstar satellite. These agreements, together with an earlier Defense Department contract with General Electric for a military communications satellite system, laid the groundwork for the testing of a range of experimental systems.[19]

The knottiest problem before the Kennedy administration was evolving a policy on how the communications satellite system would be organized. "The rivalry over systems," *Fortune* magazine noted at the time, "is chiefly important now as one of the counters in the real contest, which is how the business is to be set up and who will have a part in it."[20] In its lameduck days at the end of 1960, the Eisenhower administration had adopted a policy proposing that the government would "aggressively encourage" private industry to build the space communications network.[21]

The new Kennedy administration was disposed to accept this policy, although there was support for the idea of a government-owned system in some sectors of the New Frontier. Under such a system, the system's facilities would be available on lease to private communications concerns.[22] The prevailing sentiment, however, was in favor of some realistic combination of private and public interests in an area where both were heavily involved. International communications is traditionally a field of private-enterprise responsibility in the United States. On the other hand, the communications satellites were not just another telephone or telegraph channel which happened to operate in space. Not only was their development dependent largely on public funds and rocket launch facilities, but their operations cut across a whole new range of civil and military problems. The administration was particularly sensitive to the monopoly implications of a government-sponsored communications system placed in the hands of a small group of large international carriers. Two important groups found themselves in unlikely alliance on this point. The first of these were political liberals, in and out of Congress, who saw (in the words of a letter to the President signed by thirty-five Congressmen in August, 1961) an attempt to make AT&T "the chosen instrument of the U.S. Government to own and control civilian space communications."[23] Their allies in this viewpoint were businessmen in the aerospace equipment industry who feared that they would be frozen out of any chance to supply equipment for the new space venture if it were dominated by the telephone company and other carriers who had their own equipment-manufacturing capabilities.

All of these factors were grist for the administration's efforts to draft legislation that reflected the political, economic, and technological realities involved in the proposed space satellite communications system. There were no comfortable precedents pointing to convenient answers. The ownership decision not only was complex in itself but it would have an important bearing on the form and effectiveness of government regulation of the new venture. There were also important considerations of foreign policy to be weighed. Once the satellite system was working, only part of its operations would be in American hands.[24] The rest would be spread among a hundred or more public and private carrier systems abroad. Who would negotiate with these systems? What would be the implications of competing satellite systems, controlled by the Russians, the Europeans, or the Japanese—all of whom had the technical potential for such operations? How much should the government intervene in the system's operations with requests, for example, that the system provide unprofitable services to underdeveloped areas for political reasons? The proposed legislation would have to provide a flexible enough framework to permit the interplay of all these factors.

The administration's proposals were submitted to Congress on February 7, 1962.[25] The bill provided for the creating of a private corporation which would establish and operate American participation in the world-wide communications satellite system. The company would have a strong measure of public representation both in the sale of its stock and (as a result of a congressional amendment to the President's proposals) on the board of directors. Half of the stock in the corporation was to be available for purchase by the general public; the rest would be owned by AT&T and the other U.S. communications carriers with the proviso that no one company would own a majority. This was one of several provisions designed to allay fears of alleged domination of the new venture by AT&T and the other big international carriers. No company participating in the venture could have more than two seats on the corporation's board of directors. (The legislation as finally approved provided for a fifteen-man board with three members appointed by the President of the United States, six elected by the public stockholders, and six elected by communications concerns that have invested in the corporation.)

The bill was not exactly what the international carriers wanted, nor did it satisfy the liberal bloc in Congress who continued to have fears of AT&T domination of the entire system, no matter who owned the stock. However, the general moderate tone of the proposed legislation, together with its innovating proposals for combining public and private interests in a space enterprise, was well received in Congress. It was finally passed —after a short filibuster by a group of Senate liberals—on August 17.[26]

The Communications Satellite Act of 1962 had the useful effect of giving form and definition to the whole communications satellite venture. There may have been advantages in postponing legislation on the subject until more was known about the technological problems involved in satellite systems, as the Senate liberals proposed in their debates. However, these were outweighed by the practical necessity of channeling the powerful economic and political interests involved in the venture. The result was a law that provided a useful meld of high-flying space technology and down-to-earth politics.

On October 4, the President named a board of incorporators to organize and initially to run the corporation, under the chairmanship of Philip L. Graham, president of the *Washington Post* and chairman of the board of *Newsweek* magazine. The other incorporators were men prominent in business, banking, law, and labor. By the end of 1962, the group was deeply involved in the organization of the new venture. "It is," said one, "like being ordered to organize a world-wide airline six months after the Wright brothers first flew."

The new corporation had its problems cut out for it but none were more crucial than three which were as complex, one within another, as a set of Chinese boxes. The first of these was to get a fair determination of which of a half-dozen satellite systems was best suited for the space communications network that the corporation will operate. The second was to get this system into operation. The third, and possibly the most complex, was to sort out the political and economic problems involved in connecting this American system with hundreds of telephone, television, and telex networks throughout the world.

On February 1, 1963, the Communications Satellite Corporation was officially incorporated and, later in the month, the board of incorporators chose Leo D. Welch, chairman of the Standard Oil Company (New Jersey) to be chairman and chief executive officer of the firm. It also chose Dr. Joseph V. Charyk, undersecretary of the U.S. Air Force, to be the Comsat corporation's president. The new venture began operations in the Georgian-styled main house at Tregaron, a wooded hilltop estate in northwest Washington once owned by millionare Joseph E. Davies. From here the company began the job of starting from nothing a two-hundred-million-dollar private enterprise whose province was outer space and whose operating tools were still largely experimental. Although it was a profit-seeking enterprise, not even its most optimistic supporters expected it to turn a profit for years. This did not seem to bother the thousands of investors who snapped up five million shares of the corporation's first public stock issue in June, 1964. Comsat became one of the market's glamor securities, doubling in value within a short time after it was offered for sale.

The investors' optimism was further buoyed by the general success of the first generation of experimental communications satellites. The first two repeater satellites placed in orbit—AT&T's Telstar and RCA's Relay—had intermittent power supply failures but otherwise they performed as planned. The synchronous-orbiting Hughes satellite, Syncom, first placed in orbit in the spring of 1963, had mechanical difficulty but the second one, orbited several months later, was a complete success.

The early satellites made communications history in hundreds of experiments. These tests involved the transmission and reception of television, telephone, telegraph, teletype, wirephoto, facsimile, and other types of communication. During 1963, the Telstar and Relay satellites provided intercontinental coverage of the death of Pope John XXIII, the coronation of his successor, the June visit of President Kennedy to Europe, and, five months later, his funeral services in Washington. In July, Telstar was used by the CBS network to conduct a four-nation "Town Meeting of the World," involving an international discussion between former President Eisenhower and three European leaders—Jean Monnet, Anthony Eden, and Heinrich von Brentano. Through these and other broadcasts, hundreds of millions of people on both sides of the Atlantic were made aware of the possibilities of global television.

Meanwhile, the satellite corporation was adjusting to its unique new role as a government-sponsored private firm operating in a field where the ground rules were still to be set. The misgivings expressed by both political liberals and conservative businessmen during the debate on the Comsat bill were abated but not completely halted. In the meantime, students of government and the law were studying the possible effect of precedents set by the new corporation.[27] The possibilities of conflict between the interests of the new firm and government regulatory agencies were illustrated in August, 1963, when the corporation found itself in a controversy with the Federal Communications Commission over alleged delays in the issuance of the firm's stock issue.[28]

Another problem which faced the Comsat corporation was the doubts cast by technologists and businessmen alike on the long-range economic role of communications satellites. In February, 1963, testifying before a Senate committee, James Dingman, a Bell System executive, said that his company believed that it could install by 1966 an all-transistorized underseas cable for telephone and telegraph traffic which could handle ten times the traffic of cables then existing. Such a cable would adversely affect the volume of communications carried by space satellites over such heavily-trafficked areas as the North Atlantic.

The corporation's main problem was that its activities promised to revolutionize the high-stakes international communications business. The fact that the leading American carriers owned half the company's stock did not end the possibility of conflict between themselves and Comsat. The carriers disputed Comsat's attempt to gain control over the ground relay stations which would serve the global satellite network from various points in the United States. The potential users of the satellite system, particularly the TV networks and press associations, challenged the right of the carriers to monopolize the lucrative position of middlemen between Comsat and themselves. Several of them, including the Associated Press and the *Washington Post*, took steps to deal directly with the Comsat corporation. Finally, both the corporation and the carriers were faced with the threat by two firms, United Press International and the American Broadcasting Company, to buy and operate their own satellites.[29]

A more radical proposal, involving all of these factors, was put forward by RCA's elder statesman, David Sarnoff, in May, 1965. Renewing a suggestion he had made several years earlier, Mr. Sarnoff proposed a single U.S. common carrier organization in the international field so that this country could compete more effectively with government-monopoly carriers abroad.[30]

The manner in which these varied problems are resolved will have an important influence on the future of American activities in space communications. However these domestic issues are only one aspect of the U.S. involvement in a world-wide satellite communications system. Another aspect involves relations with over a hundred countries around the world who, as both receivers and senders of messages through the new system, have an important stake in its management and operations.

Soon after the first successful Telstar experiment in 1962, the U.S. government and the satellite corporation drew up plans for an international agreement defining the relationship between the corporation and foreign carriers. It soon became apparent that many governments—notably those in Western Europe—had misgivings about granting a private American corporation such a key role in the politically and economically sensitive field of world-wide communications. The Europeans recognized that the American lead in comsat technology gave the U.S. a decisive position in this field. They were afraid that this American dominance would freeze their own electronics industries out of the potentially profitable market for supplying materials for the new system. These factors were behind their early proposals for a substantial European role in the control of the new global network. Other proposals called for operation of the system by an international organization under United Nations rather than United States auspices.[31]

The American government took a firm line against these suggestions in a series of international conferences on the subject during the first half of 1964. American delegates stated this country's intention to proceed with the development of a world-wide communications system using the management and technological resources of the Comsat corporation. In one observer's view, the American attitude was that "the time to climb aboard the American-driven space communications bandwagon is now."[32] In July, 1964, an eighteen-nation conference reached agreement on international ownership and management of the new system. The agreement provided that initial ownership of the global enterprise would be shared by the eighteen nations and the Vatican with the United States having a preponderant financial interest and also effective voting control over most aspects of the enterprise. The U.S. Communications Satellite Corporation was designated as the system's manager, operating under a twelve-man international policy committee. The agreement was a carefully developed balance of American and foreign interests, permitting the United States to move ahead with the development of the comsat network while giving foreign countries a large measure of participation in the system's operation.[33]

By the summer of 1965, forty-five nations had signed the comsat agreements, giving the new communications system access to countries on every continent. Whether the American vision of a single world-wide system will be sustained is, however, still a moot question. One of the little-noticed provisions of the agreements calls for a review of the situation in 1969. By that time the United States may find itself sharing the space communications field with several other nations—Japan, the Soviet Union, and a half-dozen European countries.

The Europeans have already made it clear that they intend to compete with U.S. technology in space communications. Six West European nations and Australia set up the European Launch Development Organization (ELDO) in 1961 to finance and construct a purely European rocket program. Among ELDO's duties is to assist experiments sponsored by the ten-nation European Space Research Organization (ESRO); communications satellites are high on the list of ESRO's development projects. ELDO's original rocket development plan called for a five-year, 196-million-dollar program capable of lofting its first rocket in 1966 from Australia's Woomera testing range. The French, Germans, and British were assigned the task of building the rocket. Italy was made responsible for the satellite payload while Belgium and the Netherlands provide telemetry and ground guidance equipment. By 1965, however, the program was running behind schedule. Despite the delay there was little doubt that the Europeans would eventually have both the rocket power and the payload technology to become a factor in communications satellite operations. Political prestige considerations, together with European industry's desire to get into space technology, were powerful incentives. If the ELDO program is successful, the net result will be to give the Europeans a greater future say in world-wide communications satellite arrangements.[34]

In 1965 the Japanese government announced that development work was proceeding on a Japanese-designed communications satellite, scheduled to be put into operation within a few years.

A more formidable challenge to the American concept of a unified system is the possibility of a competing Soviet system. Soviet scientists discussed their plans for such a network as early as 1957.[35] During the late fifties and early sixties, however, there was relatively little discussion of the subject in Soviet output. Western observers did not doubt Russian capabilities in this field. These capabilities were proven in April, 1965, when the first Soviet comsat was successfully placed in orbit, serving as an experimental active repeater link between Soviet cities.

American policy from the start has advocated the inclusion of all nations in one global satellite system for communications. This includes Communist countries. In the congressional debate on the subject, the Kennedy administration even raised the touchy issue of Chinese Communist participation in an American-built communications satellite system. In answer to a congressman's statement opposing "equal time for Red China, financed at the United States taxpayers' expense," Edward R. Murrow, then director of the U.S. Information Agency, said: "This would be a two-way street. If the Chinese were prepared to say we would get words and pictures from the satellites to their sets, and they could get words and pictures from the satellite to our sets, I would have no doubt where the advantage would lie at the end of the day."[36]

In December, 1962, the Russians agreed in principle to a program of three cooperative space experiments with the United States as part of a UN-sponsored program of international cooperation in space. One of the projects involved space satellite communications. Under the agreement, communications experiments were to be conducted utilizing the American Echo A-12 satellite. The agreement also set up a planning mechanism "for the working out with other nations of a project for an experimental global system of space communications."[37]

After long negotiations, final agreement on this limited program was announced in August, 1963. However there were considerable differences of opinion over further cooperative efforts. One of the stumbling blocks was the Soviet insistence that a legal code governing the use of space be agreed to by both parties before a major program of cooperation began. The original Soviet version of such a code included a prohibition against using space for profit-making ventures such as those planned by the new American communications satellite corporation. In September, 1962, Soviet negotiators at the United Nations indicated that they might soften their stand on this issue.[38] The Soviet code would also prohibit propaganda activities and the collection of intelligence data in space—two restrictions that would also be unacceptable to the United States.[39]

The August, 1963, agreement, therefore, did not signal a major change in the general Russian policy of noncooperation with the United States in space activities. Past experience suggests that they will keep their own cooperative activities in communications satellites within narrow limits until they have strengthened their own technological lead in this field so that they can compete on a roughly equal footing with the United States.

The Soviet government did show a definite interest in the possibility of participating in the 1964 communications satellite agreement. While negotiations were still in progress, American government and Comsat corporation representatives met with Russian authorities to discuss the possibilities of such participation. According to reports at the time, the Russians were impressed by U.S. success in enlisting support for the agreement, particularly among the Europeans, and they were considering ways in which to reduce U.S. influence in the agreement. One course would have been to sign the agreement themselves, an option they chose not to take although, as members of the International Telecommunications Union, they were eligible to participate. Soviet propaganda has meanwhile taken a dim view of the agreement, emphasizing the consortium's dependence on a capitalistic organization for its management and the alleged U.S. dominance of the committee running the consortium's policy affairs.

The Russians have decided, for the time being, to stay outside the consortium. What they will do in the future is, of course, not easily predicted. They have three choices. They can join the system and try to modify it to their own ends, or they can set up their own system in competition with the present one. Finally, they can orbit their own comsats and then propose to integrate them with the present system.

The prospect of developing their own satellite television system for political purposes must be a tempting one for the Soviet government. Russian spokesmen have given few hints of their plans in this field. However, an interesting insight on the possibilities open to them has been provided by science writer Arthur C. Clarke, the same Mr. Clarke who started the whole discussion about communications satellites back in 1945. Regarding Soviet satellite television, he has written:

> Consider the following flight of imagination which might be entitled: "how to conquer the world without anyone noticing":
>
> By 1970, the Russians have established the first satellite TV relays high above Asia, broadcasting in several languages so that more than a billion human beings can understand the program. At the same time, in a well-organized sales campaign spearheaded by demonstrations, Russian trade missions have been flooding Asia with cheap transistorized, battery-powered receivers. There is scarcely a village which cannot afford one and it doesn't cost the U.S.S.R. anything; it even makes a small profit on the deal. And so millions who have never learned to read, who have never seen a movie, who have no rival distractions, fall under the hypnotic spell which even ostensibly educated nations have been unable to resist. Good entertainment, rapid (if slanted) news reporting, Russian-language lessons, instructional programs of do-it-yourself type useful to backward communities, quiz programs in which the first prizes are usually trips to the Soviet Union—it takes little imagination to see the pattern. In a few years of skillful propaganda, the uncommitted nations would be committed. It may be no exaggeration to say that priority in establishing the satellite communications system may determine whether, fifty years from now, Russian or English is the main language of mankind. . . .[40]

Mr. Clarke's imagination has led him to the outer limits of the possibilities facing the Soviet leadership in this field. It is possible to accuse him of journalistic hyperbole but only at the risk of ignoring some of the opportunities that global TV offers the rulers of a powerful totalitarian system whose ultimate aim is world domination.

Despite these threats, the dominant fact about global communications by satellite in the 1960's is the long technological lead the United States has in this field. This lead was further confirmed in April, 1965, with the launching of the Early Bird, the first satellite to be used for full-scale commercial operations. Early Bird was a dramatic technological advance over its predecessors, the Hughes-built Syncom satellites.

Placed into position on a synchronous orbit, hovering off the coast of Brazil, Early Bird provided round-the-clock relay facilities for North Atlantic communications traffic. Among other attributes, it offered U.S. and European television networks an opportunity to make long-range plans for intercontinental transmissions. During Early Bird's first experimental month, networks on both sides of the Atlantic utilized it for a wide variety of programs, ranging from news shows to live coverage of an art auction in London. In one memorable program on May 2, 1965, cameras in thirty different locations from Mexico City to Skansen, Sweden, gave viewers in Europe and North America a breathtaking panorama of the possibilities opened up by the new satellite. Once the experimental period was over and the new satellite began commercial operations, television networks were faced with determining just how much use they would make of the new facility.

Their programing decision was compounded by a dispute over the cost of satellite television. The Communications Satellite Corporation filed a rate schedule with the Federal Communications Commission which called for payments of up to 5,245 dollars an hour for TV transmissions. Such prices, the National Broadcasting Company announced, "will preclude TV usage of the satellite system." Moreover, the Comsat fees only covered transmission between its ground station in the United States and the satellite. The fees from the satellite down to European ground stations were regulated by European postal authorities, and they proposed fees which were even higher than those of the Comsat corporation. Faced with the threat of a boycott by the TV networks on both sides of the Atlantic, both the U.S. and European operators of the satellite system took steps to revise their rate schedules downward. Despite this move, satellite-TV charges were high enough to force American and European networks to modify their earlier optimistic estimates about large-scale use of satellite transmissions.

Reviewing the American networks' experience with satellite telecasts, *Variety* offered the following wry report on their attitude in July, 1965:

> Television's romance with astronomy has turned out to be only a flirtation. What cooled off the heavenly affair was not only the stratospheric costs for the use of the Comsat satellite but also an evaporation of the stardust. In the cold light of dawn, the plaything-in-the-sky begins to look like a prosaic, although remarkable, electronic tool of limited fascination and use. . . . A live direct carry from the satellite presents all the same hazards and limitations of any live television—the static setting, the restricted scope of the cameras, the inevitability of flubs and errors—the very production headaches that made a godsend of video tape. And since, because of international time differences, most Early Bird programming has to be previously taped anyway; and since, where entertainment and cultural shows are concerned, it matters to no one that the presentation comes a week or a month after the taping, benefitting in the interim from judicious editing, the old method of the jet carry is still the more feasible.[41]

Commercial television's use of the transatlantic comsat system during 1965 confirmed that TV-by-satellite will be largely devoted to news coverage. News meets the twin criteria for any attempt to broadcast live programs over long distances—a sense of immediacy and a substantial degree of audience interest. The Eurovision regional network has been the pioneer in this type of international reporting, with programs ranging from floods in Holland to the Vatican Ecumenical Council. Aside from their technical virtuosity in linking television stations throughout the continent, Eurovision's managers have shown considerable imagination in meeting the programing problems of a multinational network, providing an important reservoir of experience for the new satellite link.

The random pattern of special-events news programs that will dominate satellite-TV transmissions for the time being could lead to the establishment of daily regularly scheduled news programs relayed by satellite. Eurovision has already had considerable experience with just such an international news relay, providing its national networks with a pictorial summary of the day's news, transmitted via cable and microwave facilities each afternoon. Eventually a similar visual "pickup" of late-breaking news could be arranged for the earth-circling communications satellites. The pickups could be scheduled several times a day to take into account time differentials around the world and to provide adequate representation from all parts of the globe. One of the residual benefits of such a system would be to put news reporting from Asia and Africa on a more balanced basis than it has ever been.

Aside from the commercial networks, the other prospect for American participation in satellite-TV broadcasting is through the government. This would involve a television version of radio's Voice of America. The government's overseas information arm, the U.S. Information Agency, already has an extensive television operation which provides program materials on film or tape to stations in over eighty countries. The USIA's position on this subject was outlined several years ago by its then director, Edward R. Murrow: "I think it is reasonable to suggest that the national interest demands that we (in USIA) use the system. Reflect, if you will, on the impact around the world of instantaneous live television coverage of the launching of a man in orbit. Dwell upon the lessons of freedon that will attend the worldwide live television coverage of an American election."[42]

The question arises where propaganda transmissions are compatible with the other purposes the U.S. has set for the communications satellites. There is a case for the proposition that we will be setting a dangerous precedent by using the satellites for propaganda. It can be argued that, in the interests of world peace and understanding, such special nationalistic pleading should be barred from the satellites. However, this reasoning ignores certain hard facts. One of them is that one man's propaganda is another man's information program. A large percentage of the programs relayed by the satellite TV system will be, to a greater or lesser degree, presentations of national viewpoints, *i.e.*, propaganda. The United States will be doing no more or no less than most countries in the satellite network when it transmits government-sponsored programs. In foreign countries, television is usually owned or controlled by the local government. These governments are not generally going to permit transmission of programs which are harmful to their hoped-for international image; they are going to review their satellite TV output with more than half an eye on elements of national prestige.

Another factor is that any so-called propaganda programs prepared by the U.S. Information Agency will have to be acceptable to television networks in other countries. Unlike short-wave radio, satellite television transmissions will be channeled through local networks, not directly to home receivers. In the expensive business of satellite broadcasting, such programs will have to be low-keyed enough in their propaganda approach to make them palatable to foreign stations. The fact that USIA already places thousands of programs on foreign television every year is indication enough that expertise is not lacking in this sector of the U.S. overseas information program.

The most effective approach for any USIA satellite TV efforts will probably be to complement the live special-events coverage of the American commercial networks. The agency can play a particular role in seeing that such coverage is extended to TV stations in Asia, Africa, and Latin America. Here is where coverage by American commercial TV will probably be weak, and yet it is here where coverage will be most important from a prestige and informational viewpoint.

The agency may also eventually play a role in extending television coverage into Communist areas. Given the present parlous state of television program exchange arrangements with the Soviet Union, the opportunities for providing such coverage for Russian TV will be limited for a number of years. The prospects for exchanges with Eastern European countries are, however, somewhat brighter. The other possibility, limited now by technological considerations, is direct broadcasting from an orbiting satellite to home receivers, without the necessity of having the signal pass through a ground relay station for retransmission. The next generation of communications satellites will include machines with enough power capacity to do this. An RCA feasibility study announced several years ago describes such a satellite, receiving its power from a compact atomic-powered reactor plant capable of generating up to sixty kilowatts of electricity. Placed into equatorial orbit, each satellite will transmit signals into home television receivers within an area of three million square miles.[43] Other direct-broadcast satellite proposals have been made since then.

The prospect of broadcasting a television signal directly into Soviet homes is certainly an intriguing one. The Russian government can, of course, be counted upon to develop countermeasures to any such breach of their barriers against information from the outside, similar to jamming devices used in the past against Western radio stations.

The reality of direct broadcasts from satellites to home receivers is, however, a long time in the future. It may, in fact, never materialize because of the political and legal questions involved. The Soviet Union and other Communist countries will not be the only ones to claim that such broadcasting is a breach of their national sovereignty under the vague set of United Nations resolutions prohibiting the use of outer space for hostile actions against other nations. There have already been indications from European countries that they would not look with favor on a direct-broadcasting satellite system which interferes with their internal control over telecommunications facilities.

The more important immediate prospect is for the steady growth of a satellite-based global television system, linked to national and regional networks on all continents. Public interest in the idea of world-wide television is high. There has, however, been little concrete discussion of how it would be carried out.

In part this is a reflection of the doubts expressed about its practicality. Predictions about the high cost of global television have also had their dampening effect, as have more specific questions about the technical difficulties involved in linking local networks.

Added to this is the general confusion about the organization and purpose of such a network. In exploring these factors, the American government, the new Comsat corporation, and the U.S. television industry will be involved in a new kind of space-age diplomacy for which there are few precedents. One such precedent has resulted from the way in which early satellite telecasts have been arranged between this country and Europe. Without benefit of grand design, the early Telstar, Relay, and Early Bird transmissions were arranged by informal committees in Washington and in Britain, France, and other European countries. Some of these transmissions were simple country-to-country exchanges; others involved programs carried by the networks of twenty or more countries. Relays in Europe were usually arranged by Eurovision's parent organization, the European Broadcasting Union.

Although this relatively informal arrangement worked well in the early years of satellite telecasting, it seems likely that a more formal organization for coordinating television exchanges may be needed, particularly when the exchanges are extended beyond the North Atlantic area. For political prestige reasons, the United States has a stake in seeing that satellite television capabilities are extended to Latin America, Asia, and Africa. Some countries in these areas—Japan, Australia, and Brazil—will be ready in a short time to be linked to the global satellite system through their own ground relay stations. This linking will move more slowly in less developed countries that are just beginning to build up their communications systems.

One of the policy questions facing the United States is that of possible economic and technical assistance to help newly developing countries link themselves to the communications satellite system. In a July, 1961, policy statement, President Kennedy listed as one of the government's responsibilities in this area a pledge to provide "technical assistance to newly developing countries in order to help attain an effective global system as soon as possible."[44] This concept was not included in the administration's February, 1962, legislative proposals to Congress, probably out of deference to congressional sensitivities about accepting long-range foreign aid commitments.

It might be appropriate for the United States to propose to all of the technologically advanced countries using the satellite system that a fixed percentage of the system's profits be allocated for technical assistance to countries which need help in linking their telecommunications system to the world system. In any event, it will be useful, if only for psychological reasons, to bring underdeveloped countries with fledgling television systems into the discussions on a world network as early as possible.

What type of organization is best suited for coordinating the operations of a world satellite television network? One suggestion is that this coordination take place under some form of United Nations sponsorship. This could be done, according to proponents of the idea, by an international commission which would set technical and operational standards for the network as well as serving as coordinator for international telecasts. Such an organization would give the space television project a supranational framework which would seem in line with the high purpose of the venture. It would also undercut suspicions of alleged American domination of the project.

There would, however, be certain policy disadvantages for the United States in such an arrangement. International control could inhibit American use of the satellite television network for our own purposes, such as the transmission of commercial programs or of government-sponsored propaganda programs. Following the neutral tradition of the United Nations in informational affairs, the proposed television organization might set program standards which discouraged the transmission of alleged controversial material in order to shield national sensitivities of its member networks—in other words, censorship might be fostered.

A more practical approach to organizing the satellite television system involves European-American cooperation. Proposals have been made that the American networks and the European Broadcasting Union take the initiative in forming a world broadcasting union which would oversee the problems of satellite telecasting. Concrete suggestions for such an organization were made by several leading American broadcasters at the European Broadcasting Union's annual meeting in New York in October, 1962, shortly after the first round of experimental transatlantic telecasting via the Telstar satellite had been completed.[45] Similar proposals have been advanced since then. Although these plans varied in content, they all were based on the realistic assumption that, for a number of years, the most active area of television exchanges will be across the North Atlantic. A loose federation of American and European television systems, not tied directly to government-to-government negotiations, could provide a flexible administrative umbrella under which both private and government-controlled networks as well as individual stations could operate. The organization could later be expanded as satellite and microwave links make it possible to connect American and European networks with regional networks on other continents.

All of these projections are based on the assumption that there will be reasonable freedom from censorship and from blatant propaganda in the operation of the world television system. Certainly it is in the best American interest that this happen. There will, inevitably, be domestic pressures in this country for special-interest controls applied to satellite television. This was demonstrated in extremis by the September, 1962, resolution of the Women's Christian Temperance Union that liquor advertising be barred from satellite transmissions.[46] The danger of banning "Old Grandad" from outer space may never arise, but other pressures may. These will include nationalist pressures within the United States to use satellite television aggressively to present "the American image," or to deny its use to certain nations for political reasons. Similar pressures may arise in other countries.

There is, fortunately, little support either in the government or in the two major political parties for such sentiments. However, it will be important for us to remain firm in our commitment to free and open discussion in satellite television as in other media outlets. The traditional policy of presenting ourselves in the spirit of Oliver Cromwell's instructions to his portrait painter—"warts and all"—applies here as elsewhere. The American attitude in this regard will determine whether the communications satellites serve our need for a vigorous exchange of ideas between men and nations or whether they merely transmit pretty pictures on ceremonial occasions. We acted in our best interests, for example, when European television networks were permitted to use Telstar to cover the "March on Washington" rally in August, 1963, supporting civil rights legislation and the ending of racial discrimination. The sights and sounds of two hundred thousand Americans, white and Negro, gathering peacefully in the capital for redress of their grievances showed Europeans a side of our civil rights revolution that has tended to be overshadowed by more violent events.

Another important part of this commitment will be our willingness to accept the televised images of other nations on our own television screens. Satellite television is a two-way street. The American commercial networks will have to make their program schedules available for frequent transmissions from abroad. More than any other single factor, this will be the measure other countries will apply to our claim that we do not intend to use the satellite television system for narrow purposes.

This willingness to listen is as important a part of our democratic tradition as the desire to be heard. The world television system now being formed provides us with the technological means for expanding this dialogue in a new and dramatic way. Whether we choose to use it for such high purposes remains to be seen. If we do not, the fault—by way of paraphrase—will lie not in our Telstars but in ourselves.

12

Balance
Sheet

One day within the next twenty years a TV antenna will be raised in the most isolated village in Africa. And there will no longer be any remote places. All the trivia and profundities that one man can pass on to another will be open to Everyman, staring at his living room screen.

For many this prospect conjures up images of automated Big Brother conformity. For others it augurs well for a more peaceful international order. The fact that intelligent men can draw such contradictory conclusions from the same set of facts is a rough indication of television's power and of our difficulties in understanding it. The reality of TV's global influence lies, in fact, somewhere between 1984 and Utopia.

The United States has special responsibilities in defining the potentials of world-wide use of the medium. Historically, we have set the pace of television's development both as a lightweight entertainment medium and as an instrument of informational and cultural exchange. We have a stake in the medium as a positive force serving a changing international order.

Our own national interests will be strongly influenced by our ability, through TV, to bring the sights and sounds of American life to overseas audiences. Equally important will be television's role in giving this vast audience a new image of their own societies in a fast-changing world. The flickering screen can confront them with the realities of a new world order and their

283

relationship to it. Or it can shield them from this reality and their responsibilities by offering them a bland diet of escape programs and inane chatter.

We can affect the quality of world television to a limited but significant degree. Whatever we do will be determined largely by the activities of our own domestic television system. We cannot have one standard of conduct for television at home and another for our actions abroad. Ours is a glass-house culture, highly visible to the outside. Attempts to offer the rest of the world a sanitized version of American life at any level have always been self-defeating. The tone of our commitment to television's development as a positive international force will be set primarily by the commercial television industry and its activities here.

The question, then, is whether U.S. television is capable of representing our full national interests abroad. For the present, the answer must be a qualified no. Fault cannot be found with the technical and commercial achievements of U.S. television; American industry is the world leader in these areas. The weaknesses lie in programing limitations. We produce more television programs for export than all other nations combined; in 1966 over eighty million dollars' worth of programs were sent to over ninety countries. American programs dominate the most popular listening hours in many foreign countries because of high production quality and entertainment value.

By and large our television exports are useful, if bland, portrayals of various segments of American life. The claim that they represent a poor image of America is largely overdone. The record is better than most critics of U.S. television are willing to concede, but it still falls considerably short of a reasonable ideal. What the networks produce and sell is not always the best or the most representative either of American life of or television's potential. We need to be represented on overseas television by something more than the standard formula of cowboy serials, detective films, pratfall comedies, and an occasional news documentary. An overseas viewer would be hard put to believe, from what he sees on his screen, that contemporary America is a leader in the lively arts such as drama, architecture, painting, and sculpture, or to understand the workings of our economic system or our current struggle to build a truly democratic multiracial society. These subjects are seldom raised in the bland products that make up most of the U.S. television export package.

Censorship of allegedly "bad" television exports is no solution; it raises many more problems for a free society than it might settle. Proposals for official government subsidy to encourage a higher level of program exports, advanced in some quarters, are both politically unrealistic and otherwise unworkable. What is needed is a greater diversification of program sources within the domestic television industry. Already, signs point to such a development. The commercial networks and their affiliated stations will continue to be dominant, both politically and economically; but their dominance will be modified during the next decade by several newer forms of television operations.

Outstanding among these new forms are educational television (ETV), subscription or pay television (STV), and ultra-high-frequency channel television (UHF). Individually, none of these outlets will match the influence of the three large networks. Collectively, however, they will add a large measure of variety and competition to the American TV scene. Educational TV, already represented by more than a hundred community stations, will continue to expand and to improve in ways that will give greater dimensions to public-service television. Pay television promises to provide a high level of top-quality entertainment. Several hundred new UHF stations will complement network-controlled VHF outlets, with schedules emphasizing specialized programs for smaller audiences. Television will then be an instrument better serving both majority and minority interests.

Diversification will expand the spectrum of programs and other services available to foreign stations. The commercial networks and the Hollywood film syndicators may have a somewhat smaller share of the total export market, but the market will still be enormously profitable to them, given the steady increase in the number of overseas outlets and the popularity of American network products. The standardized light entertainment that is the networks' stock-in-trade will still get the lion's share of the overseas market. However, foreign stations also will be able to shop for programs covering other aspects of American life, produced by the operators of subscription television, educational TV, and other new elements.

But aside from these signs of developmental trends, there are a number of specific steps the United States should take to strengthen our over-all position in international television:

1. *There should be closer liaison arrangements between the industry and government to assure unified American policy, whenever practical, in international TV matters.* With the development of communications satellites and regional networks, the politics of international television are becoming increasingly complex. The U.S. networks and other elements of the TV industry find themselves often at a practical disadvantage in negotiating with state-controlled television organizations in other countries.

The United States is often inadequately represented in such negotiations simply because it does not speak with one voice as do the other countries. In the European Broadcasting Union, U.S. interests are represented by seven television organizations, only one of which (the U.S. Information Agency) represents the official government position. Although the views and the interests of all seven coincide more often than not, the members seldom speak as a a united group. The result is needless downgrading of American influence in discussions of EBU policy and programing matters in which both U.S. industry and the government have an interest.

The answer to this problem lies in *ad hoc* arrangements between government and industry to assure, whenever possible, a concerted American approach. The main stumbling block to such arrangements is the industry's wariness concerning any form of official control over its overseas operations. Informal consultative machinery could be devised, however, to facilitate group decisions among the government and the major networks as well as other American TV organizations such as the National Educational Television network, commercial television film producers and syndicators, electronic equipment manufacturers, and independent television stations. Any of the participants in discussions could be free to dissociate itself from any such group decision.

2. *The United States should take the lead in forming an Inter-American Broadcasting Union.* Latin American countries have made several attempts to form a regional organization patterned on the European Broadcasting Union. They have failed mainly because they lacked a strong organizational push. The United States should vitalize this lagging effort, for its success could improve regional communications throughout the hemisphere. U.S. initiative in such a project should be worked out in ways that would quell any Latin suspicions that we might dominate the new organization. Our interests are best served by deferring to Latin sensitivities in this regard. A good working model can be found in the activities of the American Broadcasting Company (ABC) in encouraging five Central American countries to set up a regional network.

Development of a full hemisphere network could be stepped up through the use of communications satellites set up on a north-south axis. With television firmly established in most Latin American countries, such a network could greatly enhance our political and cultural relations with countries to the south and north.

3. *The American government and the television industry should establish firm policies regarding TV broadcasting by communications satellites.* This subject could be an important continuing item on the agenda of the government-industry consultative committee proposed above. Although the 1962 congressional legislation setting up the Communications Satellite Corporation specifies that the U.S.-constructed satellite system should have a clear-cut public-service function, no one has clearly defined what this function is. The corporation has put its operational emphasis on those services (telephone, teletype, etc.) which eventually promise a profitable return on the investment made by its thousands of stockholders. Television ranks relatively low on the list of profitable uses of satellite transmission time. In this instance, however, profit margins and political factors do not jibe. Because of its highly visual nature, television will be a key element in the public image of the American-built satellite system. Our national claims to responsibility in developing and

operating a world-wide comsat system will depend to a large extent on television, whether it is a profitable item of business or not.

Foreign attitudes on this issue will become crucial for us by 1969 when the present interim agreement on international use of the communications satellite system will be reviewed by the more than forty nations currently involved. Negotiations for a permanent arrangement at that time will determine whether the United States will continue its pre-eminence in a world-wide communications satellite system. At present, many nations—including some of our oldest allies—are reluctant to give such a major role in developing a world-wide comsat system to a privately controlled American corporation. Our willingness to take a broad view of comsat television capabilities, over and above profit-and-loss considerations, could play an important part in convincing foreign public opinion of our adequacy to act responsibly within the private enterprise system.

4. *American educational television should be encouraged to take a more positive role in cooperating with overseas ETV efforts, particularly in devoloping countries.* After a dozen years of trial-and-error experimentation, American ETV is the world leader in technical, administrative, and programing techniques for television teaching. The Japanese may make more intensive use of educational TV, but they cannot equal the American range of experience at all levels of this new and exciting teaching tool. The fruits of our experience should be made more readily available to educators and broadcasters abroad, particularly in Asia, Africa, and Latin America. By sharing our knowledge, we could strengthen educational systems in developing areas. By adapting our ETV programs for local use, we could offer to millions of students abroad a balanced, objective picture of the world around them, including the United States. In so doing, we could achieve significant political impact in correcting some of the fanciful mythologies that overseas students have about us.

The obstacle here is financing. Most U.S. educational TV systems operate on a deficit or on the thin edge of solvency. They are dependent largely on yearly appropriations from a variety of public and private sources. There are, however, precedents for making funds available to ETV groups for overseas work. A good case can also be made for involving the federal government more directly in this field. While congressmen and educators are generally reluctant to see federal funds used for direct curriculum assistance in the United States, their fears of Washington control over local education do not apply abroad. The government has already made some significant moves in this direction with its limited ETV technical-assistance projects in Nigeria and Colombia.

5. *The U.S. government should explore more intensively the direct use of television as a tool of modernization in developing countries.* Our efforts to assist television in developing countries are now concentrated on use of the medium as a classroom teaching tool. We could initiate new pilot projects to measure TV's usefulness as a conscious instrument of social change, orienting people of all ages to their individual and collective responsibilities in a rapidly changing society. The countries selected for these pilot projects would have to be chosen carefully. The danger of any intensive use of television as a social weapon is its potential as an instrument to support dictatorial regimes in the developing areas. It can be argued, for intance, that Egypt's President Nasser is employing television as a modernization tool because of its extensive schedule of popular education programs; it is also true that Egyptian television is a propaganda instrument, restricting the *political* modernization of the country.

Despite the risks, further experimentation is justified. Any powerful instrument can be dangerous, but the power of television will be needed to break the chains of ignorance and fear that impede the modernization process.

6. *The U.S. government should consider more seriously the potentialities of television as an informational and cultural tool directly supporting its political objectives.* Every American program that appears on overseas television affects, in some small degree, the international political fortunes of the United States. Overseas prejudices are confirmed, or modified, each time Danny Kaye, Lucille Ball, the Ben Cartright clan, or other such familiar faces are shown on overseas TV screens. These popular stars make television the most influential carrier of the American image to

vast audiences throughout the world. Also contributing to the image is a more specialized type of program whose purpose is to support directly U.S. foreign-policy objectives. These are the programs prepared for overseas showings by the U.S. Information Agency, overseas information and cultural arm of the American government.

USIA has been in the business of overseas television since 1953 when it inaugurated a small TV operation as a subsection of the radio Voice of America. The agency's television service has expanded steadily since then; its studio facilities in Washington serve posts in over eighty countries. However, the agency TV budget is less than a fifth of the funds allotted to the Voice of America. There is a reasonable doubt whether this disparity accurately reflects the relative roles radio and television should be playing in the U.S. overseas information program.

Short-wave radio is still USIA's most important media operation directed toward Eastern Europe, the Soviet Union, Cuba, Communist China, and other areas where the agency is unable to conduct the usual information and cultural activities such as libraries and film showings. The Voice of America is also important in certain areas of Africa and Asia where, in the absence of television, radio broadcasting is the most influential mass medium. In all other parts of the world, however, the rapid expansion of TV facilities has had the uniform effect of reducing the hours of radio listening. USIA has increased the ratio of its television operations to the point where TV now accounts for about 10 percent of its annual media operations budget. The question remains whether this is an accurate reflection of television's potential for keeping overseas audiences informed on matters directly affecting U.S. foreign policy.

7. *The United States should resist attempts to restrict the free flow of news and other information over international television channels.* Censorship is a continuing threat to the full development of television as a world medium. The classic example of what can happen may be found in the history of international short-wave radio. Despite attempts during the twenties to organize this medium as a genuine instrument for the free exchange of information, radio evolved primarily as a propaganda weapon in

the service of competing nationalisms. Television could fall into a similar trap. The temptation is strong in many nations to restrict participation in global television to national prestige programs. Communist and other totalitarian regimes can be relied upon to impose restrictions. Even in many free world countries, the tradition of freedom of expression in broadcasting is more limited than it is here. Much of the free-swinging discussion that takes place on American radio and TV would be considered slanderous in other democratic countries. The United States will have to press hard to release these inhibitions against full discussion when the ground rules for international telecasting are made. Every country, including our own, will want to use international television for prestige propaganda purposes. Our concern should be to assure that the new global channels are also open to programs which offer independent viewpoints on a wide range of subjects.

Aside from reaffirming our tradition of free discussion, an "open channels" policy should prove useful in strengthening information links between the free world and Communist countries. The leadership in those countries undoubtedly will want to make use of comsat and other international TV channels to bring the story of "Socialist achievements" to free world audiences. We should encourage them to do so, provided two ground rules are observed. The first is that there should be equality in the amount and type of programs exchanged between Communist and free world nations. The second is that neither side should be allowed to impose arbitrary censorship on exchanges. Given the rapid expansion of television in Communist-dominated areas, we have everything to gain through a widened, unfettered dialogue which will reduce the psychological and informational barriers separating us from men and women in these areas.

While we are extolling the virtues of the free flow of ideas, we should make sure that we are practicing what we preach in our own TV activities overseas. We are not immune to the temptation to put our own best national foot forward and to try to slide past the less complimentary facts. It would be a mistake for us to succumb to this temptation. Our commitment to an open society would be compromised. The Italian author Cesare Pavese once wrote: "America is the gigantic theater where, with greater

candor than elsewhere, is being played out the drama of us all."
If we believe that our democratic pluralistic society has lessons
for the rest of the world, we have no choice but to present
ourselves as we are.

During the coming decades we share with the rest of mankind
the need to create a more stable world order, moving beyond the
present restraints of a nuclear stalemate and of social and economic disorder. This new order will be stillborn if we do not make
good use of the available implements of world communications.
Hundreds of millions of ordinary men and women must be made
aware of the facts of a new age and of the alternatives facing us.
Television will be only one of the forces in this massive effort to
get the beginnings of a consensus. We can use this unique instrument as nothing more than the greatest entertainment circus of
all time. Or we can employ it fully as a sight-and-sound interpreter of the problems we face, capable of reaching more people
than has ever been possible with any other information medium
ever invented. The choice is ours.

Appendix:

Overseas Television:
A Statistical Summary

TABLE 1. Growth of Overseas Television by Areas 1955–1964

TV SETS

	Western Europe	Eastern Europe	Near East & South Asia	Africa	Far East	Latin America & Caribbean	Total
12/55	6,018,400	1,063,200	200	5,000	259,700	619,000	7,965,500
12/56	8,364,100	1,481,800	800	5,000	487,600	1,190,000	11,529,300
12/57	11,341,200	2,349,000	4,100	11,000	1,124,000	1,560,800	16,390,100
12/58	14,676,500	3,321,000	11,200	25,000	2,530,500	2,314,500	22,878,700
12/59	19,053,900	5,303,900	45,800	43,800	5,118,000	2,524,600	32,090,000
12/60	23,816,800	7,404,600	150,900	69,300	7,946,200	3,553,600	42,941,400
12/61	29,189,000	9,406,000	306,000	96,000	10,241,000	4,522,000	53,760,000
12/62	33,581,700	11,404,000	408,400	128,300	14,796,800	5,182,700	65,501,900
12/63	39,033,200	15,283,400	724,800	250,100	18,894,700	6,142,800	80,329,000
12/64	45,931,600	19,704,000	938,800	277,100	20,977,200	6,645,700	94,474,400

TV STATIONS

	Western Europe	Eastern Europe	Near East & South Asia	Africa	Far East	Latin America & Caribbean	Total
12/55	85	32	1	2	7	32	159
12/56	133	50	2	3	18	54	260
12/57	274	78	4	3	27	61	447
12/58	469	122	6	4	63	75	739
12/59	678	190	9	7	110	94	1,088
12/60	918	268	11	10	162	119	1,488
12/61	1,312	381	18	12	187	137	2,047
12/62	1,463	577	29	18	400	154	2,641
12/63	1,803	878	35	32	511	185	3,444
12/64	2,321	1,169	40	40	841	217	4,628

Source: United States Information Agency.

TABLE 2. OVERSEAS TELEVISION
Stations and Receivers by Areas
January 1–December 31, 1964

| | TRANSMITTING STATIONS[1] | | RECEIVERS IN USE | |
AREAS	1/1/64	12/31/64	1/1/64	12/31/64
Western Europe	1,803	2,321	39,033,200	45,931,600
Eastern Europe	878	1,169	15,283,400	19,704,000
Near East & South Asia	35	40	724,800	938,800
Africa	32	40	250,100	277,100
Far East	511	841	18,894,700	20,977,200
Latin America & Caribbean	185	217	6,142,800	6,645,700
World Total[2]	3,444	4,628	80,329,000	94,474,400

[1] For breakdowns of type of stations, see Table 3.

[2] Except U.S., Canada and Armed Forces stations abroad. There were an estimated 67,100,000 TV sets in use in the U.S. and 4,950,000 sets in Canada at the end of 1964.

SOURCE: United States Information Agency.

TABLE 3. OVERSEAS TELEVISION
Stations and Receivers by Countries
December 31, 1964

| | TRANSMITTING STATIONS | | | |
COUNTRIES	Programing	Other	Total	RECEIVERS IN USE
Western Europe				
Austria	2	52	54	584,600
Belgium	2	12	14	1,440,600
Denmark	1	15	16	1,163,300
Finland	3	43	46	651,000
France	2	281	283	5,582,000
West Germany	13	653	666	10,024,000
Gibraltar	1	1	2	3,500
Iceland[1]	—	—	—	5,000
Ireland	1	8	9	283,000
Italy	2	748	750	5,406,300
Luxembourg	1	4	5	17,200
Malta	1	—	1	27,000
Monaco	1	1	2	13,000
Netherlands	2	5	7	1,848,500
Norway	1	55	56	408,100
Portugal	2	13	15	150,000
Spain	2	155	157	1,200,000
Sweden	3	103	106	2,013,700
Switzerland	3	51	54	494,600
United Kingdom	3	75	78	14,616,200
TOTAL	46	2,275	2,321	45,931,600

[1] These sets tune in to the local U.S. Armed Forces Station.

TABLE 3 (*continued*)

COUNTRIES	TRANSMITTING STATIONS			RECEIVERS IN USE
	Programing	Other	Total	
Eastern Europe				
Albania	1	—	1	1,000
Bulgaria	1	18	19	120,000
Czechoslovakia	10(a)	260	270	1,899,000
East Germany	10(a)	246	256	2,800,000
Hungary	1	8	9	685,000
Poland	8(a)	49	57	1,700,000
Rumania	10(a)	18	28	330,000
USSR	150(a)	300	450	11,800,000
Yugoslavia	3(a)	76	79	369,000
TOTAL	194	975	1169	19,704,000
Near East and South Asia				
Aden	1	—	1	4,000
Bahrein[1]	—	—	—	7,000
Cyprus	1	—	1	9,000
India	1	—	1	700
Iran	2	—	2	100,000
Iraq	1	—	1	170,000
Israel[1]	—	—	—	13,500
Jordan[1]	—	—	—	500
Kuwait	1	1	2	25,000
Lebanon	2	3	5	126,000
Pakistan	2	—	2	1,700
Qatar[1]	—	—	—	2,500
Saudi Arabia	1	1	2	18,000
Syrian Arab Republic	1	4	5	39,000
Turkey	1	—	1	1,000
United Arab Republic	3	14	17	420,000
TOTAL	17	23	40	938,800

[1] These sets tune in to the local U.S. Armed Forces stations or to neighboring countries.

(a) TV Centers

TABLE 3 (*continued*)

COUNTRIES	TRANSMITTING STATIONS			RECEIVERS IN USE
	Programing	Other	Total	
Africa				
Algeria	3	3	6	150,000
Congo (Brazzaville)	1	—	1	400
Congo (Leopoldville)[1]	—	—	—	400
Ethiopia	1	—	1	4,700
Gabon	1	—	1	300
Ivory Coast	1	1	2	1,200
Kenya	1	1	2	9,900
Liberia	1	—	1	1,300
Libya[1]	—	—	—	6,000
Morocco	1	10	11	25,500
Nigeria	4	4	8	20,200
Rhodesia	2	—	2	28,400
Sierra Leone	1	—	1	500
Sudan	1	—	1	10,000
Tunisia[1]	—	—	—	5,400
Uganda	1	—	1	3,500
Upper Volta	1	—	1	200
Zambia	1	—	1	9,200
TOTAL	21	19	40	277,100

[1] These sets tune in to the local U.S. Armed Forces stations or to neighboring countries.

NOTE: A TV station was to go on the air on the island of Reunion in January, 1965.

TABLE 3 (*continued*)

COUNTRIES	TRANSMITTING STATIONS Programing	Other	Total	RECEIVERS IN USE
Far East				
Australia	46	—	46	2,324,700
Communist China	13	—	13	30,000
Hong Kong	(1)[1]	—	(1)[1]	36,500
Indonesia	2	—	2	45,200
Japan	104	634	738	17,710,000
Korea (South)	2	1	3	50,000
Malaysia (incl. Singapore)	4	—	4	114,000
New Zealand	4	4	8	238,300
Philippines	13	—	13	100,000
Ryukyu Isl. (Okinawa)	2	1	3	91,000
Taiwan	2	—	2	37,500
Thailand	5	4	9	200,000
TOTAL	197	634	841	20,977,200
Latin America & Caribbean				
Argentina	11	3	14	1,360,000
Barbados	1	—	1	2,500
Bermuda	1	—	1	13,000
Brazil	33	9	42	2,156,000
Chile	3	—	3	33,000
Colombia	2	12	14	350,000
Costa Rica	2	4	6	30,000
Cuba	2	17	19	500,000
Dominican Republic	2	2	4	50,000
Ecuador	3	—	3	40,000
El Salvador	2	1	3	27,000
French Antilles	2	—	2	2,000
Guatemala	2	—	2	45,000
Haiti	1	—	1	5,000
Honduras	1	2	3	8,000
Jamaica	1	4	5	20,000
Mexico	24	8	32	1,071,000
Netherlands Antilles	2	—	2	22,000
Nicaragua	1	1	2	6,200
Panama	3	6	9	100,000
Peru	16	6	22	210,000
Trinidad and Tobago	1	1	2	19,700
Uruguay	4	—	4	174,000
Venezuela	6	15	21	401,100
TOTAL	126	91	217	6,645,700

[1] Closed circuit service: not counted in totals.

SOURCE: United States Information Agency.

$$\left(\begin{array}{c} Notes\ to \\ Chapters \end{array} \right)$$

1. SMALL SCREEN, BIG WORLD

1. *London Observer*, September 20, 1959.

2. *Time*, April 6, 1962.

3. Speech before the Liberty Bell Award luncheon, Philadelphia, June 14, 1962.

4. It is difficult to document this view in the euphoric accounts of television's early years written largely by the industry's resident historians. However, a respected British source, former BBC television chief Sir Gerald Beadle, recalls that the two *eminences grises* of U.S. television, David Sarnoff of NBC and William Paley of CBS, separately acknowledged to him their disinterest in television during the late thirties. *Television: A Critical Review*, by Gerald Beadle (London: George Allen & Unwin, 1963), p. 41.

5. Specifically, Hitler's opening speech in the 1938 propaganda campaign against Czechoslovakia was televised in a number of Berlin cinemas. *Nazi Propaganda*, Z. A. B. Zeman (London: Oxford University Press, 1964), p. 154.

6. The survey cited is the annual Roper Poll determination of media influences in U.S. public opinion. The 1963 results are summarized in *Variety*, February 5, 1964.

7. Richard Hoggart in *Encounter* (London), January, 1960.

8. "Old School Tie is Snapped," Anthony Sampson, *Washington Post*, April 18, 1965.

9. *Life*, June 12, 1964, p. 64.

2. UP FROM ALEXANDRA PALACE

1. Although the credit for the first commercially feasible television system must go to Shoenberg and Franklyn, the contribution of John Baird—the man who lost out—deserves at least footnote mention, primarily for his single-minded efforts to force the BBC and the British government to take an active interest in television. Baird also sparked considerable interest in television in the United States through his imaginatve and successful effort to transmit television pictures across the Atlantic by short wave in 1928.

Two years earlier he had demonstrated the transmission of live images by television from one room to another in a laboratory in London's Soho district. It was probably the first public transmission of live images. See *Television, Today and Tomorrow,* by Sydney A. Moseley and H. J. Barton Chapple (New York: Isaac Pitman & Sons, 1930), pp. 2-3.

2. "The Evolution of Television 1927–1943 as Reported in the Annual Reports of the Federal Radio Commission and the Federal Communications Commission," *Journal of Broadcasting,* Summer, 1960, Vol. 4, No. 3, pp. 199-240. Also "Regulatory Influences Upon Television's Development," Robert H. Stern, *American Journal of Economics and Sociology,* July, 1963, Vol. 22, No. 3, pp. 347-62.

3. *Television: A World Survey,* Reports on Facilities of Mass Communications (Paris: UNESCO, 1952), p. 58.

4. *Ibid.,* p. 170.

5. The survey is described in *BBC Quarterly* (London), Spring, 1952.

6. For background on these developments, see "Aspects of Television in Western Europe," Committee on the Judiciary, House of Representatives, Washington, D.C., January, 1959.

7. The charge was made by Pierre Lazaroff in *Cahiers de la Télévision* (Paris), No. 1, December, 1962.

8. *New York Times,* May 27, 1964.

9. The details of this campaign are outlined in *Pressure Group: The Campaign for Commercial Television in England,* by H. H. Wilson (New Brunswick, N.J.: Rutgers University Press, 1961).

10. *Ibid.,* p. 171.

11. *Variety,* November 14, 1962.

12. A left-oriented description of the interlocking connection between political power and the British television industry is contained in *Power Behind the Screen,* by Clive Jenkins (London: Macgibbon and Kee, 1961).

13. *The New Look—A Social History of the Forties and Fifties,* by Harry Hopkins (London: Secker & Warburg, 1963), pp. 400-16.

14. *Variety,* April 1, 1965, quoting a speech by Alphonse Ouimet, president of the Canadian Broadcasting Corporation.

15. *Broadcasting Without Barriers,* by G. A. Codding (Paris: UNESCO, 1959), p. 128.

16. The legal and administrative details of the dispute between the *land* governments and Bonn are given in two articles, both entitled "Report from the Federal Republic of Germany," by Egon Wagner in *EBU Review* (Geneva), No. 67B, May, 1961, pp. 23-36, and *EBU Review,* No. 72B, March, 1962, pp. 48-52.

17. A number of such incidents are described in "West German TV— The Way Ahead," Thomas Petry, *Television Quarterly,* Vol. II, No. 3, Summer, 1963, pp. 58-66.

18. The conception of Japan as a country of adaptable but unskilled labor is disproved by the training records of postwar Japanese children. In 1962 just over 40 percent left school at the minimum leaving age of fifteen, another 45 percent remained in school until eighteen, and 10 percent were in colleges and universities. By comparison 60 percent of British children left school at fifteen and only 7 percent went on to college. *Economist* (London), September 1, 1962, p. 793.

19. "A History of the National Association of Commercial Broadcasters in Japan," Saburo Sakai, *EBU Review* (Geneva), No. 74B, July, 1962, pp. 9-12.

20. An account of Shoriki's TV activities can be found in *Shoriki— Miracle Man of Japan*, by Edward Uhlan and Dana L. Thomas (New York: Exposition Press, 1957); also in brochures issued by the Nippon Television Network Corporation, notably *How Television Came to Japan* (November, 1955).

21. A useful summary of the commercial development of Japanese television is contained in "Television in Japan Today," Sadao Mazaki, *Broadcasting*, February 12, 1963, p. 114.

22. *New York Times*, June 7, 1965.

3. EAST OF SUEZ, SOUTH OF THE RIO GRANDE

1. *Variety*, October 10, 1962.

2. *Television: A World Survey*, a booklet issued in 1952, and a supplement, issued in 1955, provide the most authoritative background material on TV's development during the late forties and early fifties. The booklet is particularly thorough in describing the situation in Cuba.

3. *Ibid.*, pp. 45-50.

4. *Ibid.*, p. 93.

5. *Variety*, October 10, 1962.

6. The best general accounts of Señor Mestre's television activities since he fled Cuba are contained in *Variety*: "TV: The Best of Gaucho," October 10, 1962; "Mestre Rides Again," January 13, 1965.

7. "Mestre Rides Again."

8. A television station had been authorized by the Bolivian government as early as 1961. Television in Paraguay is still in the "talking stage."

9. A useful summary of Malaysian TV's first two years of operations is contained in *Variety*, June 22, 1965.

10. The arguments, pro and con, are given in *The Wall Street Journal*, June 9, 1964.

11. The announcement was made originally in the Hungarian publication *Esti Hirlap* (Budapest), March 1, 1965.

12. Korean television is surveyed in *Variety*, June 2, 1965.

13. *Television: A World Survey*, p. 11. Television operations were resumed by the Moroccan government, using the old French equipment, in 1962.

14. The French and Italians were primarily interested in seeking out markets for television equipment, not in investing in overseas television operations. The Americans, British, and Japanese have been interested in television equipment sales and they have often tied their participation in overseas stations to such sales.

15. In 1965 the East Germans were reportedly negotiating the gift of television studio equipment to the Indian government, a transaction that was canceled out by the Indian acceptance of a similar offer by the West German government.

16. For an account of Roy Thomson's rise to eminence in British journalism, see *Time*, July 24, 1964, p. 71.

17. *The Annual Review for 1964 of The Thomson Organization, Ltd.* (London), p. 9.

18. *Nigeria Trade Journal* (Lagos), October–December, 1959, Vol. 7, No. 4, p. 165, contains a description of the early financial and administrative history of Nigerian television.

19. *Variety*, August 23, 1961.

20. Despite their dependence on commercial operations, the Nigerians have taken the lead in developing educational television in Africa.

21. *Variety*, March 11, 1963.

22. Interview with E. V. Badejo, director of programs, Nigerian Broadcasting Corporation, at Brandeis University, Waltham, Mass., September 24, 1962.

23. With the break-up of the Rhodesian federation in 1963, the station in Kitwe became part of the communications facilities of the new nation of Zambia.

24. Interview with Ralph Cable, Rhodesian government audio-visual officer, Brandeis University, September 25, 1962.

25. *Broadcasting*, January 11, 1965.

26. *Variety*, October 30, 1961; August 5, 1964.

27. Both Kenya and Rhodesia nationalized their TV systems in 1964, thus ending the Thomson interest in the medium there.

28. For example, Kenya's commercial TV operations included the following interests among its stockholders: National Broadcasting Co. of New York, Twentieth Century-Fox, East African Newspapers, Ltd., Nakura Press, Ltd., plus the Thomson interests. *Variety*, October 18, 1961.

29. This French involvement is described, country by country, in *La Radiodiffusion Harmonisée au Service du Développement*, by André Célarié (Paris: Les Cahiers Africains, No. 6, Editions Créations de Presse, 1963).

30. *Overseas Television Developments in 1964* (Washington, D.C.: USIA, April, 1965), p. 28.

31. *Variety*, December 23, 1964.

32. "Low-Cost National Television Comes to East Africa," William S. Halstead, *Multiplier*, staff magazine of the U.S. Agency for International Development (AID), June, 1964, pp. 22-27.

33. *New York Times*, November 10, 1964.

34. This problem is surveyed in *Developing Information Media in Africa*, Reports and Papers on Mass Communication, No. 37 (Paris: UNESCO, 1962). A more current report is found in "Meeting on the Introduction and Development of Television in Africa," a summary of a UNESCO seminar held in Lagos in September, 1964, reprinted in *Television and Adult Education* (Paris), No. 15, October, 1964, pp. 43-51. Another useful background document is *Communications Media In Tropical Africa*, a fourteen-nation survey of television and other media made for the U.S. International Cooperation Administration (ICA) in 1961 by Arno Huth.

35. *The Development of Television in the Middle East, Africa and Asia*, by A. D. Dunlap (Cambridge, Mass.: Center for International Studies, M.I.T., April, 1957), contains a useful survey of early TV developments in Iraq and neighboring countries.

36. *Variety*, January 6, 1965.

37. *New York Times,* October 10, 1964.

38. Television's role in this program is described in a Riyadh dispatch by Dana Adams Schmidt, "Saudi Arabia: Major Changes Due," *New York Times,* November 8, 1964.

39. In their anti-Nasser fervor at the time, Syrian nationalists condemned television as an "unwarranted luxury." *Overseas Television Developments in 1961* (Washington, D.C.: USIA, April, 1962), p. 27.

40. *Variety,* February 20, 1963.

41. "The Future of Television in Pakistan," A. F. Kalimullah, *CETO News,* No. 6 (London: Center for Educational Television Overseas, March, 1965), pp. 9-10.

42. Although radio began in British India as a series of private stations —including one operated by the Young Men's Christian Association—it has been a nationalized operation since the early 1930's. See "Nationalization of Broadcasting in India," J. V. S. Ramasastri, *Indian Economic Journal,* July, 1959, pp. 62-63.

43. Editorial in *Sunday Statesman* (Calcutta), April 29, 1962.

44. For a useful summary of the early fight to introduce commercial television into India, see "The Challenge of Television," a special supplement to the November 21, 1959, issue of *Eastern Economist* (New Delhi).

45. *Variety,* May 27, 1964.

46. *Washington Post,* November 10, 1964.

47. *Variety,* June 23, 1965.

4. TELEVISION'S GLOBAL NETWORKS

1. See Chapter 8 for a detailed description of this development.

2. In July, 1959, OIR's organizational title was changed to International Radio and Television Organization. For a description of postwar developments in this field, see "Origin and First Steps of the EBU Programme Committee," *EBU Review* (Geneva), No. 85B, May, 1964.

3. European national networks had three standards that had to be made compatible for international operations: the British 405-line system, French 819-line system, and 625 lines for the rest of Europe.

4. The magazine is published monthly in two separate editions, one on technical affairs and the other on administrative, legal, and programing subjects.

5. Not all of these, however, were Eurovision network programs. A large percentage of the programs sent to the United States are bilateral relays intended to service the American commercial networks' news operations.

6. During 1963, RTF provided Eurovision with 134 originations of all kinds. This was twice the number of originations of any other single member of the network. Although this record is undoubtedly due in large part to RTF's coverage of French domestic events, it is also explained by the importance of Paris as an international news center. See *EBU Review* (Geneva), No. 85B, May, 1964, p. 25.

7. A detailed statistical summary can be found in *EBU Review* (Geneva), No. 91B, May, 1965, p. 51. The discrepancy between the number of networks that originate and those that pick up Eurovision news transmissions can be explained by the fact that American, Canadian, and Eastern

European networks generally do not contribute news items to the daily Eurovision exchange but are occasional users of its services. The exchange procedures are described in detail in "The Eurovision News Transmissions —A First Step in World-wide News," J. W. Rengelink, in the same issue of *EBU Review*.

8. "Experimental Color TV Link Across Europe," *New Scientist* (London), No. 286, May 10, 1962, p. 264.

9. For a description of Eurovision's technical operation, see "Eurovision," Georges Hansen (director of the EBU Technical Center), *Telefilm International* (Los Angeles), January, 1962, p. 27.

10. For a more detailed description of Eurovision involvement in communications satellite activities, see Chapter 11.

11. Given the exigencies of politics within the Communist bloc, Albania has not become a member of Intervision. Yugoslavia has been an active member of Eurovision for a number of years; in 1964 the Yugoslavs announced that they were building a relay tower in Northern Serbia that would connect them directly with Intervision, of which they are also a member.

12. OIRT members include Albania, Bulgaria, Communist China, Cuba, Czechoslovakia, the United Arab Republic, Finland, East Germany, Hungary, Iraq, North Korea, Mali, Mongolia, Poland, Rumania, the Soviet Union, and North Viet Nam.

13. For an Intervision official's description of the organization, see "Intervision," Ales Suchy, *World Radio-TV Handbook*, O. Lund Johansen (ed.), (18th ed.; Hellerup, Denmark: 1964), p. 26.

14. The report on Intervision appeared in the Polish weekly, *Polityka*, March 23, 1963. An English translation can be found in *East Europe* (New York), March, 1964.

15. *New York Times*, April 13, 1964.

16. *Ibid.*, February 13, 1964.

17. Eleven such organizations are ABU charter members: Australian Broadcasting Commission, Broadcasting Corporation of China (Taiwan), All India Radio, Japan Broadcasting Corporation (NHK), Korean Broadcasting System, Radiodiffusion National Lao, Radio Malaysia, New Zealand Broadcasting Corporation, Radio Pakistan, Philippine Broadcasting Service, and the UAR Broadcasting Corporation (Cairo).

18. It would, however, be wrong to dismiss the proposed Asiavision network simply as a Japanese commercial venture. Its organizers have an awareness of its potential political effect. One of them declared, in a 1962 Tokyo interview with the author, that Asiavision "was something like your American Peace Corps."

19. Not the least of the problems facing the proposed Asian network would be the admission of the Chinese Communists into its activities. The Chinese Reds, who already have considerable television experience, are well aware of the propaganda potential of a link with other Asian television systems.

20. *Variety*, October 2, 1963.

21. The proposals were made at the special European Broadcasting Union meeting held in New York shortly after the launching of the first

Telstar communications satellite in 1962. There were some indications at the time that the European members of EBU resented the manner in which the Americans presented their proposals without first consulting privately with their EBU associates. See *Variety,* October 10, 1962.

5. TV POLITICS, INTERNATIONAL STYLE

1. *New York Times,* March 19, 1965.

2. The survey, made by Social Research, Inc., is summarized in *Broadcasting,* June 15, 1964.

3. *Overseas Television Developments in 1963* (Washington, D.C.: USIA Research and Reference Service, April, 1964), p. 9.

4. *Ibid.,* p. 29.

5. *Television and the Political Image,* by J. Trenaman and D. McQuail (London: Methuen Books, 1961), p. 233.

6. For a summary of the debates' effects, see "A New Tool for Politics," Rowland Evans, Jr., *The Eighth Art* (New York: Holt, Rinehart & Winston, 1962), p. 44. President Kennedy himself often credited the debates with being the decisive factor in his 1960 election.

7. *Time,* November 28, 1960.

8. *New York Times,* October 24, 1963.

9. *Variety,* July 22, 1964.

10. *Economist* (London), April 20, 1963, p. 222.

11. *Variety,* January 6, 1965.

12. *Ibid.,* November 27, 1963; November 25, 1964.

13. *New York Times,* May 28, 1964.

14. *Television: A World Survey,* pp. 115-16.

15. The BBC has a long tradition of Welsh programing, stemming in part from its charter requirement to provide such programs.

16. *Variety,* October 10, 1962.

17. *Washington Post,* March 21, 1964.

18. *New York Times,* April 26, 1964.

19. *New York Times,* October 14, 1964.

20. *Broadcasting,* September 9, 1963.

21. The formula for the calendar year 1965 limited TV political broadcasts to a total of 140 minutes, allowing 60 minutes each for the Labor and Conservative parties and 20 minutes for the Liberals. *Times* (London), December 17, 1964.

22. *Broadcasting,* June 6, 1963.

23. *Ibid.,* January 4, 1965.

24. For details, see twenty-fifth annual report of the Cinematograph Films Council (London, 1962).

25. *Variety,* November 27, 1963.

26. *Ibid.,* July 1, 1964.

27. *Ibid.,* January 8, 1964.

28. *Ibid.,* June 12, 1963.

29. *Ibid.,* June 30, 1964.

30. *New York Times,* January 19, 1965.

31. *Variety,* April 29, 1964.

32. West German TV's advertising revenue is less than 10 percent of that

of the German press, mainly because TV is limited to twenty minutes of commercials nightly. For a description of the press-radio dispute, see "Report from the Federal Republic of Germany," Egon Wagner, *EBU Review* (Geneva), No. 84B, March, 1964.

33. *Variety*, January 12, 1965.

34. A 1962 royal commission recommended that newspapers divest themselves of control of television properties as a step toward preserving diversity of opinion in Britain. *New York Times*, September 20, 1963. See also *Economist* (London), September 22, 1963, for a useful analysis of the commission's findings.

35. Quoted in *Broadcasting*, May 25, 1964.

36. *British Broadcasting Corporation Handbook* (1965 ed.), p. 161.

37. An influential minority in Canada has proposed that the CBC eliminate commercial advertising altogether on the theory that such a move would permit the corporation to serve over-all national interests better. The most influential support for the plan came from Dr. Andrew Stewart in 1964 when he was head of the Board of Broadcast Governors, the Canadian counterpart of the FCC. To no one's surprise, Canadian commercial broadcasters support the idea, too. *Variety*, June 3, 1964.

38. The figure is taken from an analysis of commercial television profits and prospects in *Economist* (London), September 21, 1963, p. 1037.

39. *Variety*, July 31, 1963.

40. For a description of USIA television's early activities, see the author's *The Strategy of Truth* (Washington, D.C.: Public Affairs Press, 1961), pp. 100-19.

41. *Radio i Telewizja* (Prague), March 15, 1964.

42. *Variety*, July 29, 1964.

43. It is relevant to note, in assessing this trend, that the BBC's second television service has generally fared badly in its attempt to win listeners from the commercial network. Its drawing power has been largely at the expense of the regular BBC television service.

6.   THREE TV STARS: CASTRO, de GAULLE, NASSER

1. *World Communications, Press, Radio, Television, Film* (Paris: United Nations Educational and Social Council, 1964); also, *Basic Facts and Figures* (Paris: UNESCO, 1962).

2. "Cuban TV: The Fidel Show," R. Hart Phillips, *New York Times*, July 23, 1961.

3. For a detailed description of the nationalization of Cuban television, see U.S. Department of State *Bulletin*, Vol. 43, No. 1105, August 29, 1960, p. 331.

4. "Cuban Television's One-Man Show," Tad Szulc, *The Eighth Art* (New York: Holt, Rinehart & Winston, 1962), pp. 100-02.

5. The Conte Aguero incident is described in detail in Department of State *Bulletin, op. cit.*, pp. 333-34.

6. Their chances were slim in any event. In February, 1959, Castro replaced the democratic 1950 Cuban constitutions, as had his dictatorial predecessor, with his own "Fundamental Law" which deprived citizens of most basic rights. See *Cuba and the Rule of Law* (Amsterdam: International Commission of Jurists, 1962).

7. Favorable atmospheric conditions in November, 1964, permitted the direct reception of most of a two-hour major speech by Castro on Miami's Channel 6.

8. Cesar Escalanta, head of the Commission of Revolutionary Orientation of the United Party of Socialist Revolution (PURS), speaking at a meeting for propaganda workers in Havana, October 14, 1964.

9. "Cuba's Fumbling Marxism," James Cameron, *Atlantic Monthly*, September, 1964, p. 96.

10. The Swiss journalist, Jean Ziegler, writing in an International Press Institute report, summarized in the *Washington Post*, February 29, 1960.

11. According to one report from Havana, Cubans must get an order from the district Committee of Defense before their TV set can be repaired. *Reporter* (New York), March 14, 1963.

12. "What Castro is Doing to Cuba," *U.S. News and World Report*, March 1, 1965.

13. *New York Times*, April 12, 1964.

14. *Variety*, June 3, 1964.

15. For an analysis of this aspect of French TV, see "Television for the General," John Weightman, *Observer* (London), February 3, 1963.

16. "Letter from Paris," *New Yorker*, October 6, 1962.

17. *Variety*, July 17, 1963. The period covered the year ending July 1, 1963.

18. The controversy is summarized in "Their Master's Voice," *Economist* (London), March 2, 1963.

19. *New York Times*, February 27, 1964.

20. *Time*, July 3, 1964.

21. *EBU Review* (Geneva), No. 85B, May, 1964, p. 25.

22. Tass European transmission, February 9, 1963.

23. *Washington Post*, July 11, 1963.

24. *Cahiers de la Télévision* (Paris), No. 1, December, 1962.

25. *New York Times*, November 5, 1962.

26. *Variety*, July 3, 1963.

27. The group sought to have television and radio broadcasting included under an old French law that requires newspaper editors to publish such rebuttals within eight days of their receipt. *Broadcasting*, January 6, 1964.

28. "Independent Deterrent," *Economist* (London), May 30, 1964, p. 945, provides an analysis of the new regulations. An English translation of the bill authorizing ORTF is given in *Television and Adult Education* (Paris), No. 13, May, 1964, pp. 31-34.

29. Colonel Nasser did not take formal charge of the new regime until April, 1954. The new government bore the stamp of his ideas and personality, however, from the beginning.

30. Middle East News Agency dispatch from Cairo, February 1, 1965.

31. A narrative account of the development of UAR broadcasting can be found in "Television in Egypt," Bahie Nassr, *Broadcasting*, June 10, 1963.

32. *Television and Radio Transmissions* (Cairo: UAR Information Department, 1961).

33. This project is described in the monograph, *A Five Year Developmental Program for the Use of Instructional Television to Extend Quality*

Education in the United Arab Republic, by I. Keith Tyler and Margaret Tyler (Cairo: Cultural Affairs Section, American Embassy, June, 1963).

34. For an Egyptian view of the medium's role in these areas, see "The Part Played by Television in Developing Countries," by Abbas Ahmed, a paper submitted by the UAR delegation to a research seminar at the Third International TV Festival, Alexandria, August, 1964.

35. From a London lecture given by Murrow in 1959. Quoted in "Television and the British General Elections," John Beavan, *EBU Review* (Geneva), No. 59B, January, 1960, p. 8.

7. U.S. TELEVISION'S OVERSEAS MARKETS

1. The programs are, respectively, "The Lucy Show" (Spanish), "Fractured Flickers" (German), "Fair Exchange" (Swedish), and "Jazz Scene U.S.A." (Polish).

2. This revenue may be as high as 150 million dollars annually.

3. *Variety,* January 22, 1964. By comparison, the overseas distribution of U.S. feature films accounts for about 55 percent of Hollywood's total syndication revenues.

4. An excellent, though somewhat dated, survey of the television film industry is *The Economics of Television Film Production and Distribution,* by Irving Bernstein, a report issued by the Screen Actors Guild in 1960.

5. *Ibid.,* p. 39.

6. *Broadcasting,* November 25, 1963.

7. A detailed account of television's early effect on Hollywood is given in "Hollywood and Television," *Times* (London), January 12, 1962. Another useful survey of this subject is contained in *Television,* September, 1963.

8. The Fremantle firm, which represents thirty independent producers and distributors abroad, claims that the Hopalong series has never failed to run in seven countries at one time since it was syndicated abroad more than a dozen years ago. *Broadcasting,* December 30, 1962.

9. *Broadcasting,* March 25, 1963. The report also notes that Canadian stations have insisted on the release of such programs before their U.S. showing to attract audiences who would otherwise see them on nearby Stateside channels.

10. For a description of the conditions that led the networks to organize TPEA, see *Broadcasting,* September 21, 1959. The existence of two trade organizations doing precisely the same work overseas mirrors domestic conflicts-of-interest within the industry. Most objective observers feel that the TPEA-MPEA split probably has adverse effects on the expansion of U.S. telefilm syndication abroad. See *Variety,* November 27, 1963.

11. The U.S. Department of Commerce lists only "Motion Picture Film Features, 16 mm., exposed or exposed and developed, 1,600 linear feet or over" in its export statistics. This category includes some television films, but certainly not all. For instance, it does not include 35 mm. film or videotape.

12. See survey by the British Institute of Practitioners in Advertising, reported in *Variety,* August 14, 1963. In 1963, the total advertising revenue of British commercial television stations was 301 million dollars according to Media Records, Ltd., *Variety,* February 26, 1964.

13. *Variety*, July 31, 1963.

14. The figures are from the annual report of the Australian Broadcasting Control Board for the year ending June 30, 1963, citing statistics of the Commonwealth Film Censorship Board. *Broadcasting*, December 9, 1963.

15. *Variety*, February 27, 1963.

16. *Ibid.*, December 18, 1963.

17. *Ibid.*, February 27, 1963.

18. *Ibid.*, March 27, 1963.

19. *Ibid.*, November 11, 1963.

20. *Ibid.*, May 15, 1963.

21. *Ibid.*, February 25, 1964. NBC also is the exclusive U.S. distributor for this coverage.

22. *Ibid.*, September 25, 1963.

23. *Ibid.*, March 11, 1964. ITN reportedly has close working arrangements with CBS-TV.

24. The smaller U.S. networks—the so-called group stations—have also begun to investigate the potentialities of the overseas market. The most active such "group" is the broadcasting division of Time, Inc. This firm purchased, and then sold, an interest in a Beirut television station in recent years. It has been interested in television operations in such diverse countries as Sweden and Pakistan. In 1963, Time Inc. also invested in a British pay-TV enterprise, British Telemeter.

25. Advertisement in *Broadcasting*, February 17, 1964.

26. *Variety*, August 23, 1961.

27. *Ibid.*, July 19, 1961.

28. *Broadcasting*, April 1, 1963.

29. *Variety*, April 14, 1965.

30. *Ibid.*, November 20, 1963.

31. *Observer* (London), December 16, 1962.

32. For details, see *Variety*, January 1, 1964.

33. Domestic Japanese TV does both. It has, for instance, its own cowboy stars, led by Jo Shishido. Out of deference to his American counterparts, he has modestly described himself as the third-fastest gun in the West. *Time*, August 3, 1962.

34. *Variety*, March 3, 1964.

35. *Broadcasting*, February 3, 1964.

36. For an interesting account of the early period of British pay-TV developments, see "Companies Get Ready for Start of Pay-TV," by "Mammon," *Observer* (London), December 9, 1962. For a discussion of the economics of British pay-TV, see *Economist* (London), January 26, 1963.

37. *Broadcasting*, November 18, 1963.

38. *Variety*, December 11, 1963.

8. COMMUNIST TELEVISION

1. The statistics on receivers are taken from *USSR in Figures* (Moscow: Central Statistical Publishing House, April, 1965), p. 102.

2. Soviet historiography claims that a Russian biologist, P. N. Bakhnetev, transmitted the first televised images in 1880. A more substantial Russian claim is that Boris Rosing of the St. Petersburg Institute of Technology designed the first television system using a cathode-ray tube as a receiver

in 1907. See *Radiotekhnika i electronika* (Moscow), No. 111, November, 1957, for a survey of the technological development of television in the USSR. An English translation of the survey is contained in *A Survey of Soviet Communications Electronics,* Paul E. Green (ed.) (Cambridge, Mass.: Lincoln Laboratory Group Report 34-76, M.I.T., September, 1958), pp. 16-18.

3. For a description of Soviet television programing at the time, see "A Survey of Programming on the Central Studios of TV, Moscow, January–June 1960," Richard Tuber, *Journal of Broadcasting,* Fall, 1960, pp. 315-25.

4. "On the tasks of party propaganda in present-day conditions," Resolution of the Party Central Committee, January 9, 1960, *Pravda,* January 10. English translation in *Current Digest of the Soviet Press,* Vol. XII, No. 2, February 10, 1960, pp. 17-23. *Current Digest* will be cited hereafter as *CDSP.*

5. "On improving Soviet radio broadcasting and on further developing television," Party Central Committee resolution reprinted in the committee's magazine *Partiinaia Zhizn* (Party Life), No. 4, February, 1960. *CDSP,* Vol. XII, No. 29, August 17, 1960, p. 10.

6. *Radio and Television in the USSR* by S. V. Kaftanov and others (Washington: Library of Congress Joint Publications Research Service, 1961), p. 30. This useful compendium of official Soviet attitudes on television and radio is a translation of *Radio i Televidenive v SSR* (Moscow: State Publishing House, 1960).

7. *Ibid.,* p. 36.

8. Interview with Juri Fokin, chief of Moscow television news broadcasting, Robert Lewis Shayon, *Saturday Review,* June 9, 1962.

9. This description is from *Soviet Life,* the official Soviet magazine distributed in the United States under the U.S.-USSR 1958 cultural agreement, Vol. 5, No. 106, July, 1965, p. 47.

10. "Finding Programs to Meet Television's Voracious Needs," G. Kazakov, *Kommunist* (Moscow), No. 8, June, 1959. *CDSP,* Vol. XI, No. 25, July 22, 1959, p. 16.

11. For a description of the 1965 program schedule on Moscow television, see "Opiate of the Masses," *Newsweek,* March 8, 1965, p. 83.

12. Kazakov, *op. cit.*

13. *Pravda,* May 7, 1959, *CDSP,* Vol. XI, No. 18, June 3, 1959, p. 7.

14. "A Word from Our Sponsor—the Kremlin," Marya Mannes, *New York Times Magazine,* March 5, 1961, p. 44.

15. *New York Times,* May 28, 1965.

16. *Ibid.,* July 18, 1963.

17. *Ibid.,* February 21, 1965.

18. Kazakov, *op. cit.,* p. 16.

19. "Literary Life in Moscow," Olga Carlisle, *New York Times Book Review,* March 14, 1965, p. 7.

20. *Variety,* October 21, 1964.

21. *Kulturni Tvorba* (Prague), September 10, 1964.

22. *Variety,* February 22, 1962.

23. For a general review of Western influences on East European TV, see "Communist Radio, TV Imitate the West," *Iron Curtain News,* No. 26, Radio Free Europe Committee, June 3, 1964, pp. 2-9.

24. *Television: A World Survey*, 1955 supplement, p. 31.

25. The television survey was reported by CTK (Czech News Agency), May 30, 1964.

26. *Zycie Gospodarcze* (Warsaw), January 30, 1965.

27. The survey was described by the chairman of the Polish Radio and TV Affairs Committee, W. Sokorski, in a talk given on Radio Warsaw, January 1, 1965.

28. The list of six serials was given in *Radio i Telewizja* (Warsaw), June 7, 1964. The attack on American programs appeared in the July 5, 1964, issue.

29. "And Now, for 25,000 Zlotys, What's the Hit on Polish TV?" David Halberstam, *New York Times*, May 9, 1965.

30. "Gomulka Decries Foreign Propaganda," *East Europe* (New York), June, 1963, p. 49.

31. *Variety*, October 7, 1964.

32. *Washington Post*, September 6, 1964.

33. For a useful summary of East German television, see "East German TV Viewers Prefer Non-political Fare," Hans Hoen, *Variety*, January 20, 1965.

34. Radio Prague, June 10, 1965.

35. *Variety*, June 16, 1965.

36. New China News Agency international service in English, December 27, 1960.

37. The loud-speaker project is described by Seymour Topping in a Hong Kong dispatch to the *New York Times*, December 4, 1964.

38. "Television in Asia," special supplement to the *Far Eastern Economic Review* (Hong Kong), January 16, 1964, p. 114.

39. *Jen-Min Jih-Pa* (*People's Daily*), Peking, August 12, 1962.

40. "On Peking's TV Screen," Lung Hao-Jan, *China Reconstructs* (Peking), December, 1964, p. 39.

9. ETV: THE EUROPEAN AND JAPANESE EXPERIENCE

1. *Broadcasting*, November 9, 1964.

2. *Ibid.*, April 12, 1965.

3. *Variety*, August 28, 1963.

4. *Ibid.*, April 21, 1965.

5. "School Broadcasting, Sound," F. N. Lloyd Williams (director of BBC school radio broadcasting), *EBU Review* (Geneva), No. 70B, November, 1961, p. 44.

6. The most famous of these early studies, *Television and the Child*, was published by Britain's Nuffield Foundation in 1958. For a summary, see Jones, *op. cit.*, pp. 43ff.

7. *Ibid.*, p. 44.

8. For a description of early development of the "Telescuola" see *La Radiotelevision Scolaire en Italie*, published by RAI, December, 1961. Also, "Telescuola Enters Its Second Year," Maria Grazia Puglisi, *EBU Review* (Geneva), No. 59B, January, 1960, pp. 12-13, and "Educational Television," Italo Nervi, *EBU Review*, No. 69B, September, 1961, pp. 14-17.

9. "Television and the Fight Against Illiteracy," Maria Grazia Puglisi, *EBU Review* (Geneva), No. 82B, November, 1963, p. 7.

10. *EBU Review* (Geneva), No. 72B, March, 1962, p. 24.

11. For a review of early French ETV efforts, see "Ten Years of School Television," Henri Dieuzeide, *EBU Review* (Geneva), No. 69B, September, 1961.

12. *New York Times*, January 19, 1965.

13. These experiments are described in two reports in UNESCO's monograph series on mass communications: *Television—An Experiment in Community Reception in French Villages*, Report No. 5, August, 1952, and *Television and Tele-Clubs in Rural Communities*, Report No. 16, July, 1955.

14. The system is described in *EBU Review* (Geneva), No. 75B, September, 1962, pp. 17-18.

15. René Dovaz, chairman of the Swiss Central Committee of School Broadcasting, in *EBU Review* (Geneva), No. 70B, November, 1961, p. 42.

16. "Third Program Choice for Viewers," *EBU Review* (Geneva), No. 88B, November, 1964, p. 43.

17. "A Background Note on BBC School Broadcasting," School Broadcasting Council for the United Kingdom, London, 1963, p. 3.

18. "Learning from Television," Peter Laslett, *Twentieth Century* (London), Autumn, 1963, pp. 58-66.

19. The 1954 Television Act authorizing commercial television provided its own pressure in this direction by requiring ITA to set up a "Children's Advisory Committee" to monitor the tone and content of programs for young viewers. "Independent Television for Schools," Noel Stevenson, *EBU Review* (Geneva), No. 69B, September, 1961, p. 24.

20. *Variety*, May 27, 1964.

21. This view is described in "The Phoney Fourth Service," *New Statesman* (London), December 15, 1961. The official ITA position is described in a pamphlet, *Educational Television*, issued by the authority in 1961.

22. *Future Prospects in Broadcasting*, by Sir Hugh Carleton Greene, the Sixth Bishop Bell memorial lecture, Workers Educational Association, Chichester, issued as BBC Publication No. 5290, 1963, p. 7.

23. Jenkins, *op. cit.*, p. 279. Leeds University has since become a major center for study and research in educational television.

24. The Cambridge experiment is described in "University Pipeline," Peter Laslett, *Guardian* (Manchester), October 18, 1963.

25. *Economist* (London), December 16, 1961, pp. 1104-05. The newspaper commented further on its proposal in its issue of May 16, 1964, p. 700.

26. *Variety*, April 14, 1965.

27. *Broadcasting*, April 6, 1963.

28. "The First Year of School Television," Hrvoje Juracic, *EBU Review* (Geneva), No. 69B, September, 1961, pp. 33-36.

29. The experiment is described in "Big Brother's TV Set," William Benton, *Esquire*, March, 1963, p. 99.

30. For a summary of these and other details of Japanese ETV, see "Television for Teaching," Yoshida Maeda (general managing director of

NHK), *Guildhall Lectures—1962* (London: Macgibbon and Kee, Ltd., 1962), pp. 63-81; also, descriptions of Japanese educational broadcasting in the following issues of *EBU Review* (Geneva): No. 60B, March, 1960; No. 70B, November, 1961; No. 75B, September, 1962; No. 82B, November, 1963; No. 86B, July, 1964.

31. For a detailed description of NHK's correspondence school project, see "Experiences of the Japan Broadcasting Corporation in the Correspondence High School Course," Michio Nagahama, *EBU Review* (Geneva), No. 82B, November, 1963, pp. 25-32.

32. Maeda, *op. cit.*, p. 72.

10. ETV: NEW TOOL FOR DEVELOPING NATIONS

1. *Airborne Television and Universal Primary Education*, by Neil Hurley, S.J. (Santiago, Chile: Centro da Investigación y Acción Social, 1964), p. 4.

2. *EBU Review* (Geneva), No. 72B, March, 1962, p. 26.

3. For a useful summary of ETV's role in Colombian education, see *New York Times* educational supplement, January 13, 1965.

4. "Technical School Television in Argentina," Carlos Alberto Duhoura, S.J., *Television and Adult Education* (Paris), No. 13, March, 1964, pp. 7-10.

5. "Schools Television in Western Nigeria," by Douglas Grant, *EBU Review* (Geneva), No. 69B, September, 1961, p. 63.

6. For a survey of the role of educational radio and television in French-speaking areas of Africa, see *La Radiodiffusion Harmonisée au Service du Développement*, by André Célarié (Paris: Editions Créations de Presse, Les Cahiers Africains, No. 6, 1963). Célarié, a French radio newsman, also discusses the modernization role of radio and television in other African countries, as well as in the Middle East, South Asia, and Latin America.

7. "Educational Television in Iran," R. S. Hadsell and Gordon Butts, *Multiplier*, U.S. International Cooperation Administration (Washington, D.C.), July/August 1961, pp. 28-31.

8. "Television in Israel," Z. E. Kurzwell, *Television and Adult Education*, No. 12, February, 1964, pp. 47-50.

9. The UNESCO project is described in *Social Education Through Television*, Reports and Papers on Mass Communication, No. 38 (Paris: UNESCO, 1963). See also "First Steps Towards Educational Television," J. C. Mathur (director-general of All-India Radio), *EBU Review* (Geneva), No. 69B, September, 1961, pp. 47-50.

10. A detailed description of the board's experiment and an evaluation of its results are contained in *The Philippines' First TV College Course*, a study issued by the board in August, 1961.

11. UNESCO's early efforts in the television field are summarized in "TV at the Crossroads," Henry Cassirer, *Television Quarterly*, Vol. II, No. 3, Summer, 1963, pp. 68-71.

12. "Aid to the Broadcasting Organizations of the Developing Countries," *EBU Review* (Geneva), No. 88B, November, 1964, p. 61.

13. See *OCORA—au service des radiodiffusions nationales africaines et malagaches* (Paris: l'office de Coopération Radiophonique, September, 1963).

14. META lists as its "cooperating agencies" in addition to the Ateneo the following organizations: U.S. Agency for International Development, Association of Christian Schools and Colleges, Bureau of Public Schools, Bureau of Private Schools, Catholic Educational Association of the Philippines, Manila City Schools, National Science Development Board, Philippine Association of Colleges and Universities, Philippine Broadcastng Service, the Asia Foundation, UNESCO National Commission of the Philippines, and the United States Information Service.

15. For a summary of earlier experiments in Philippine school broadcasting, see *School Broadcasting in the Philippines* (Manila: Bureau of Public Schools, Department of Education of the Republic of the Philippines, 1964).

16. "School Broadcasting," Henri Dieuzeide, *EBU Review* (Geneva), No. 88B, November, 1964, p. 16.

11. TELEVISION SIGNALS FROM SPACE

1. A summary of early satellite accomplishments is contained in *Communications Satellite Experiments*, House Report No. 2560 (Washington: House of Representatives Committee on Science and Astronautics, December 2, 1962), p. 5.

2. "Communications Satellite Act of 1962," Hearings before the Committee on Foreign Relations, U.S. Senate, August 3-9, 1962, p. 126.

3. *Variety*, July 2, 1961, reporting remarks by FCC Commissioner T. A. M. Craven.

4. "Communications Satellite Act of 1962," testimony by USIA Director Edward R. Murrow, p. 128.

5. *Communications Satellites: Technical, Economic and International Developments* (Washington: Staff report of the U.S. Senate Committee on Aeronautical and Space Sciences, February 25, 1962), p. 133.

6. *Ibid.*, p. 102.

7. See *Outlook for Television* by Orrin E. Dunlap, Jr. (New York: Harper & Bros., 1932), pp. 79-85, for a summary of this and other long-distance, short-wave experiments in the television field.

8. Appendix to the second annual report of the Federal Radio Commission for 1928, Washington, D.C. Brief submitted by Dr. Alfred N. Goldsmith, chief broadcast engineer of the Radio Corporation of America, pp. 252-55.

9. "Extra-terrestrial Relays: Can Rocket Stations Give World-wide Radio Coverage?" Arthur C. Clarke, *Wireless World* (London), October, 1945, pp. 305-08.

10. "Orbital Radio Relays," Dr. John R. Pierce (communications research director, Bell Telephone Laboratories), *Jet Propulsion*, April, 1955, pp. 153-57.

11. *Communications Satellites: Technical, Economic and International Developments*, pp. 37-39.

12. A breakdown of these appropriations is contained in U.S. Senate Committee on Commerce Report No. 1584, Calendar No. 1544, June 11, 1962, p. 50.

13. *Communications Satellites: Technical, Economic and International Developments*, p. 65.

14. *Ibid.,* p. 28.
15. *Ibid.,* p. 64.
16. *Ibid.,* p. 193.
17. *Ibid.,* p. 42.
18. This excludes consideration of the "Project Score" satellite, which transmitted voice relay and teletype relay signals on ninety-seven different occasions after it was orbited in December, 1958.
19. *Communications Satellites: Technical, Economic and International Developments,* pp. 193-94.
20. *Fortune,* July, 1961, p. 255.
21. *New York Times,* December 31, 1960.
22. *Communications Satellites: Technical, Economic and International Developments,* p. 45.
23. *Ibid.,* p. 160.
24. This point was made by Frederick R. Kappell, board chairman of AT&T, in a speech in San Francisco, December 1, 1961.
25. The bill was introduced in the Senate by Senators Robert Kerr and Walter Magnuson (S. 2814) and in the House by Rep. George F. Miller, Jr. (H.R. 10138). The bill and the President's letter of transmittal are reproduced in *Communications Satellites: Technical, Economic and International Developments,* pp. 263-69.
26. The filibuster, led by Senators Wayne Morse and Estes Kefauver, was ended by the first cloture vote to pass the Senate in over thirty years.
27. A useful summary of the pros and cons of the new corporation is contained in "Some International Aspects of Communications Satellite Systems," by Dr. Samuel D. Estep of the University of Michigan Law School, reprinted in the *Congressional Record,* July 9, 1963, p. 11572. An incisive analysis of the system is contained in "On the Effects of Communications Satellites," Dallas W. Smythe, *Communications Explosion,* Paper No. 9, Program of Policy Studies in Science and Technology, The George Washington University, Washington, D.C., June, 1965, and its companion piece, "The Role of Communications Technology in Democracy," Neil P. Hurley, S.J., *ibid.*
28. "Heads of Satellite Firm Politely Tell Off FCC," *Washington Post,* August 6, 1963.
29. The implications of this move are described in *The Wall Street Journal,* May 17, 1965.
30. *Variety,* June 2, 1965.
31. *New York Times,* November 13, 1963.
32. *Washington Post,* February 10, 1964.
33. Two agreements were signed in connection with the formation of the new consortium. The first was an intergovernmental agreement establishing organizational principles for the new venture and setting up an International Interim Communications Satellite Committee having over-all responsibility for the space segment of the program. The second agreement involved the communications entity of each of the countries party to the first agreement. The Communications Satellite Corporation was the entity designated by the United States. For the texts of both agreements, see U.S. Department of State *Bulletin,* Vol. 51, No. 1313, August 24, 1964, p. 281.

34. European space policies and projects are authoritatively surveyed in *Air Force,* June, 1965, pp. 59-77.

35. A number of these predications, made shortly after the launching of the first Sputnik, are reprinted in *East Europe* (New York), April, 1958, p. 28.

36. *New York Times,* July 15, 1961, reporting on remarks made by Mr. Murrow before the House Committee on Science and Astronautics.

37. *Ibid.,* December 6, 1962.

38. *Ibid.,* September 14, 1963.

39. For a description of Soviet points of view on a space legal code, see "Soviet Attitudes Towards International Space Law," Robert D. Crane, *American Journal of International Law,* Vol. 56, 1962, p. 685. See also, "Conflicts Peril Space Agreement," *New York Times,* April 27, 1963.

40. *Holiday,* September, 1959, pp. 49-50.

41. *Variety,* July 7, 1965.

42. "Communications Satellite Act of 1962," p. 128.

43. *New York Times,* November 7, 1961. A technical description of the RCA proposal is contained in *A System for Direct Television Broadcasting Using Earth Satellite Repeaters,* Donald S. Bond (ed.) (Princeton, N.J.: Radio Corporation of America, David Sarnoff Laboratories, July, 1961).

44. "Statement of the President on Communications Satellite Policy," July 24, 1961, reproduced in *Communications Satellites: Technical, Economic and International Developments,* p. 45.

45. *Variety,* October 31, 1962.

46. *New York Times,* September 12, 1962.

A Note on
Research

Television developed so swiftly that it has yet to be given its proper status in mass-communications research and studies. This situation will undoubtedly change in the coming years. In the meantime, a note on the research that went into the making of this book might be useful to students of the subject.

My primary research sources were personal interviews and correspondence with television experts from over thirty countries. Interviews were done on the spot in the Middle East, the Far East, and Europe. I also talked with television specialists brought to this country under the State Department's cultural exchange program. Dr. Louis Cowan and his staff at Brandeis University's Communications Research Center were most helpful to me in arranging interviews with these visitors while they attended the center's seminars on television.

My second major source was the American television industry's trade press. The most fruitful of these sources is *Variety*, the lively journal of the entertainment industry whose coverage of overseas media developments dates from before World War I. Television is "show biz" both here and abroad; *Variety* is the most accurate and objective chronicler of its activities. Other American trade journals which provide continuing coverage of overseas television developments include *Broadcasting, Television, Printer's Ink, Advertising Age, Telefilm International, Television Digest,* and *Television Age.* The last-mentioned journal has a semiannual issue featuring overseas developments in the medium. At the scholarly level, the best American sources are *Television Quarterly,* published by Syracuse University's Newhouse Communications Center for the National Academy of Television Arts and Sciences, and *Journal of Broadcasting,* published at the University of Southern California.

Overseas, a number of specialized "little magazines" devoted to television studies have appeared in recent years. In Britain, the British Film Institute sponsors a quarterly magazine, *Contrast,* which chronicles the successes and foibles of the medium in Britain. In 1964, a group of Italian intellectuals founded a TV-film quarterly named *TVC.* The French *Cahiers de la Télévision* offers a well-edited, highbrow critique of Gaullist TV. Another Paris publication, *Culture et Télévision* (with an English-language edition, *Television and Adult Education*), is a primary source for material on the medium's worldwide educational value. This subject is also covered by a British magazine, *CETO Review,* issued quarterly in London by the Center for Educational Television Overseas.

Basic information—statistical and otherwise—can be found in several reference works. *World Radio-TV Handbook* is a yearly almanac of world broadcasting developments published by O. Lund Johanson in Hellerup, Denmark. Mr. Johanson relies heavily, and somewhat uncritically, on information supplied to him by broadcasting organizations throughout the world. The best American estimates on world television are contained in the annual *Television Factbook* published by *Television Digest.* Another useful source is the yearly research report on overseas television developments issued by the U.S. Information Agency, individual copies of which may be obtained by writing to the agency in Washington, D.C.

Developments in individual countries are chronicled in handbooks issued by local broadcasting organizations. In Britain, both the BBC and the Independent Television Authority put out such handbooks every year. Most other European broadcasting organizations have a similar service; one of the best is issued in English by JRT, the Yugoslav state broadcasting organization. Japan's state-chartered NHK network publishes an English-language version of its annual handbook, together with a monthly review, *NHK—Today and Tomorrow.* The National Association of Commercial Broadcasters in Japan (NAB) also issues an annual English-language handbook.

An indispensable source of information on world-wide television is *EBU Review,* published six times a year by the European Broadcasting Union in Geneva. French and English editions of the magazines are issued in two parts, one covering purely technical matters and the other, administrative, legal, and programing subjects. Although its editorial emphasis is on European television, *EBU Review* covers the medium's progress in all parts of the world. Its special numbers on educational TV are the standard references on this subject. A bimonthly review, available in French and English, is published by EBU's Communist counterpart, the International Radio and Television Organization (OIRT) in Prague.

All of the major television systems abroad now have their own research units. Many of them also rely on survey services offered by local advertising agencies and polling oganizations. It has been several decades since Sir John Reith, the first chief of the BBC, declared that "the real degradation of the BBC started with the invention of that hellish department which is called Listener Research." BBC audience studies are now a highly institutionalized part of the corporation's activities, but Sir John's suspicions about such activities linger on at the BBC and other television organizations. There is certainly not the hushed reverence assigned to audience surveys that one finds in many sectors of the industry in this country. No overseas country has developed the range of television surveys conducted in this country—from the well-known Nielsen and Trendex Polls to the Jack Mabley "plumber's poll." (Mr. Mabley, a Chicago newsman, once documented the fact that Chicago's water pressure fell substantially during TV commercials and proved that many Chicagoans deserted their sets at such opportune moments.)

A number of American polling organizations have extended their survey activities abroad. One important telefilm distributor, Screen Gems, in 1965 branched out into the surveying business through a Japanese subsidiary, Audience Studies, Inc. However, the bulk of surveying is done by such local organizations as Britain's Television Audience Measurement (TAM), Canada's Bureau of Broadcast Measurement, and Australia's George Patterson, Ltd.

The bookshelf literature on world television is still very narrow. The best over-all survey of early television developments, up to 1955, is contained in a UNESCO publication, *Television: A World Survey*, issued originally in 1952 in the UNESCO series "Reports on the Facilities of Mass Communication." Both it and a supplement issued in 1955 are now out of print; they are, however, indispensable guides to the medium's early development abroad. UNESCO presently issues a regular survey of all world media entitled *World Communications: Press, Radio, Television, Film*, as well as specialized monographs on television developments in educational and cultural fields.

The only general survey of world television that has come to my attention is "La Télévision dans le Monde—Organisation Administrative et Financière," by François Pigé, a 1962 University of Paris doctoral thesis describing television organizations in thirty countries. While the work is highly detailed in describing television in Europe, it is weak in covering other areas of the world.

The British have shown the greatest initiative in documenting the growth of television and in measuring its influence. The best single study written about the politics of television is *Pressure Group* by H. H. Wilson, a Princeton University professor who describes the manner in which a small group of politicians, backed by a well-organized lobby, ended the BBC's traditional broadcast monopoly in 1954 by successfully maneuvering a bill authorizing commercial television through a reluctant Parliament. The subject is also covered in a left-wing-oriented volume by Clive Jenkins, *Power Behind the Screen*. The medium's effect on political elections is documented in *Television and the Political Image*, a 1961 study by Joseph Trenaman and Denis McQuail, published under the auspices of the Television Research Unit of the University of Leeds. One can only hope that in the coming years American scholars will recognize the need for similar studies of the impact that television has had on our own society.

Selected Bibliography

Ahmed, Abbas. *The Part Played by Television in Developing Countries.* A paper submitted by the United Arab Republic delegation to the Third International Television Festival, August, 1964.

Aliskey, Marvin. "Spain's Press and Broadcasting: Conformity and Censorship," *Journalism Quarterly,* No. 39, Winter, 1962.

Altman, Wilfred, Denis Thomas, and David Sawers. *TV: From Monopoly to Competition.* Hobart Paper No. 15. London: Institute of Economic Affairs, 1962.

American Broadcasting Company International Inc. *Television in the Space Age.* Proceedings of the first Worldvision Symposium held in Washington, D.C., under the auspices of ABC International, March 21, 1965.

Annuaire du Spectacle: Théatre, Cinéma, Radio, Télévision. Fifteenth edition, Paris: 1960.

Apple, R. W. "What Telstar Cannot Do," *Saturday Review,* September 8, 1962.

Associated Rediffusion. *School Report—The First Four Years.* London: 1961.

Barnell, M. "TV Spreading Fast Through Central America," *Barron's,* June 4, 1956.

Barber, Russell B. "European Broadcasting Union: Structure and Function," *Journal of Broadcasting,* Spring, 1962.

Baruch, R. "Don't Rap U.S. Television Exports," *Broadcasting,* April 16, 1962.

Beadle, Sir Gerald. *Television: A Critical Review.* London: George Allen & Unwin, 1963.

Beaver, John. "Television and the British General Elections," *EBU Review* (Geneva), No. 59B, January, 1960. Analysis of the 1959 general elections.

Belsen, William. *Research for Programme Planning in Television.* London: Associated Television, Ltd., 1960.

Benton, William. "Big Brother's TV Set," *Esquire,* March, 1963. Soviet television.

Bernstein, Irving. *The Economics of Television Film Production and Distribution.* Los Angeles: Screen Actors Guild, 1960.

321

Bond, Donald S. (ed.). *A System for Direct Television Broadcasting Using Earth Satellite Repeaters.* Princeton, N.J.: Radio Corporation of America, David Sarnoff Laboratories, July, 1961.

Boyer, Sir Richard. "TV in Perspective," *Australian Quarterly,* September, 1957.

Braunthal, G. "Federalism in Germany: The Broadcasting Controversy," *Journal of Politics,* August, 1962.

Briggs, Asa. *The History of Broadcasting in the United Kingdom.* Vol. I, *The Birth of Broadcasting;* Vol. II, *The Golden Age of Wireless.* London: Oxford University Press, 1965.

British Broadcasting Corporation. *BBC Audience Research in the United Kingdom—Methods and Services.* London: 1961.

————. *BBC Educational Broadcasting.* Report to the delegates to the second World Conference on School Broadcasting, Tokyo. London: April, 1964.

————. *British Broadcasting Corporation Handbook.* 1964 edition, London.

————. *Outlook—BBC Educational Programmes for Adult Listeners and Viewers.* London: 1963.

————. *The Public and the Programmes.* London: 1959. Audience research report.

————. *Radio and Television Broadcasts to Schools and Colleges, 1964–1965.* London. Brochure.

British Information Services. *Sound and Television Broadcasting in Britain.* London: Reference Division, Central Office of Information, August, 1963.

Brown, Donald E. "Radio and TV—An Annotated Bibliography," *Journalism Quarterly,* No. 34, Summer, 1957. Covers the period 1946-57.

Brown, M. L. "Italian TV Sponsors' Problems: Twenty Seconds to Sell Every Eight Days." *Printer's Ink,* February 15, 1957.

————. "London TV Letter: Commercial Developments in England," *Printer's Ink,* October 5, 1956.

————. "Pattern of England's New Commercial TV Comes Into Focus," *Printer's Ink,* March 18, 1955.

Cameron, James. "Cuba's Fumbling Marxism," *Atlantic Monthly,* September, 1964.

Canadian Broadcasting Corporation. *What the Canadian Public Thinks of the Canadian Broadcasting Corporation.* Ottawa: 1963.

Carlisle, Olga. "Literary Life in Moscow," *New York Times Book Review,* March 14, 1965. Role of television in Soviet intellectual life.

Casaneuve, Jean. *Sociologie de la Radio-Télévision.* Paris: Presses Universitaire de France, 1964.

Casaneuve, Jean, and Jean Oulif. *La Grande Chance de la Télévision.* Paris: Calmann-Lévy, 1963.

Cassirer, Henry R. *Television Teaching Today.* Paris: UNESCO, 1960.

————. "TV at the Crossroads," *Television Quarterly,* Summer, 1963.

Célarié, André. *La Radiodiffusion harmonisée au service du développement.* "Les Cahiers Africains," No. 6. Paris: Editions Créations de Presse, 1963. Documents French use of radio and television in West Africa.

Chen Shih-ping. "TV Comes to Taiwan," *Free China Review,* November, 1962.

Clarke, Arthur C. "Extra-terrestrial Relays: Can Rocket Stations Give World-wide Radio Coverage?" *Wireless World* (London), October, 1945.

Codding, George A. *Broadcasting Without Barriers.* Paris: UNESCO, 1959.

Crane, Robert D. "Soviet Attitudes Towards International Space Law," *American Journal of International Law,* Vol. 59, 1962.

Crossman, R. H. S. "Thoughts of a Captive Viewer," *Encounter* (London), August, 1962.

Current Digest of the Soviet Press (New York). "Finding Programs to Meet Television's Voracious Needs," translated from *Kommunist* (Moscow), No. 8, June, 1959, in Vol. XI, No. 25, July 22, 1959.

————. "On Improving Soviet Radio Broadcasting and on Further Developing Television," Resolution of the Party Central Committee, translated from *Partiinaia Zhizn* (Party Life), No. 4, February, 1960, in Vol. XII, No. 29, August 17, 1960.

————. "On the Tasks of Party Propaganda in Present-Day Conditions," Resolution of the Party Central Committee, January 9, 1960, translated from *Pravda,* January 10, 1960, in Vol. XII, No. 2, February 10, 1960.

Della Porta, Glauce. "RAI-TV: The Italian Radio and Television Corporation," *Review of Economic Conditions in Italy,* November, 1956.

Department of State (Washington, D.C.) "Foreign Policy Aspects of Space Communications." Statement by Secretary of State Dean Rusk before the Senate Foreign Relations Committee, August 6, 1962. Department of State *Bulletin,* August 27, 1962.

————. "U.S. Agrees to Discuss Exchange of Radio-TV Exports with USSR," Department of State *Bulletin,* September 2, 1957.

Diamon, Leslie A. W. "Bringing Radio and Television to Northern Nigeria," *EBU Review* (Geneva), No. 93B, September, 1965.

Dieuzeide, Henri. "The Bright Green Blackboard—TV Education in France," *Réalités* (Paris), English-language edition, July, 1963.

————. "School Broadcasting," *EBU Review* (Geneva), No. 88B, November, 1964.

————. *Teaching Through Television.* Paris: Organization for European Economic Cooperation, Office for Scientific and Technical Personnel, 1960.

————. "Ten Years of School Television," *EBU Review* (Geneva), No. 69B, September, 1961. Reviews French educational television efforts.

Dizard, Wilson P. *The Strategy of Truth.* Washington: Public Affairs Press, 1961.

Doherty, D. M. "TV in Japan," *Sponsor,* June 6, 1959.

————. "TV in Thailand," *Sponsor,* June 20, 1959.

————. "TV Italiana," *Sponsor,* March 28, 1959.

Duhoura, S.J., Carlos A. "Technical School Television in Argentina," *Television and Adult Education* (Paris), No. 13, March, 1964.

Dunlap, A. D. *The Development of Television in the Middle East, Africa and South Asia.* Cambridge: Center for International Studies, Massachusetts Institute of Technology, April, 1957. Mimeo.

Dunlap, Orrin E., Jr. *Outlook for Television.* New York: Harper & Bros., 1932.

Eastern Economist (New Delhi). "The Challenge of Television," special supplement, November 21, 1959.

East Europe (New York). "Gomulka Decries Foreign Propaganda," June, 1963. Publication of Radio Free Europe Committee.

Eckert, Gerhard. "TV in Germany," *Gazette* (Amsterdam), November 1, 1959.

European Broadcasting Union (Geneva). "This is the EBU," 1962. Pamphlet.

EBU Review (Geneva). "Aid to the Broadcasting Organizations of the Developing Countries," No. 88B, November, 1964.

————. "Origins and First Steps of the EBU Review Committee," No. 85B, May, 1964.

Fabian Society. *The Future of Broadcasting*. Fabian Research Series, No. 138. London: Victor Gollanz, February, 1950.

Far Eastern Economic Review (Hong Kong). "Television for Asia," special supplement, January 16, 1964.

Ford Foundation. *ETV: A Ford Foundation Pictorial Report*. March, 1961.

————. *Instructional Television in the Public Schools—Fact Sheet*. April, 1964. Mimeo.

————. *Roots of Change: The Ford Foundation in India*. November, 1961.

Friedman, Richard. "Commercial TV in Japan," *Journal of Broadcasting*, Summer, 1959.

Frutkin, A. W. "International Programs of NASA," *Bulletin of the Atomic Scientists*, May, 1961. Discusses early communications satellite programs of the National Aeronautics and Space Agency.

Fund for the Advancement of Education and the Ford Foundation. *Teaching by Television*. First edition, May, 1959; second edition, January, 1961. New York. Pamphlet.

Furu, Takeo. *Television and Children's Life—A Before-After Study*. Tokyo: Radio and Television Culture Research Institute, Japan Broadcasting Corporation, 1962.

"Genet." "Letter from Paris," *New Yorker*, March 7, 1964. Discusses French use of television in election campaigns.

————. "Letter from Paris," *New Yorker*, March 17, 1962. Discusses General de Gaulle's use of television.

Givton, Hanoch. "Introducing Television Into Israel," *EBU Review* (Geneva), No. 93B, September, 1965.

Grant, Douglas. "Schools Television in Western Nigeria," *EBU Review* (Geneva), No. 69B, September, 1961.

Green, Paul E. (ed.). *A Survey of Soviet Communications Electronics*. Lincoln Laboratory Group Report 34-76. Cambridge, Mass.: Massachusetts Institute of Technology, September, 1958. Includes translations of Soviet technical reports on communications electronics.

Greenberg, D. S. "Cooperation in Space: Soviet Scientists and Politicians Appear to Have Different Views," *Science*, November 24, 1961.

Greene, Sir Hugh Carleton. *Future Prospects in Broadcasting*. Sixth Bishop Bell Memorial Lecture, Workers Educational Association, Chichester. London: British Broadcasting Corporation Publication No. 5290, 1963.

Hadsell, R. S., and G. K. Smith. "Educational Television in Iran," *Multiplier*, U.S. International Cooperation Administration, 1961.

Hagerstown (Md.) Board of Education. *Closed Circuit Television: Teaching in Washington County, 1958-59.* March, 1959. Pamphlet.

Halstead, William S. "Low-Cost National Television Comes to East Africa," *Multiplier,* U.S. International Cooperation Administration, June, 1964.

———. "TV in the USSR," *Atlantic Monthly,* June, 1960.

Hans Bredau Institute for Radio and Television (Hamburg University). *Internationales Handbuch für Rundfunk und Fernsehen.* Fourth edition, 1960.

Hansen, George. "Eurovision," *Telefilm International* (Los Angeles), January, 1962.

Hoen, Hans. "East German TV Viewers Prefer Non-political Fare," *Variety,* January 20, 1965.

Hoggart, Richard. "The Uses of TV," *Encounter* (London), January, 1960.

Hopkins, Harry. *The New Look—A Social History of the Forties and Fifties.* London: Secker & Warburg, 1963. Discusses impact of television in postwar British life.

Hourdin, Georges. "Une révolution socio-culterelle: la Télévision," *Le Monde* (Paris), September 8, 10, 11, 1963.

Hull, W. H. N. "The Public Control of Broadcasting," *Canadian Journal of Economic and Political Science,* February, 1962. Discusses problem as it relates to Canada and Australia.

Hurley, S.J., Neil. "Airborne Television and Universal Primary Education." Santiago, Chile: Centro da Investigación y Acción Social, 1964. Mimeo.

———. "The Role of Communication Technology in Democracy," in *Communications Explosion,* Report No. 9, Program of Policy Studies in Science and Technology. Washington, D.C.: George Washington University, June, 1965.

Hutber, P. "Licenses to Print Money: Commercial Television in Britain Has Been a Smashing Success," *Barron's,* January 9, 1961.

Huth, Arno. *Communications Media in Tropical Africa.* Washington: U.S. International Cooperation Administration, 1961. Government-financed study of media in fourteen African countries.

Independent Television Authority. *ITV 1965—A Guide to Independent Television.* London: January, 1965.

Indian Ministry of Information and Broadcasting. *Report of the Mass Communications Study Team Sponsored by the Ford Foundation.* New Delhi: 1963.

Intam, Ltd. *The Intam Commercial Television Data Book.* Second edition, London: 1960. Basic facts about television advertising in 39 countries.

International Commission of Jurists. *Cuba and the Rule of Law.* Amsterdam: 1962.

International Federation for Information Processing. *The Information Revolution,* special supplement to *New York Times,* May 23, 1965.

Iron Curtain News. "Communist Radio, TV Imitate the West," No. 26, New York: Radio Free Europe Committee. June 3, 1964. Mimeo.

Japan Broadcasting Corporation (NHK). *NHK in Charts and Diagrams.* Yearbook of Nippon Hoso Kyokai. 1960——.

Jenkins, Clive. *Power Behind the Screen.* London: Macgibbon & Kee, 1961. Study of ownership control and motivation in British commercial television.

Johansen, O. Lund (ed.) *World Radio-TV Handbook*. Eighteenth edition, Hellerup, Denmark: 1964.

Journal of Broadcasting. "The Evolution of Television 1927-43, as Reported in the Annual Reports of the Federal Radio Commission and the Federal Communications Commission," Summer, 1960.

Juracic, Hrvoje. "The First Year of School Television," *EBU Review* (Geneva), No. 69B September, 1961. Educational TV in Yugoslavia.

Kaftanov, S. V. and others. *Radio i Televidnive v USSR*. Moscow: State Publishing House, 1960. Translated as *Radio and Television in the USSR*. Washington: Library of Congress Joint Publications Research Service, 1961.

Kalimullah, A. F. "The Future of Television in Pakistan," *CETO News*, No. 6. London: Center for Educational Television Overseas, March, 1965.

Karmatz, F. N. "Television," *New Republic*, February 27, 1956. Discusses television in the Soviet Union.

Konkoly, Coleman. "Eurovision: TV at Its Best," *Free World Review*, Summer/Fall, 1959.

Kurzwell, Z. E. "Television in Israel," *Television and Adult Education* (Paris), No. 12, February, 1964.

Larkin, S.J., Leo H. *Educational Television for the Ateneo de Manila: A Preliminary Study*. New York: Fordham University, May, 1960. Mimeo.

————. *A Report on Educational Television for the Philippines*. Manila: Ateneo de Manila University, January, 1961. Mimeo.

Laslett, Peter. "Learning from Television," *Twentieth Century* (London), Autumn, 1963.

————. "University Pipeline," *Guardian* (Manchester), October 18, 1963. Description of experimental closed-circuit television in British universities.

Lear, John. "Ever Stranger Pictures in the Sky: Global TV," *Saturday Review*, September 8, 1962.

Lerner, Daniel. *The Passing of Traditional Society*. Glencoe, Ill.: Free Press, 1958.

Linz, C. C. "Television and Education," *Australian Quarterly*, September, 1958. Describes educational television in the United States, the United Kingdom, and France.

Lloyd Williams, F. N. "School Broadcasting (Sound)," *EBU Review* (Geneva), No. 70B, November, 1961. Describes radio educational broadcasting in the United Kingdom.

Lower, A. R. M. "The Question of Private TV: A Powerful New Medium Has Created a Life-and-Death Crisis for the Canadian Cultural, Economic and Political Community," *Queen's Quarterly*, Kingston, Ontario: Queen's University, Summer, 1953.

Lung Hao-Jan. "On Peking's TV Screen," *China Reconstructs* (Peking), December, 1964.

McCormack, T. H. "Canada's Royal Commission on Broadcasting," *Public Opinion Quarterly*, Spring, 1959.

McLuhan, Marshall. *The Gutenberg Galaxy*. Toronto: University of Toronto Press, 1962.

————. *Understanding Media*. London: Routledge & Kegan Paul, Ltd., 1964.

McNaught, Kenneth. "The Failure of Television in Politics," *Canadian Forum*, August, 1958.

Maeda, Yoshineri. "Television for Teaching," *The British Association Granada Guildhall Lectures, 1962*. London: Macgibbon and Kee, 1962. Describes Japanese experience in educational television.

Malko, G. "Australian Television," *Saturday Review*, August 11, 1962.

"Mammon." "Companies Get Ready for Start of Pay-TV," *Observer* (London), December 9, 1962.

Mannes, Marya. "A Word from Our Sponsor—The Kremlin," *New York Times Magazine*, March 5, 1961.

Marks, Leonard H. "The Role of Broadcasters in Space Communications," *EBU Review* (Geneva), No. 84B, March, 1964.

Martinez, A. M. "TV in Latin America," *Advertising Agency*, October, 1951.

Marx, E. A. "Status of TV in Europe," *Commercial and Financial Chronicle*, December 17, 1953.

Masaka, Ikuta. "Television in Japan," *Gazette* (Amsterdam), November 1, 1960.

Mast, Benjamin V. "Impact of Television on Control of Broadcasting in Canada," *Journal of Broadcasting*, Summer, 1959.

Mathur, J. C. "First Steps Towards Educational Television," *EBU Review* (Geneva), No. 69B, September, 1961. Discusses experimental educational TV in India.

Mazaki, Sadao. "Television in Japan Today," *Broadcasting*, February 12, 1963.

Millikan, Max, and Donald L. M. Blackmer. *The Emerging Nations*. Boston: Little, Brown & Co., 1961.

Moir, Guthrie, and John Lord. "Teaching by TV," *New Commonwealth*, September, 1959. Discusses proposed educational television plan for Western Nigeria.

Mole, J. W. "Canada's TV Problems," *Commonweal*, May 20, 1960.

Moseley, Sydney, and H. J. Barton Chapple. *Television, Today and Tomorrow*. New York: Isaac Pitman & Sons, 1930.

Moses, C. "Australian Television Booming," *Broadcasting*, February 17, 1958.

Muggeridge, Malcolm. "Tele-politics," *New Statesman*, August 9, 1963.

Nassr, Bahie. "Television in Egypt," *Broadcasting*, June 10, 1963.

National Association of Commercial Broadcasters in Japan. *Japanese Commercial Radio and Television Broadcasting Industry Today: The 1960-61 Pictorial Handbook of the National Association of Commercial Broadcasters in Japan*. Tokyo.

———. *NAB Handbook*. Tokyo: 1963———.

National Educational Television Conference, Toronto, May 23-26, 1961. *The Role of Television in Canadian Education*. Toronto: University of Toronto, 1961.

Nervi, Italo. "Educational Television," *EBU Review* (Geneva), No. 69B, September, 1961. Describes Italian school television efforts.

Newell, Ray. *Who Watches TV in Australia?* Issued by the Australian Broadcasting Commission. Undated. Mimeo.

New Scientist (London). "Experimental Color TV Link Across Europe," No. 286, May 10, 1962.

New Statesman (London). "The Phoney Fourth Service," December 15, 1961. Critical of British ETV efforts.

Newsweek. "Opiate of the Masses," March 8, 1965. Description of Soviet television programs.

New York City Board of Education. *Closed Circuit Television: A Report of the Chelsea Project.* 1962.

Nickus, Fritz, and Joachim Schafer. *Tele-Radio Europa—Handbuch fur Funk- und Fersehwerbung.* Frankfurt/Main: 1959.

Nigerian Government Commission on Post-School Certificate and Higher Education. *Investment in Education* (The "Ashby Report"). Lagos: 1960. Discusses possibilities of educational television in Nigeria.

Nippon Television Network Corporation. *How Television Came to Japan.* Tokyo: 1955. Pamphlet.

Office de Coopération Radiophonique. *OCORA.* Paris: August, 1963. Description of the French government's system for assisting radio and television organizations in underdeveloped countries.

Panter-Downes, Mollie. "Letter from London," *New Yorker*, July 14, 1962. Analyzes British reaction to the Pilkington report.

Parasher, S. C. "Three Decades of Broadcasting," *March of India* (New Delhi), February, 1958. Description of All-India Radio broadcasting organization.

Paulu, Burton. "Audiences for Broadcasting," *Journalism Quarterly*, Summer, 1955. Compares reactions of British and American audiences to similar broadcasts.

——. *British Broadcasting: Radio and TV in the United Kingdom.* Minneapolis: University of Minnesota Press, 1956.

Petry, Thomas. "West German TV—The Way Ahead," *Television Quarterly*, Summer, 1963.

Philippine National Science Development Board. *The Philippines' First TV College Course for Credits.* Manila: August, 1961. Pamphlet.

Phillips, R. Hart. "Cuban TV: The Fidel Show," *New York Times*, July 23, 1961.

Pierce, John R. "Communications Satellites," *Scientific American*, October, 1961.

——. "Hazards of Communications Satellites," *Bulletin of the Atomic Scientists*, May, 1961.

——. "Orbital Radio Relays," *Jet Propulsion*, April, 1955.

Pigé, François. *La Télévision dans le Monde—Organisation Administrative et Financière.* Paris: Société Nationale des Entreprises de Presse, 1962.

Planning (London). *TV in Britain.* Survey report issued by the British research organization, PEP. March 24, 1958.

Pool, Ithiel de Sola. "The Mass Media and Politics in the Modernization Process," in *Communications and Political Development.* Lucian Pye (ed.). Princeton, N.J.: Princeton University Press, 1963.

Puglisi, Marie Grazia. "Telescuola Enters Its Second Year," *EBU Review* (Geneva), No. 59B, January, 1960.

——. "Television and the Fight Against Illiteracy," *EBU Review* (Geneva), No. 82B, November, 1963.

Pye, Lucian (ed.). *Communications and Political Development.* Princeton, N.J.: Princeton University Press, 1963.

Qualter, T. H. "Politics and Broadcasting: Case Studies of Political Interference in National Broadcasting," *Canadian Journal of Economic and Political Science,* May, 1962. Case studies of British and New Zealand examples are discussed.

RAI (Italian Radio and Television Broadcasting Corporation). *I Programmi Televisivi nelle Opinioni della Pubblico.* Fifth survey published by RAI in its audience research notebooks. Turin: 1962.

―――. *La Radiotélévision Scolaire en Italie.* Rome: December, 1961.

Raisor, Timothy. "Pilkington: Why and What Next," *Statist* (London), July 9, 1962.

Ramasastri, J. V. S. "Nationalization of Broadcasting in India," *Indian Economic Journal,* July, 1959.

Ratkowski, G. "Eurovision: Some Technical Aspects," *Gazette* (Amsterdam), No. 3/4, 1962.

Rengelink, J. W. "The Eurovision News Transmissions―A First Step in World-wide News," *EBU Review* (Geneva), No. 91B, May, 1965.

Rock, Vincent. "World-wide Television and the National Interest," Program of Policy Studies in Science and Technology. Washington, D.C.: George Washington University, February, 1965.

Rosen, George. "Mestre Rides Again," *Variety,* January 13, 1965. Survey of Latin American television.

―――. "TV―The Best of Gaucho," *Variety,* October 10, 1962. Survey of Argentine television.

Ross, Gordon. *Television Jubilee: The Story of 25 Years of BBC Television.* London: W. H. Allen, 1961.

Rudzki, Jerzy. "Polish Television and Rural Youth," *Television and Adult Education* (Paris), No. 16, January, 1965. TV listenership survey by the director of research at the Warsaw Academy's Institute of Philosophy and Sociology.

Sakai, Saburo. "A History of the National Association of Commercial Broadcasters in Japan," *EBU Review* (Geneva), No. 74B, July, 1962.

Sarnoff, Robert. "Exported Shows Not Harmful," *Broadcasting,* June 18, 1962.

Schecter, Amy. "TV in the USSR," *New World Review* (Moscow), June, 1951.

School Broadcasting Council of the United Kingdom. *After Five Years―A Report on BBC School Television Broadcasting.* London: September, 1962. Pamphlet.

―――. *A Background Note on BBC School Broadcasting.* London: 1963. Pamphlet.

Schramm, Wilbur. *Mass Media and National Development.* Stanford, Calif.: Stanford University Press, 1964.

―――, and Gerald Winfield. "New Uses of Mass Communications for the Promotion of Economic and Social Development," in *Communications: United States Papers Prepared for the United Nations Conference on the Application of Science and Technology for the Benefit of Less-developed Areas.* Vol. XII. Washington, D.C.: Government Publications Office, 1962.

Scupham, John. *Broadcasting and Education.* BBC Lunch-time Lectures, Second Series. London: British Broadcasting Corporation, November 13, 1963. Pamphlet.

Shayon, Robert Lewis. "Change of Diet," *Saturday Review,* May 14, 1960. Discussion of French television.

———— (ed.). *The Eighth Art.* New York: Holt, Rinehart and Winston, 1962. Twenty-three American and foreign critics, including Mr. Shayon, examine television's prospects.

Skornia, Harry J. *Television and Society: An Inquest and Agenda for Improvement.* New York: McGraw Hill, 1964.

Smith, Leonard. *Half Decade—An inside story.* London: 1961. Chronicle of the first five years of operations of Associated Rediffusion, Ltd., one of the British commercial television firms, issued under the firm's imprint.

Smythe, Dallas W. "Communications Satellites," *Bulletin of the Atomic Scientists,* February, 1961.

————. "On the Effects of Communications Satellites," in *Communications Explosion,* Paper No. 9. Program of Policy Studies in Science and Technology. Washington, D.C.: George Washington University, June, 1965.

Snare, Austin. "The Development and Problems of Australian Broadcast Services," *Journal of Broadcasting,* Winter, 1962/63.

Solvay Institute of Sociology. *La Télévision: The Verbatim Account of the Proceedings of the XVIII Semaine Sociale Universitaire, 21-26 March 1960.* Brussels: The Free University of Brussels, 1961. A significant European attempt to assess television's impact at the social level.

Spry, Graham. "The Decline and Fall of Canadian Broadcasting," *Queen's Quarterly.* Kingston, Ontario: Queen's University, Summer, 1961.

Stanford University Institute of Communications Research. *Educational Television—The Next Ten Years.* 1962. Report on the future of educational television in the United States, prepared under the auspices of the U.S. Office of Education.

Stern, Robert H. "Regulatory Influence upon Television's Development," *American Journal of Economics and Sociology,* July, 1963.

Stevenson, Noel. "Independent Television for Schools," *EBU Review* (Geneva), No. 69B, September, 1961. Review of ETV activities of British commercial stations.

Suchy, J. T. "British Television and Its Viewers," *Journalism Quarterly,* Fall, 1954.

Swatkovsky, Andrew. "The Soviet Attitude on Outer Space," *Problems of Communism* (Washington), May/June, 1960.

Szulc, Tad. "Cuban TV's One-Man Show," *The Eighth Art.* Robert Lewis Shayon (ed.). New York: Holt, Rinehart and Winston, 1962.

Television Age. "TV in Orbit." A special issue devoted to international television. July 19, 1965.

Television and Adult Education (Paris). "Meeting on the Introduction and Development of Television in Africa," No. 15, October, 1964. Report of a UNESCO seminar held in Lagos, Nigeria, September, 1964.

Television Factbook. 1964 edition. Washington: Television Digest.

Television Information Office. *Television and Education: A Bibliography.* New York: December, 1960. Pamphlet.

Thomson Organisation, Ltd. *The Annual Review for 1964*. London: Thomson Organisation, Ltd., Thomson House, 1965.

Times (London). "Hollywood and Television," January 12, 1962.

Tokyo Broadcasting System (TBS). *TV Comparograph of Network Programs*. Tokyo: 1962.

Toynbee, Arnold. "Message for Mankind from Telstar," *New York Times Magazine*, August 12, 1962.

Trafford, I. "Risk and Reward: Commercial TV Has Paid Off Handsomely in Great Britain," *Barron's*, November 24, 1958.

Trenaman, Joseph, and Denis McQuail. *Television and the Political Image*. London: Methuen, 1961. Study of television's impact on the 1959 general elections in Great Britain.

Tuber, Richard. "A Survey of Programming on the Central Studios of TV, Moscow, January–June 1960," *Journal of Broadcasting*, Fall, 1960.

Tyler, I. Keith, and Margaret Tyler. *A Four-Year Developmental Program for the Use of Instructional Television to Extend Quality Education in the United Arab Republic*. American Embassy, Cairo. June, 1963. Mimeo.

Uhlan, Edward, and Dana L. Thomas. *Shoriki—Miracle Man of Japan*. New York: Exposition Press, 1957.

United Arab Republic Information Office. *Television and Radio Transmissions*. Cairo: 1961. Pamphlet.

United Kingdom Colonial Office. *Sound and Television Broadcasting in the Overseas Territories—1964 Handbook*. Sixteenth edition, London: Information Department, Colonial Office, 1964.

UNESCO. *Adult Education Groups and Audio-Visual Techniques*. Reports and Papers on Mass Communication, No. 25. Paris: 1958.

———. *Current Mass Communication Research I—Bibliography of Books and Articles on Mass Communication Published since 1 January 1955*. Paris: December, 1956.

———. *Developing Information Media in Africa: Press, Radio, Film, Television*. Reports and Papers on Mass Communication, No. 37. Paris: 1962.

———. *Developing Mass Media in Asia*. Reports and Papers on Mass Communication, No. 30. Paris: 1960.

———. *Film and Television in the Service of Opera and Ballet and of Museums*. Reports and Papers on Mass Communication, No. 32. Paris: 1961.

———. *The Kinescope and Adult Education*. Reports and Papers on Mass Communication, No. 26. Paris: 1958.

———. *Mass Media in the Developing Countries. A UNESCO Report to the United Nations*. Reports and Papers on Mass Communication, No. 33. Paris: 1961.

———. *Report of the Meeting: Meeting of Experts on Development of Information Media in Latin America, Santiago, Chile, 1-13 February 1961*. UNESCO/MC/41. Paris: May 31, 1961.

———. *Rural Television in Japan*. Paris: 1960.

———. *Screen Education. Teaching a Critical Approach to Cinema and Television*. Reports and Papers on Mass Communication, No. 42. Paris: 1964.

————. *Social Education Through Television: An All India Radio-UNESCO Pilot Project.* Reports and Papers on Mass Communication, No. 38. Paris: 1963.

————. *Space Communications and the Mass Media.* Reports and Studies on Mass Communication, No. 41. Paris: 1964.

————. *Study of the Establishment of National Centres for Cataloguing of Films and Television Programmes.* Reports and Papers on Mass Communication, No. 40. Paris: 1963.

————. *Television: A World Survey.* Reports on the Facilities of Mass Communications. Paris: 1952; supplement, 1955.

————. *Television and Tele-clubs in Rural Communities.* Reports and Papers on Mass Communication, No. 16. Paris: July, 1955.

————. *World Communication: Press, Radio, Television, Film.* 1964 edition, Paris.

United States House of Representatives. *Chronology of Missile and Astronautic Events.* Report of the Committee on Science and Astronautics. House Report No. 67. March 8, 1961.

————. *Commercial Applications of Space Communications Systems.* Committee on Science and Astronautics. House Report No. 1279, October 11, 1961.

————. *Communications Satellite Experiments.* Report of the Committee on Science and Astronautics. Serial V. December 3, 1962.

————. *The Next Ten Years in Space.* Staff report of the Select Committee on Aeronautics and Space Exploration. 86th Congress, 1st Session. House Document No. 115. 1959.

————. *Proposed Studies on the Implications of Peaceful Space Activities for Human Affairs.* Report of the Committee on Science and Astronautics. March 24, 1961.

————. *Satellites for World Communications.* Committee on Science and Astronautics. Report No. 343, May 7, 1959.

————. *Space Handbook: Astronautics and Its Applications.* Staff report of the Select Committee on Astronautics and Space Exploration. 86th Congress, 1st. Session. House Document No. 86. 1959.

United States Senate. *Antitrust Problems of the Space Satellite Communications System.* Hearings before the subcommittee on antitrust and monopoly, Committee on the Judiciary. Part 1: March 29, 30, April 4 and 5, 1962; Part 2: April 6, 10, 11, 12, and 17, 1962.

————. *Communications Satellite Act of 1962.* Hearings before the Committee on Foreign Relations. August 3, 6, 7, 8, and 9, 1962.

————. *Communications Satellites: Technical, Economic and International Developments.* Staff report prepared for the use of the Committee on Aeronautical and Space Sciences, February 25, 1962.

————. *Policy Planning for Space Telecommunications.* Staff report prepared for the Committee on Aeronautical and Space Sciences. December 4, 1960.

————. *Report Together with Minority Views: To Accompany H.R. 11040, Communications Satellite Act of 1962.* Committee on Commerce. June 11, 1962.

United States Information Agency. *Overseas Television Developments*. Annual review of global television developments, issued each April since 1959. Washington, D.C.

———. Twelve Years of Communist Broadcasting, 1948–1959. Simon Costikyan (ed.). Washington, D.C.: 1960.

U.S. News and World Report. "What Castro is Doing to Cuba," March 1, 1965.

USSR Central Statistical Publishing House. *USSR in Figures*. Moscow: April, 1965.

Victoria School Broadcasts Advisory Committee. *Television for Schools: Report on Experimental Mathematics Programme*. Victoria, Australia: 1961.

Wagner, Egon. "Report from the Federal Republic of Germany," *EBU Review* (Geneva), No. 67B, May, 1961.

———. "Report from the Federal Republic of Germany," *EBU Review* (Geneva), No. 72B, March, 1962.

Wallace, Mike. "TV in Russia: A Really Hard Sell," *New York Times Magazine*, January 18, 1959.

Watson, J. "United Nations TV," *Television Magazine*, October, 1958.

Weightman, John. "Television and the General," *Observer* (London), February 3, 1963. Critique of television in de Gaulle's France.

Welch, F. X. "International Regulation of Communications in the Space Age," *Public Utility*, October 22, 1959.

Williams, Frederick. "The Soviet Philosophy of Broadcasting," *Journal of Broadcasting*, Winter, 1961/62.

Wilson, H. H. *Pressure Group: the Campaign for Commercial Television* [in Great Britain]. New Brunswick, N.J.: Rutgers University Press, 1961.

World's Press News and Advertising Review. *International Commercial Television Rate and Data Book, 1961-62*. London: 1961. Successor to the INTAM annual commercial television data book. Covers all countries outside North America.

Worsnop, Richard. *Peaceful Use of Outer Space*. Washington: Editorial Research Reports, June 27, 1962.

Yench, John. "Role of Radio and Television in the Philippines," *American Chamber of Commerce Journal* (Manila), December, 1960.

Yugoslav Institute of Journalism. *JRT Yearbook 1964*. Dr. Ivke Pustisek (ed.). Belgrade: 1965. Annual handbook of the Yugoslav state radio and television broadcasting system.

Zeman, Z. A. B. *Nazi Propaganda*. London: Oxford University Press, 1964.

Zinder, Harry. "Television in Israel." *Gazette* (Amsterdam), No. 1, 1961.

Index

ABC. *See:* American Broadcasting Company
ABC International Co.: interest in regional networks, 98-99
Accra, 67
Adams, Kenneth: quoted, 117, 169
Adenauer, Konrad: attempt to set up national West German network, 39
Adult education by TV: in Great Britain, 218-19; Argentine experiments with, 233-34; UNESCO experiment in India, 238
Advertising, TV: in Japan, 44; threat to newspaper revenues in West Germany 122; American advertising activities on overseas TV, 161, 167
Advertising Age, 317
Advertising agencies: role in introduction of British commercial TV, 32; interest of U.S. agencies in overseas TV business, 167
Advertising controls by overseas TV systems: British regulations, 32; West European examples, 117
Africa: 5; growth of TV in, 48, 64-70; U.S. TV investment in, 63; interest in regional network, 77, 98-99; TV language difficulties, 113; U.S. telefilm exports to, 162; educational TV in, 227, 235-36
Agency for International Development (AID), 248
Albania, 186, 192
Alexandra Palace, London, 22-23
Alexandria, UAR: TV festival in, 153
"Alfred Hitchcock Presents," 196
Algeria: 72; accepts TV assistance from UAR, 152
Algerian war: French TV coverage of, 28, 142, 145
Allen, Fred: quoted, 7

Alliance for Progress, 233
Alliance of Television Film Producers, U.S., 158
All-India Radio, 74, 244-45
American Broadcasting Company: investments in Latin American TV, 54; operations of "Worldvision" subsidiary, 64; interest in Lebanese TV, 71; sponsors Arab TV network, 98; sponsors Central American network, 99; range of overseas activities, 164, 167
"American image" on overseas TV: role of TV and films in projecting it to foreign audiences, 5, 8; Polish attacks on, 196; influenced by communications satellite, 257, 281
"Americanization" of foreign TV, actions against: in Canada, 36; in Australia, Great Britain, Japan, West Germany, Brazil, Mexico, and Sweden, 109; British views on, 169
American Telephone & Telegraph Company: prewar experiments with TV, 23; role in communications-satellite project, 261, 263, 265, 267
Anglo-American Corporation: South Africa, 69
Arabian-American Oil Company (ARAMCO), 71, 237
Arab Television Network: plans for, 5, 98-99, 152
ARD, West German TV network, 39
Argentina: 48, 51, 53; transmissions to Uruguay, 99; market for U.S. TV films, 160; overseas telefilm sales, 170; educational TV in, 233
Armed Forces Radio and Television Service, U.S.: operations in Korea, 59
Arms control: TV as a factor in, 252
Asahi Shimbun, Tokyo, 122

335